W9-AGX-588

PROFESSIONAL ETHICS IN EDUCATION SERIES

Kenneth A. Strike, EDITOR

The Ethics of School Administration, Third Edition
Kenneth A. Strike, Emil J. Haller, and Jonas F. Soltis

"Real World" Ethics:
Frameworks for Educators and Human Service Professionals,
Second Edition
Robert J. Nash

Justice and Caring:
The Search for Common Ground in Education
Michael S. Katz, Nel Noddings, and Kenneth A. Strike, Editors

Ethics in School Counseling
John M. Schulte and Donald B. Cochrane, Editors

The Moral Base for Teacher Professionalism
Hugh Sockett

Ethics for Professionals in Education:
Perspectives for Preparation and Practice
Kenneth A. Strike and P. Lance Ternasky, Editors

The Ethics of Multicultural and Bilingual Education
Barry L. Bull, Royal T. Fruehling, and Virgie Chattergy

The Ethics of Special Education
Kenneth R. Howe and Ofelia B. Miramontes

Classroom Life as Civic Education:
Individual Achievement and Student Cooperation in Schools
David C. Bricker

THE
ETHICS
OF
SCHOOL
ADMINISTRATION

THIRD EDITION

KENNETH A. STRIKE
EMIL J. HALLER
JONAS F. SOLTIS

Teachers College, Columbia University
New York and London

Published by Teachers College Press, 1234 Amsterdam Avenue, New York, NY 10027

Copyright © 2005 by Teachers College, Columbia University

All rights reserved. No part of this publication may be reproduced or transmitted in any form or by any means, electronic or mechanical, including photocopy, or any information storage and retrieval system, without permission from the publisher.

Library of Congress Cataloging-in-Publication Data

Strike, Kenneth A.
    The ethics of school administration / Kenneth A. Strike, Emil J. Haller, Jonas F. Soltis.—3rd Ed.
        p. cm. — (Professional ethics in education series)
    Includes bibliographical references.
    ISBN 0-8077-4573-1 (pbk. : alk. paper)
        1. School management and organization—Moral and ethical aspects—United States—Case studies. 2. School administrators—Professional ethics—United States—Case studies. 3. Pluralism (Social sciences)—United States—Case studies. I. Haller, Emil J. II. Soltis, Jonas F. III. Title. IV. Series.
LB2806.S73 2005
371.2'00973—dc22   2004058897

ISBN 0-8077-4573-1 (paper)

Printed on acid-free paper
Manufactured in the United States of America

12   11   10   09   8   7   6   5   4   3

Contents

Preface   ix

A Note to the Instructor   xi

Chapter 1   Administration and Ethical Thinking   1

    A Case   1
    Purposes of This Book   2
    The Nature of Ethical Inquiry   3
    Learning Moral Reasoning   6

Chapter 2   Intellectual Liberty   7

    A Case   7
    Dispute   9
    Concept: Freedom of Expression   9
    Analysis: Ethical Decision Making   14
      The Principle of Benefit Maximization   17
      The Principle of Equal Respect   17
    Conclusion   18
    Additional Cases   20
      Equal Time?   20
      Two Black Swans   23
      The Last Straw?   27

Chapter 3   Individual Freedom and the Public Interest   30

    A Case   30
    Dispute   31
    Concept: Personal Liberty   32
    Analysis: The Nature of Moral Judgments   37

Conclusion		43
Additional Cases		44
Tiger! Tiger! Burning Bright		44
Pregnant		47
The Aryan Brotherhood		49

Chapter 4   Equal Educational Opportunity — **52**

A Case	52
Dispute	54
Concept: Equality	54
Analysis: Moral Experience	60
Conclusion	63
Additional Cases	64
Can Mathematicians Reason?	64
Bigotry?	67
Little School, Big Problem	71

Chapter 5   Educational Evaluation — **75**

A Case	75
Dispute	77
Concept: Due Process	78
Analysis: Respect for Persons	81
Conclusion	85
Additional Cases	86
A Letter of Recommendation	86
A Matter of Standards	88
A Problem of Grades	90

Chapter 6   Educational Authority and Accountability: Community, Democracy, and Professionalism — **93**

A Case	93
Dispute	96
Concepts: Accountability, Democracy, Community, and Professionalism	97
Analysis: Objective Moral Reasoning	109
Conclusion	115
Additional Cases	115
Democracy in Action	116
A Problem of Policy: Retaining Pupils at Jackson Elementary	118
Accountability Meets Community at Ruebens Flats	122

Chapter 7   **Diversity: Multiculturalism and Religion**   **127**

A Case   127
Dispute   130
Concepts and Issues   131
Radical Diversity   *134*
Consequentialist and Nonconsequentialist Views
on Diversity   *138*
Pros and Cons   *141*
Persons and Citizens   *146*
Additional Cases   149
A Christmas Quarrel   *149*
Understanding Infibulation   *150*
The People of the Corn   *155*

Chapter 8   **Supplemental Cases**   **159**

Case # 1:   Friendly Support or Sexual Harassment?   161
Case # 2:   Abuse? Neglect? Or Nothing to Worry
About?   162
Case # 3:   The Rumors About Taylor Roberts   164
Case # 4:   Honors Courses and Board Policy   166
Case # 5:   A Matter of Honesty   169
Case # 6:   A Matter of Integrity   170
Case # 7:   Merit or Mercy?   172
Case # 8:   A Conflict of Interest   173
Case # 9:   Exploitation   174
Case # 10: Borrowed Property?   176
Case # 11: An Office Affair   178
Case # 12: Societal and Individual Good   179
Case # 13: Job References for Students   180
Case # 14: Confidentiality, Obligations, and Friendship   181
Case # 15: Loyalty   182
Case # 16: Are Schools More Important Than Sewers?   183
Case # 17: BANG! Zero Tolerance   184
Case # 18: Hiding Bad News at Hindemith High   186

Annotated Bibliography   **191**

About the Authors   **196**

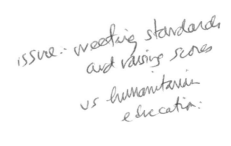
issue: meeting standards and raising scores vs humanitarian education.

Preface

The second edition of *The Ethics of School Administration* made two important changes to the first edition. It added a chapter discussing religious and cultural diversity, and it added case material discussing sexual harassment and child abuse. This third edition adds material that refocuses the discussion of legitimate authority and democracy on accountability. School leaders are increasingly required to emphasize meeting standards and raising test scores. At the same time leaders must respect the professional judgment of teachers, make their schools into learning communities, and get parents and members of the larger community involved and invested in their schools. These demands create significant role conflicts for leaders. To address these concerns, we have substantially revised Chapter 6, now entitled, "Educational Authority and Accountability: Community, Democracy, and Professionalism," and we have added new case material. In Chapter 8 we have added new cases on zero tolerance policies and integrity in reporting data. The third edition of *The Ethics of School Administration* maintains the successful format of the first two editions. After introducing readers to our subject in Chapter 1, each of Chapters 2–7 begins with a case and a dispute. Next the key ethical concepts required to discuss the case are presented and applied to the case. Finally, we discuss what light the argument of the chapter sheds on the nature of ethical decision making and ethical reasoning, and include three additional cases. In Chapter 8 we provide 18 supplementary cases on the topics of the book.

    The Ethics of School Administration is one of a set of books in the Teachers College Press series Professional Ethics in Education. All of the books in this series will aim at helping educators and the education profession to examine and reflect on the ethical issues and controversies that are a normal and routine part of educational practice. We believe that this is an especially important task as education seeks to mold itself more on the model of a self-governing profession. Our world is not one in which eternal verities or the moral sentiments of a cohesive community can easily govern conduct in public institutions. Educators who wish to be responsible for the practice of education must therefore be equipped to take individual responsibility for thinking through defensible positions on difficult ethical questions. We hope to assist in that endeavor.

The present volume, *The Ethics of School Administration*, is intended to help teach a range of ethical concepts that are important to the practicing administrator. Its ample case studies and detailed analyses should provide practitioners with information and skills needed for a knowledgeable approach to thinking through the ethical problems they encounter in the course of their work.

The Ethics of School Administration is largely modeled on Strike and Soltis, *The Ethics of Teaching*, which is part of the Teachers College Press Thinking About Education Series. The editor of that series, Jonas F. Soltis, is also one of the co-authors of this book. We have found the format of the books in the Thinking About Education Series to be quite effective in teaching and have modified it only slightly here, largely by expanding the case material and organizing it topically. Readers who appreciate the content and approach *of The Ethics of School Administration* will also enjoy *The Ethics of Teaching* and the other books in the Thinking About Education Series.

Kenneth A. Strike
Editor, Professional Ethics in Education Series

A Note to the Instructor

The purpose of this book is to teach some ethical concepts that are important to educational administration as well as something of the process of ethical reasoning. To this end we have built the book around cases. We believe that ethical reasoning is a skill and that its acquisition requires practice. It is not enough merely to have students read the text. We believe that it is important that cases be thoroughly discussed in class, and we think that it is entirely in order that writing assignments be built around them as well.

We have provided a generous selection of cases that may be used for these purposes. Each substantive chapter begins with a case that is referred to throughout the chapter. Each chapter concludes with several other cases dealing with the issues of that chapter. Finally, at the end of the book we have provided a set of additional cases that are not linked to the topics of specific chapters and that deal with a wide range of ethical issues.

We have tried to construct these cases so that they contain genuine moral dilemmas. Thus it will not be apparent, at the outset, that there is a clearly right response to the case. For this reason they should make good material for discussion.

We believe, however, that it is important that these discussions have a certain character. And we believe that the instructor is vitally important to the effective use of cases. Students are often inclined to approach ambiguous cases by simply stating what they feel should be done. When other students produce different responses, they are apt to conclude that the matter is unresolvable and that everyone is entitled to his or her own opinion. We have also found that the first time around students will frequently miss much of what is at stake in the case.

It is therefore important that students be encouraged to formulate the moral principles that underlie their initial reactions to these cases and that these principles be subject to criticism. It is the process of judging cases against principles and of criticizing and reformulating moral principles that constitutes the art of moral reflection. This is the way students are going to become capable of sophisticated moral reasoning.

The role of the instructor in using these cases is thus Socratic. It consists in drawing out responses from students. But it also consists in criticizing students' initial responses and helping them to formulate views that are more adequate and more thoroughly considered. This book contains an account of the process of ethical reasoning. It is equally an account of how ethical issues can be profitably discussed and argued about. It should provide the instructor with a useful account of what a fruitful classroom discussion is like. Finally, the role of the instructor consists in establishing a classroom climate in which everyone feels free to participate in the process of criticism and debate.

CHAPTER 1

Administration and Ethical Thinking

A CASE

Janet Russel, the principal of Haven Elementary School, sat staring out the window. It was a pleasant late spring day. A pair of robins had built a nest in a tree a few feet away, and she could see them darting in and out with an occasional worm or grub. She would have liked to see if the babies were observable from a vantage point closer to the window. But she would have to wait to investigate later.

The feathered domestic tranquility outside provided counterpoint to the absence of tranquility inside. Mr. and Mrs. Taylor were still talking, but Ms. Russel was only half listening. Great attention was not required. She had heard it several times already this week. In fact, she heard it every year at this time. Each spring after the class assignments for next year went home, parents, moved by some primordial urge to secure any marginal advantage for their children, began to migrate toward the school, twittering in frenzied agitation about the placement of their fledglings.

The usual speech went like this: "We know, Ms. Russel, that you work hard to match students to teachers. In the past we have appreciated your attention to the special needs of our child. But this year we think you are wrong. We know our child better than you, and we are sure that our child will do much better with Ms. Tarkington than with Mr. Booth. We would appreciate it if you would make the change."

The first speech was usually polite and tactful. But any resistance escalated matters to a more stressful level. There was the friends-in-high-places ploy. It was hard to believe that school board members and the superintendent of schools had so many personal friends. And of course there were the parents-have-rights and the unresponsive-school-administrators ploys.

The problem was that every parent was right. Their child would do better with Ms. Tarkington than with Mr. Booth. Ms. Tarkington was the local superteacher. Children blossomed in her class. Mr. Booth, on the other hand, was—well—undistinguished. Both teachers had reputations in the community. Parents knew.

What could Ms. Russel say? She could not admit that one teacher was far superior to the other. Principals did not do that. She had to be supportive of all her staff. Parents understood that intuitively. Nobody ever came in and said, "I want the best teacher for my child." Euphemisms were the order of the day. After much evasion the parents would leave with her promise to think it over.

She had already thought it over. Obviously she could not simply put every child whose parents requested it in Ms. Tarkington's class. Having one class of 35 children and another of 15 would be noticed. Nor could she move enough children out of Ms. Tarkington's class to compensate for the children transferred in. That would be unfair. It would give an advantage to those children whose parents were willing to come in and lobby on their behalf. It was not surprising that these were usually the parents of middle-class children, who tended to be the most successful in school. To grant parental wishes would be to segregate the class on socioeconomic lines and to systematically assign the least able children to the poorest teacher. Given a choice, Ms. Russel would prefer to do the opposite. Yet she had to grant that parents did have a right to some say about the education of their children. She always listened to their requests, and she granted them whenever she could. But she did not think she ought to do so in this case. Parents' rights or not, it just was not fair.

PURPOSES OF THIS BOOK

Ms. Russel has a problem. It is not just an administrative problem; it is also a moral dilemma regarding a clash between rights and fairness. What makes some administrative problems ethical ones, and how can administrators reach justifiable decisions about moral matters? Asking these questions raises others. How do ethical questions differ from factual questions? What is moral or ethical decision making like? Is ethical reasoning really possible? Are not our moral values merely matters of personal choice? Are they not relative to our culture? Can there be objective answers to ethical questions? If so, how do we decide such questions?

In this book we will deal with these basic philosophical questions in the practical context of educational administration. We have a number of objectives in doing so. First, we want to persuade you that objective ethical reasoning is both possible and important for educational administrators. Ethical decisions are not just matters of personal preference. Deciding how to place children, given two teachers of differing ability, is not a matter of taste, like deciding whether to have ice cream or chocolate cake.

Instead, we will show you that it is possible to make ethical decisions based on good reasons that others can accept even if such decisions go against their preferences.

In saying that objective ethical reasoning is possible, however, we do not mean to claim that there is always one right answer to every moral dilemma. Ethical situations often require that hard choices be made under complex and ambiguous circumstances. It is difficult to be sure that we have made a good decision. At the same time, one choice is often better than another. In the case above, for example, Ms. Russel believes that it is morally better to assign children to classes fairly, rather than to concede to parents the right of choice. We agree with her. We also believe that it is possible to give reasons for our choices, to decide objectively on the basis of these reasons, and to persuade others who are willing to judge our evidence fairly that our views are correct. If we are open-minded and reasonable people, we must also grant that sometimes we will be persuaded to change our own minds. Moral reasoning has a moral point, and it can help us to make better and more justified moral decisions if we see the moral point. Ms. Russel seems to sense the importance of morally justifying her acts. At least her comment that "it just wasn't fair" suggests that she does. But "it just wasn't fair" is not much of a justification. As a professional, she needs to be able to specify what being fair means in this context, and she needs to be able to articulate her reasons to others.

Therefore, another of our major purposes in this book is to help you learn how to engage in ethical reflection and justification. Not that you do not already know how. After all, people engage in ethical reflection all the time. But we do think that we can help you to do it better. Part of our task will be to sensitize you to the kinds of moral issues that arise in the normal activities of administrative life. That is one of the reasons we will use cases extensively in this book. We also believe that we can help you to state some ethical principles and arguments more clearly and bring them to bear on your own decisions where principles conflict in actual situations. As a consequence, we expect that you will be a better administrator.

THE NATURE OF ETHICAL INQUIRY

What makes Ms. Russel's administrative problem a *moral* dilemma? We are going to talk about the characteristics of moral issues in more detail in the next chapter, but let us make a start here. Ms. Russel's dilemma has the following characteristics. First, it concerns what is the *right* thing to do, not just the most expedient or least trouble making, but the *fair* or *just* thing. Moral issues are usually characterized by certain kinds of language. Words such as *right*, *ought*, *just*, and *fair* are common. Moral issues concern our duties and obligations to one another, what constitutes just or fair treatment of one another, and what rights we each have.

Second, Ms. Russel's dilemma cannot be settled by the facts. Facts are relevant in deciding moral questions, but they are not sufficient in deciding them. Ms. Russel knows what the consequences of her choices will be. She knows that if she fulfills parental assignment requests, those children who have less aggressive parents or who are less academically able will end up with the poorer teacher. But that does not solve her moral problem. It does not tell her what is a fair way to assign students to teachers. Nor does it tell her what rights parents should have in the education of their children. The facts here are insufficient to allow her to decide. She also needs to bring some moral principles—principles about fairness and rights—to bear on her decision.

Finally, Ms. Russel finds herself in a moral dilemma because her moral sentiments conflict. This is a typical characteristic. She has appealed intuitively to two moral principles at the same time, although she has not stated either with much clarity. On one hand, she has appealed to a principle of fairness. It is not fair for the weakest students to have the poorest teacher. On the other hand, she has recognized the principle of parents' rights. Parents do have a right to a say about the education of their children. Even without further clarification of these principles, given the facts of the case, it is apparent that they conflict. To resolve her dilemma, Ms. Russel needs to be clearer about these two principles and how they are justified. She also would have to have some idea about the priorities of such principles when they conflict.

These characteristics of Ms. Russel's dilemma suggest some of the general features of ethical reasoning. One part of ethical reasoning is the application of principles to cases. Applying moral principles to cases requires expressing and clarifying the principles and finding out the relevant facts about the cases. For example, the principle of fairness to which Ms. Russel is appealing might be based on the idea of equality of educational opportunity. This would mean that the educational resources made available to children should not depend on such irrelevant characteristics as family background, race, or socioeconomic class. Once we understand the facts of the case, however, we find that these would be the deciding characteristics if Ms. Russel granted parental requests for the assignment of their children to teachers. Middle-class children would end up with the better teachers.

In order to perform this task of aptly applying principles to facts, we may also have to inquire into the justification of the principle. This is another aspect of ethical reasoning. Why should we accept the principle of equality of educational opportunity? What purposes does it serve? We may not be able to understand the exact nature of its application until we have a clear idea of its point and rationale.

Often, in thinking about these questions, we are led to ask further questions of a different and more complex sort. How should we decide between conflicting ethical principles? How in general do we justify ethical principles? What is the nature of moral evidence? How do we distinguish moral from nonmoral claims? And can we construct a general ethical theory that orders our ethical principles under some general view of the Good Life?

The differences among these ethical questions are not sharp. They seem easily to lead into one another. Nevertheless, they do seem to differ in roughly the following way. One set of questions (i.e., how to apply the principle of equal opportunity) seems directly concerned with what we ought to do in a specific situation. We want to know how we should act and why we should act that way, here and now, in these circumstances. The concern is for the morally correct choice and its justification in a specific context. The next set of questions (i.e., how to resolve conflicts between ethical principles) seems to be more general. They are about our process of moral reasoning itself. Here we need to describe our process of justification and to understand how it is possible for us to engage in productive ethical reflection in any situation. We are not so much concerned with the justification of particular actions as with the justification of our moral principles and our ethical theories. We seek to locate our particular moral principles in a general view of the moral life that orders our principles and tells us how to decide when they conflict.

Philosophers often mark the difference between these concerns by calling the first set *ethical* questions and the second set *meta-ethical* questions. We are not going to use those terms after this chapter, but the two sorts of questions are reflected in the structure of this book. In each of the next five chapters you will find four sections, two dealing with ethical issues and two with meta-ethical issues. First there will be a "Case" that, like the case of Ms. Russel in this chapter, sets up the ethical dilemma. Next there will be an imaginary "Dispute" that lays out some of the ethical issues in the case in an intuitive way. Disputes will be similar to the kinds of discussions that occur in a dorm room or in a teachers' lounge when people sense something is morally amiss and argue over what is ethically problematic. Next will come a discussion of the particular ethical "concepts" that are important to thinking about the meta-ethical issues of the case. In these discussions, we will explore the meaning and justification of such principles as liberty, equality, and due process. Finally, in a section headed "Analysis," will come a meta-ethical discussion of the general features of moral reasoning and moral theories. Each chapter ends with some additional cases and questions for your further reflection on the major concepts treated in the chapter.

LEARNING MORAL REASONING

We have adopted this organization because of our convictions about how people can learn moral reasoning. We use cases because part of the process of moral reflection is learning how to apply principles to real problems. Part of learning to think is learning to see the world through useful concepts. We employ disputes because we believe that your intuitive moral reactions, your feelings about what is right and wrong, and your initial attempts to describe the principles that underlie your feelings are an important initial source of moral data. Much of ethical reasoning is an attempt to state and test systematically and accurately the principles that underlie one's "gut" reactions. In the section called "Concepts," we will discuss such educationally important concepts as intellectual and personal liberty, equality, due process, and democracy. What do they mean? Why should we accept them as principles to guide ethical decision making? These discussions get at the substance of ethical reasoning but also raise some meta-ethical issues. Finally, in the section titled "Analysis," we will raise a number of other meta-ethical issues. These issues are important for understanding how ethical reasoning progresses. We raise them because it has been our experience as teachers of professional ethics that it is impossible to get very far with a discussion of an ethical question before these issues become important. In our classrooms, questions such as "Isn't that just your personal opinion?" or "Aren't you trying to impose your values on us?" occur during the first hour. (They are probably thought of during the first minute.) If we are to help people think constructively about ethical issues, we will have to help them think about such meta-ethical issues as well.

Ultimately, then, the purpose of this book is to help administrators and prospective administrators think through some of the ethical problems they encounter in doing their jobs so that they may become more responsible and ethical as administrators. Our focus will be on some major concepts used by administrators in ethical reasoning and on the process of ethical reflection itself. Human beings are moral agents. They are responsible for their choices, and they have a duty to make choices in a morally responsible way. Thus it is crucial that people be able to reflect ethically on their choices and their actions. This is especially important when individuals have power and influence over the lives of others. We can think of few areas where it is more important than in the administration of schools.

CHAPTER 2

Intellectual Liberty

A CASE

Paul Robinson, principal of Sutton High, was sitting in a chair in the superintendent's office, but he knew he was really on the carpet. Dr. Higgins was holding a copy of the morning paper. The paper was conspicuously folded to reveal the "Letters to the Editor" section. As Paul knew from his own inspection of the paper at breakfast, the phantom letter writer had struck again.

At least today he wished Eliza Fitzgerald was a phantom. But she was all too real. She had a busy pen, which she frequently employed to inform the good citizens of the district of the alleged foibles of the administrators and teachers of their local schools. Last year it had been the athletic program. Student athletes, in her view, received easy grades to keep them eligible. The year before it had been the English program in the middle school. Why, oh why, she had wondered, did she continue to have to correct the writing of the newly arrived freshmen? If only the middle school teachers were as competent as she.

Needless to say, she was not an especially popular figure at the middle school. Perhaps her comments were resented because they were usually true. Ms. Fitzgerald was not only the district's most noteworthy character, she was also its foremost English teacher. Numbered among her students were several newspaper editors and an award-winning novelist. Students returning to class reunions spent a great deal of time rehearsing Fitzgerald stories. She was a legend of sorts. Students wore her dressing-downs and her D- grades like purple hearts. They were proud of the sarcasm and abuse she had heaped on their sentence fragments and mangled paragraphs. And they knew she cared for them.

This year she had elected to go after big fish. The district was in the process of negotiating a new contract. Negotiations were at a crucial and sensitive phase. Moreover, the relations between administrators and teachers had become strained. The teachers had initiated a job action and were "working to rule"—doing the minimum their contract required. Administrators had responded by tightening up on the rules teachers worked to. Teachers had to show up on time and dared not leave early. Lesson plans were checked carefully and were frequently returned for correction. The air was filled with technicalities and litigiousness.

Ms. Fitzgerald was distraught about the effect this tense atmosphere was having on the education of "her" students and on the welfare of "her" school. Her response was a literary hand grenade to the local paper that scattered verbal shrapnel at everyone in sight. She had devoted special attention to Dr. Higgins and the union representative, Mr. Twist, comparing one to Shylock and the other to Silas Marner. For those who missed the literary allusions, she had left little doubt that she believed that the love of money was the root of a great evil in the district. Teachers and administrators had sold their birthright as educators to squabble over a mess of pottage.

Dr. Higgins might have triumphed over the allusion to Shylock. Indeed, it seemed that he had only a vague notion of who Shylock was. But he cared greatly for the success of the negotiations, and he was most apprehensive about the possibility that Ms. Fitzgerald's letter would make them more difficult. Moreover, Ms. Fitzgerald had weakened her case in Dr. Higgins's eyes by allowing a widespread rumor about the negotiations to creep into her letter. She had helped spread the idea that the district was insisting on a merit-pay provision in the contract. Dr. Higgins had, of course, talked about merit pay to some community groups. Indeed, this was a ploy on his part to secure a higher level of cooperation from the union. But, in fact, the district had made no such proposal to the union. Thus, Ms. Fitzgerald had allowed an error to spoil her legendary reputation for getting it right. Dr. Higgins was livid.

He had a simple suggestion. Paul Robinson was to tell Ms. Fitzgerald to shut up. Any further letters on the topic would be regarded by the district as insubordination, and Ms. Fitzgerald would be dealt with accordingly.

Paul had grave reservations about saying this to Ms. Fitzgerald. It would only make her worse, and he had considerable doubt as to who would end up dealing with whom. It did not pay to underrate Ms. Fitzgerald. Moreover, Paul had vague recollections from his undergraduate days that notions such as free speech and a free press were important in our society. He wondered if the attorney whom the district kept on retainer had earned his fee lately. But Dr. Higgins was not in a mood to be reasonable. He wanted Ms. Fitzgerald silenced and was not taking "no" for an answer. Thus, Paul lifted himself from Dr. Higgins's carpet and started back to his office to call Ms. Fitzgerald onto his. He had few illusions about his ability to keep her there.

DISPUTE

A:　People have a right, a basic right, to speak their piece no matter what. That is what freedom of speech means in our society.

B:　No, it doesn't. You can't publicly say false and malicious things about people. That's libel. And in the United States, you can't preach violent overthrow of the government. That's sedition. Even in a democratic society, there have to be some constraints on free speech.

A:　Oh, I don't mean those things; I mean freedom to state your opinion even if it is disagreeable to those in authority.

B:　But what if your opinion is wrong and contains falsehoods or is just plain stupid?

A:　As judged by whom? That's the whole point. Opinions and ideas can't be censored or suppressed in a free society. There has to be the presumption that the truth will win out only if there is free competition among ideas.

B:　That sounds great in theory, but what if your personal opinion is harmful to the welfare of others?

A:　How can opinions hurt people? That's ridiculous!

B:　No, it isn't. Suppose you are someone in authority, a policeman or a teacher, say. Suppose, in your opinion, people from a certain ethnic group are stupid, crafty, and dishonest. Don't tell me you wouldn't treat them differently!

A:　Sure, you might, but just saying they are "stupid, crafty, and dishonest" isn't harmful. It is only harmful when you act on your beliefs. It is important to see that we are talking about free speech, not about actions. Acts can be harmful, not words.

B:　I'm not sure that just saying things like that about people isn't harmful. If I were the police commissioner or the superintendent of schools, I'd make a rule against the use of derogatory language regarding any ethnic group by my staff, wouldn't you?

A:　No. There can never be a good reason to constrain free speech.

B:　Then what about libel and sedition?

CONCEPT: FREEDOM OF EXPRESSION

Dr. Higgins and Paul Robinson are about to challenge Ms. Fitzgerald's right to express her views about school district matters to the public. Dr. Higgins believes he has good reason to do this, that it is necessary in order to permit the negotiations between the district and the union to go smoothly. He is doing it for the good of the district. The sooner the negotiations are settled, the sooner everyone can get back to running the schools and teaching students. Everyone will be better off.

Will everyone be better off? Is this a sufficient reason to threaten Ms. Fitzgerald with disciplinary action should she write another letter? The issue is one of intellectual freedom. In a free society people are supposed to be free to hold their own opinions and to express them. But why should this be their right, and what are the limits on a person's right to express his or her views?

At the outset, it is important to distinguish between the right to hold an opinion and the right to express it. Generally, we may assume that the right to believe what one wants is absolute. No one has a right to tell us what we may believe. Part of the reason for this is that beliefs do not have consequences for people, other than those who hold them, so long as they are not expressed or acted upon. But to say or to write something is to act. So actions based on our beliefs may have consequences for the welfare of others. Thus the freedom to act on our opinions and beliefs cannot be absolute. We must inquire into its limits.

Note that in these comments we have already made some important ethical assumptions. We have assumed that people have a right to be the authors of their own beliefs. Why assume this? And we have assumed that a person's actions can be regulated only when they injure the welfare of others. Is this correct, and why should we believe it?

It does seem that the harmfulness of some speech acts can be a reason for limiting freedom of expression. Supreme Court Justice Oliver Wendell Holmes wrote that the right to free speech does not give one the right to yell "fire!" in a crowded theater. It seems reasonable, then, that if the immediate consequence of some expression of opinion is that the lives and property of others will be endangered, then that is a good reason to forbid it.

On the other hand, the view that the expression of ideas can be restricted because some harm might result seems quite dangerous to the values of free speech and a free press. Often people believe that the views of those who disagree with them are dangerous and harmful. Indeed, some ideas *are* dangerous and harmful. For example, the belief that the members of some races or religions are inherently inferior has been and continues to be a cause of much human suffering. But if we are willing to repress ideas simply because they are potentially harmful, we will do great violence to freedom of expression. Politicians often believe that the views of their opponents are dangerous and harmful. If potential harm or danger is allowed as a good reason for repressing speech, free and open debate about matters of public policy will soon disappear. Indeed, if Dr. Higgins's opinion that Ms. Fitzgerald's letter will harm negotiations were to count as a good reason for suppressing her right to express her views on matters of educational policy, then we would not need to inquire further to decide the issue raised in the case. It is true that Ms. Fitzgerald has endangered sensitive negotiations. Her letter may perpetuate the unpleasant tensions in the schools and damage the educational process. What more do we need to know?

We hope you will agree that we do need to know more. The fact that an idea is harmful or that someone believes that it is harmful is not a sufficient reason to forbid its expression. If we believe otherwise, we will end up eliminating free discussion about very many issues, especially those that are most important.

Why should we so value free expression? What is its point and justification? To address these questions, we should consider some classical arguments for freedom found in John Stuart Mill's essay, "On Liberty."

First, if any opinion is compelled to silence, that opinion may, for aught we can certainly know, be true. To deny this is to assume our own infallibility.

Secondly, though the silenced opinion may be an error, it may and very often does, contain a portion of the truth; and since the general or prevailing opinion on any subject is rarely or never the whole truth, it is only by the collision of adverse opinions that the remainder of the truth has any chance of being supplied.

Thirdly, even if the received opinion be not only true, but the whole truth, unless it is suffered to be, and actually is rigorously and earnestly contested, it will, by most of those who receive it, be held in the manner of a prejudice, with little comprehension of its rational grounds. And not only this, but fourthly, the meaning of the doctrine itself will be in danger of becoming lost or enfeebled, and deprived of its virtual effect on the character and conduct; the dogma becoming a mere formal profession, inefficacious for good, but cumbering the ground and preventing the growth of any real and heartfelt conviction from reason and personal experience. (Mill, 1859/1956, p. 64)

Here Mill provides us with some of the more powerful arguments for free expression. Free expression is a condition of inquiry and the discovery of the truth. We can never refine or improve our ideas if we do not permit them to be challenged. Ideas are tested in debate. Truth is best sought by a process of criticism and debate. Not only that, but if our ideas are not contested we soon lose sight of why we held them and, eventually, of their full meaning. Untested ideas degenerate into platitudes and clichés and cease to affect action.

We might consider the case of Ms. Fitzgerald in the light of Mill's arguments. Educational policy in our society is made democratically. Members of school boards and state legislators, those who make most educational policy, are elected. How are voters to vote intelligently about matters of educational policy without information? And how can they refine their thinking about matters of educational policy unless educational issues are debated? Moreover, who is better placed to inform the public about educational issues than teachers? One might argue, then, that Ms. Fitzgerald has performed a public service by informing the public of her views on a matter of interest to them. She has generated debate and discussion on an important matter. Will not the public be better informed and have a more reasonable view of the issues on her account? Ms. Fitzgerald is simply exemplifying the process of free and open debate that Mill so ably argues for, with the results that Mill anticipated.

One reason for protecting the right of free expression, then, is because criticism and debate are conditions of rationality itself. The public store of tested ideas is enlarged, and rational public decision making is improved. We cannot make competent decisions without free expression.

A second reason for valuing freedom is that it promotes personal growth. Here, too, Mill speaks eloquently.

> He who lets the world, or his own portion of it, choose his plan of life for him has no need of any other faculty than the ape-like one of imitation. He who chooses his plan for himself employs all his faculties. He must use observation to see, reasoning and judgment to foresee, activity to gather materials for decision, firmness and self-control to hold to his deliberate decision. And these qualities he requires and exercises exactly in proportion as the part of his conduct which he determines according to judgment and feeling is a large one. (Mill, 1859/1956, pp. 71–72)

Personal growth requires freedom. Participation in the processes of reflection, argument, and deliberation that go into the evaluation of ideas not only improves the ideas, it also enhances the intellectual competence of the participants. Thus, Ms. Fitzgerald not only has informed the public about an important issue, but by stirring up a debate she has contributed to the growth and competence of the participants. Perhaps Dr. Higgins does not now feel greatly improved by Ms. Fitzgerald's letter. But on another day, when the dust has settled, he may be willing to admit that she helped him see how his actions affected students and made him a better superintendent as a consequence.

Freedom of expression thus contributes to the refining of ideas, to competent decision making, and to personal growth. Are these reasons why we should value free expression? It seems self-evident that better ideas, competent decision making, and personal growth are valuable. Nevertheless, our grasp of the reasons for free expression may be enhanced by further exploring the reasons undergirding these values. Let us ask, then, why we should value better ideas, competent decision making, and growth.

One response is that we should value these things because they contribute to the overall welfare of society and its members. If the capacity of society or of individuals to evaluate ideas, make better decisions, and grow is enhanced, we will all be better off. People will make more sensible decisions. More people will get more of what they want. We will all be happier as a result. Thus free speech and a free press are ultimately of value because they contribute to human welfare and human happiness.

Another sort of response is possible. Here the ultimate value to be realized is not happiness, but the realization of individual moral agency. Human beings are free moral agents. This means not only that they are able to make decisions about themselves, but also that they have the responsibility to do so. When people are responsible for their choices, they have a duty to make their choices wisely.

Now, if I have a duty as a moral agent to make responsible choices, I also have an interest in the availability of the resources that will enable me to choose wisely. Other human beings, as moral agents, also have this interest. Insofar as we are obligated to respect one another's status as moral agents, this is an interest that we each must respect. This means that I and others have a right to necessary information. It may also mean that I have a right to expect that I can freely discuss ideas with others or benefit from the discussions and debates of others. If I am to make competent choices, I will need the best ideas and information I can obtain. If free speech, a free press, and freedom of information are important in making ideas available to me, then, as a moral agent, I have a right to these things. Finally, as a moral agent, I have a right to the conditions that make it possible for me to evaluate and choose between competing ideas. One of these conditions is the free and open debate of ideas. Another is an education that teaches such evaluative skills.

From the perspective of this argument, we may wish to claim that Ms. Fitzgerald has done a service to the voters of her district, who are eventually to be faced with the need to make a responsible choice as to whom they will support in school board elections or as to what policies they will advocate. She has helped them to be more responsible in fulfilling their civic duties.

Both of these arguments make a strong case for such institutions as free speech, a free press, and freedom of information. The first argument emphasizes the social utility of these institutions. The second emphasizes their importance to the individual faced with the moral requirement to make responsible choices. Ms. Fitzgerald may have served both of these purposes.

Is this a sufficient case for Ms. Fitzgerald? Shall we conclude that she has or should have a right to write her letters to the editor and that it is improper for Dr. Higgins or Paul Robinson to attempt to stop her? At this point such a conclusion would be premature. We must also consider whether there are other rights or interests that conflict with Ms. Fitzgerald's freedom to write her letters.

Dr. Higgins is sure to argue that there is an important right that conflicts with Ms. Fitzgerald's right to take advantage of the free press. There are sensitive negotiations in progress. Ms. Fitzgerald's letter may have an adverse effect on these negotiations. If negotiations break down and teachers strike, would not the students' right to an education suffer? Is this not a sufficient reason to curtail Ms. Fitzgerald's literary excesses? Moreover, her letter contained some factual errors. Does the right of a free press include the right to be wrong? Can Ms. Fitzgerald be allowed to jeopardize the negotiations with her mistakes? We are not going to consider these issues in depth, but we do have two observations on them.

First, we believe that rights, in general, are not absolute. Often they can conflict with other rights or with other important interests. In this case, Ms. Fitzgerald's ideas and her letter may well have adverse consequences for the negotiations, and, if the negotiations are harmed and the tensions between administrators and teachers continue, the children of the district may have their right to an education infringed upon. We must, then, address the question of how to balance the right of intellectual freedom against other rights and interests.

Second, however, we must also insist that intellectual freedom is a most important right in our society. We have already stated the basic arguments for it. It serves important considerations of social utility and individual responsibility. Thus, if there are other considerations that may be balanced against it and that are sufficiently weighty to tip the scales against free speech or a free press, they must be very weighty indeed. Are there such weighty considerations in favor of suppressing Ms. Fitzgerald?

ANALYSIS: ETHICAL DECISION MAKING

What do educational administrators do? How would one characterize their role? Obviously there is no one answer to these questions. Administrators are decision makers. They are leaders. They are organizers. They facilitate the work of faculty. They make up budgets, hire and evaluate teachers, and allocate resources. They deal with students, parents, and school boards.

Many, perhaps all, of these administrative tasks involve an ethical component. If the administrator is a leader or a decision maker, questions arise as to whether decisions are made fairly or democratically. If administrators allocate resources, they must do so justly and equitably. If they evaluate teachers, they must do so fairly and humanely. If they discipline students, their punishments must be just. Note the words: *just, fair, equitable, humane.* Ethics seems to be part of the job. Administrators who are seen as unfair, unjust, inhumane, or capricious in their decisions usually buy themselves a great deal of trouble in their jobs. Indeed, it has been our experience that administrators are just as likely to fail because they are seen as unjust as they are to fail because they are seen as inefficient. The administrator who is unfair will soon be faced with a hostile faculty and an angry community. Ethics is part of the job. Indeed, it is an essential part of the job. Administrators deal with fairness, equality, justice, and democracy as much as they deal with test scores, teachers' salaries, parents, and budgets.

If this is so, then it is surprising that few universities offer courses on administrative ethics. If ethics is part of the job, why is ethical decision making not a part of the training of school administrators? One response to this question might be that administration is a science and so should not deal with values. As for decision making, the best guide to our actions, so the argument goes, is well-confirmed scientific research that connects actions with their consequences. Boards and the public determine ends, educators the means to achieve the desired ends. It is science that tells us what decisions and actions will bring about policies and goals deemed by others to be desirable. This seems to be the view of administration that is assumed in many of the leading textbooks.

Perhaps so. Yet the science of administration, if there is one, still seems insufficient. It is not clear that any amount of scientific inquiry can tell us whether an evaluation is fair, whether a decision is democratic, or whether some allocation of resources is equitable. Indeed, sometimes we can know what the consequences of our actions will be but not know if the action itself is right. A moral residue seems to be left. We need to make moral as well as management judgments.

But moral judgments are value judgments! How can we learn *how* to make them correctly? Often the phrase "that's a value judgment" is used to halt conversations. It appears to mean that the matter in question is something about which there is no right or wrong answer. It is all just a matter of opinion. It depends on our tastes or our feelings. Thus there is no point in talking about it further. No rational resolution of value issues is possible.

If this were true, it would explain why ethics is not a part of the study of administration. There is nothing to study; that is, there is no relevant body of knowledge. There is only how people happen to feel or what they happen to believe is right or wrong. There is nothing to be learned and known. We might, of course, scientifically study what people believe about what is right or wrong, and this might help us deal with them more successfully, but there is no method of inquiry suitable for determining whether any ethical view or decision really is correct.

Is this true? One of the purposes of this book is to persuade you that it is not. Part of the problem, we think, is the sloppy use of such phrases as "value judgments." We think that moral claims are not value judgments in the sense of being only personal or group preferences. But that is a topic for the next chapter. Here we should note that in the "Concepts" section of this chapter we seemed perfectly capable of producing objectively compelling reasons for moral claims. We argued that as moral agents and in order to promote social well-being, people ought to have a right to intellectual liberty. If you accept that basic argument, then it follows that people are entitled to their own opinions and beliefs and that they are entitled to express them or publish them. Free speech and a free press promote the public welfare and individual responsibility. We also suggested that these rights might need to be balanced against other rights and interests.

All of these claims are moral claims. Moreover, we gave arguments for them. Perhaps you were not persuaded by everything we had to say, but we are willing to bet that it did not seem to you that there was something strange or wrong about the very fact that we were trying to argue for moral claims rather than merely express our preferences or our beliefs. In the real world, when we are not doing philosophical exercises, we all manage to have cogent moral discussions all the time. We give and listen to arguments about what is right or wrong with no suspicion that such matters are simply "value judgments" and thus merely matters of taste.

This suggests a strategy. We propose a working hypothesis, to be tested in the remainder of the book: namely, that moral arguments and moral discussions have a valid function in our lives and in our institutions. That is, we tentatively assert that sometimes it is possible to decide, as a result of hearing arguments and weighing evidence, that some actions are right and others wrong. In other cases that are, perhaps, not so clear, it is still possible to decide that some choices are morally preferable to others. If we accept this working hypothesis that moral discourse has a valid function in reaching ethical decisions, then we can focus on the question of how it is that we can and do successfully discuss moral matters with one another. If we can give a plausible account of how we actually proceed to have meaningful moral discussions, perhaps we will not have to have our conversations stopped by "that's a value judgment."

Let us look more closely at our discussion about Ms. Fitzgerald's right of free expression. How did we argue for that right? We did so by appealing to two different moral principles. On the one hand, we appealed to the good of the public interest. We argued that free expression helps people to make better decisions and that, as a consequence, all people are better off. Second, we appealed to the moral principle of individual responsibility. We said that since people are moral agents and responsible for their choices, they have a right to expect that those condi-

tions that provide for the opportunity of responsible choice will be ful-
filled. And we said that the right to information was one such condition.
These arguments, in turn, presuppose two even more fundamental moral
conceptions. They are *the principle of benefit maximization* and *the principle
of equal respect for persons.*

The Principle of Benefit Maximization

The principle of benefit maximization holds that, whenever we are
faced with a choice, the best and most just decision is the one that results
in the most good or the greatest benefit for the most people. Thus the
principle of benefit maximization judges the morality of our actions by
their consequences. It says that the best action is the one with the best
overall results. It does not directly tell us what is to count as a benefit or
a good. That requires additional reflection. It merely says that once we
know what is good, the best decision is the one that maximizes good outcomes. If, for example, the production of happiness is thought to be a basic
good, then the principle of benefit maximization indicates that we should
make those decisions and engage in those actions that result in the greatest
happiness for the greatest number. You may have heard this version of the
principle of benefit maximization referred to as "utilitarianism."

The Principle of Equal Respect

The principle of equal respect requires that we act in ways that respect the equal worth of moral agents. It requires that we regard human
beings as having intrinsic worth and treat them accordingly. The essence
of this idea is expressed in the Golden Rule. We have a duty to accord others the same kind of treatment we expect them to accord us. The principle
of equal respect can be seen as involving three subsidiary ideas.

First, the principle of equal respect requires us to treat people as *ends*
rather than *means.* This means that we may not treat them as though they
were simply means to further our own goals. We must respect their goals
as well. We cannot treat people as though they were things, mere objects,
who are valued only insofar as they contribute to our welfare. We must
consider their welfare as well. People cannot be treated as though they
were nothing more than instruments to serve our purposes.

Second, when we are considering what it means to treat people as
ends rather than means, we must regard as central the fact that persons *are
free and rational moral agents.* This means that, above all, we must respect
their freedom of choice. And we must respect the choices people make
even when we do not agree with them. Moreover, it means that we must
attach a high priority to enabling people to decide responsibly. It is impor-

tant that people have the information and the education that will enable them to function responsibly as free moral agents.

Third, no matter how people differ, as moral agents they are of *equal value*. This does not mean that we must see people as equal insofar as their abilities or capacities are concerned. Nor does it mean that relevant differences among people cannot be recognized in deciding how to treat them. It is not, for example, a violation of equal respect to pay one person more than another because that person works harder and contributes more. That people are of equal value as moral agents means that they are entitled to the same basic rights and that their interests are of equal value. Everyone, regardless of native ability, is entitled to equal opportunity. Everyone is entitled to one vote in a democratic election, and every vote should be worth the same as every other vote. No one is entitled to act as though his or her happiness counted for more than the happiness of others. As persons, everyone has equal worth.

CONCLUSION

We want you to notice a few important things about the principles of benefit maximization and equal respect. First, we suspect that both principles (in some form) are part of the moral concepts of everyone who is reading this book. These are the sorts of fundamental moral principles that everyone appeals to at some time or another in making moral arguments. We may have formulated them in a way new to you, but the ideas themselves will be familiar. They form part of our common ethical understandings. We appealed to both principles in arguing about freedom of expression. We held that free expression results in more knowledgeable and more competent decisions and that such decisions make everyone better off. This argument appeals to the principle of benefit maximization. We also argued that, as responsible moral agents, people are entitled to the resources that help them to make more competent decisions. This appeals to the principle of equal respect. Both principles were involved in the argument. One, the other, or both seem to appear in most moral arguments. They are part of our everyday ethical thinking.

Second, both principles seem dependent upon each other. Neither is sufficient by itself. The principle of equal respect requires us to value the welfare of other people; that is, we must value their well-being equally to our own and equally to that of others. But to value the welfare of ourselves and of others is to be concerned with benefits. Indeed, it is to be concerned with maximizing benefits. We will want people to be as well off as possible.

Conversely, the principle of benefit maximization seems to presuppose the principle of equal respect. Why, after all, must we value the welfare of others? Why not insist that only our happiness counts, or that our happiness is more important than the happiness of others? Answers to these questions will quickly lead us to affirm that people are of equal worth and that, as a consequence, everyone's happiness is to be valued equally. Thus, our two principles seem intertwined.

Third, however, the principles may also conflict. There are times when it appears that if we are to follow the logic of the principle of benefit maximization, we must violate the principle of equal respect and vice versa. Suppose, for example, that Dr. Higgins is right in that further letters from Ms. Fitzgerald will, in fact, destroy the negotiations and harm the education of the children of the district. The principle of benefit maximization, then, may lead us to the conclusion that Ms. Fitzgerald should be silenced for the good of all. If we are to respect her as a person, however, we must respect her right to express her views even if she might harm the negotiations. To hold otherwise would be to treat her as though she were only a means to the end of the welfare of others.

So even if we are obligated to give each principle its due, sometimes we must decide which is to take precedence. To do that we need to see not only how they are related to each other, but also how they differ. One of the differences between the principle of benefit maximization and the principle of equal respect is the regard they have for the consequences. For the principle of benefit maximization, all that matters is consequences. The sole relevant factor in choosing between courses of action is to decide which action has the best result. But for the principle of equal respect, consequences are not always decisive. What is decisive is that our actions respect the dignity and worth of the individuals involved. We are required to respect people's rights even if in doing so we choose a course that produces less benefit than some other possible action. Thus the crucial question that usually characterizes a conflict between the principle of benefit maximization and the principle of equal respect is this: When is it permissible to violate a person's rights in order to produce a better outcome?

Often philosophers call ethical views that are dominated by the principle of benefit maximization *consequentialist* theories. Such theories rely solely on consequences to judge the morality of an action. By contrast, for *nonconsequentialist* theories, consequences are not decisive. Nonconsequentialists are not oblivious to consequences. However, the crucial thing that makes an action a moral action for the nonconsequentialist who takes as basic the principle of equal respect is that the action taken gives first consideration to the value and dignity of persons. Sometimes this will lead a nonconsequentialist to prefer an action that respects a person's rights over an action that produces the best consequences.

In subsequent chapters, we will show you how consequentialists and nonconsequentialists might reason about the various ethical issues in administration that we shall deal with. We believe that the tension between these two views is a common feature in the kinds of ethical dilemmas administrators face. We also believe that understanding them will help you become a better diagnostician of moral dilemmas and a better ethical decision maker.

ADDITIONAL CASES

Equal Time?

It had seemed like a good idea at the time. Now Dr. Sam Turner wasn't so sure. He had to admit that Mr. Foster of ESTA had a point. Maybe the board of education brochure had been a political statement. But he didn't see why the school district had to provide Foster's antitax group with "equal time" when doing so could very well send the budget vote down in defeat. Why should he assist a group opposed to badly needed improvements in East Salem's schools? As he saw it, his job as the district's superintendent was to improve the education of kids, not make it worse.

This latest town-gown flap, like so many others in East Salem, involved money. The district was a relatively poor one, a condition made worse by recent cuts in state funds. It had to struggle to provide a quality education to its students. Part of that struggle involved convincing district taxpayers that their already high tax rate should be made even higher. If the schools were going to provide a decent computer education program, if they were going to give teachers a much deserved raise, and if they were going to initiate the new math curriculum, money would be required. Sam Turner had worked hard to convince a skeptical board of education that it should propose a 14% tax increase to district voters to cover the costs of these items, as well as to cover the continually rising costs of its regular programs.

The board had gone along with Sam's proposal, though several members were highly dubious of the plan. They pointed out that budget votes in East Salem were always touch and go and seemed to be getting more so. Last year the voters had passed the budget by the slimmest margin yet. Since then, one of the larger manufacturing plants in town had closed. Unemployment was up. It didn't seem like a good time to hit people with a substantial boost in their taxes. One board member thought that they might face a major tax revolt—a revolt that would not only defeat the new initiatives but also make it more difficult to get them approved next year. It might also create serious problems for all future attempts to improve the district's programs. She had pointed out that at present the community's opposition to school improvements and higher taxes was largely unorganized. Asking for 14% might be enough of a catalyst to create a permanent, organized, and powerful opposition. Nevertheless, Sam convinced the board, and the proposed tax increase was announced.

Sam also convinced the board of the need to mount a sustained effort to inform the voters of the wisdom of the increase. As part of that effort, Sam had written a carefully worded brochure describing how the district would use the money and the benefits students would receive as a result. In it he had pointed out, for example, that at present only a very few of the district's pupils had access to a computer and that the new program would give every secondary student a chance to become computer literate—an essential skill in today's world. He had also called attention to the fact that the East Salem salary schedule was the lowest in the region and that the district couldn't expect to attract competent staff at current salaries. The brochure was printed and mailed, at the district's expense, to every voter in town.

Two weeks later Mr. Foster appeared in Sam's office. He was, he said, the president of the newly created East Salem Taxpayers' Association. The association had formed, he explained, to monitor the uses of citizens' tax dollars and to inform community residents of inefficiency, waste, and misuse of their money. Toward that end, the association had prepared a brochure, a copy of which Foster gave to Sam, along with the request that Sam have it printed and mailed to every voter in East Salem—at the district's expense.

Sam was impressed with the association's handiwork. Whoever had written the pamphlet had done a good job. It was well phrased; with a few exceptions the facts were correct, the arguments were cogent, and the rhetoric was very persuasive. It was likely to convince a lot of people. And it was entirely given over to refuting, point by point, Sam's case for raising taxes.

For example, it agreed that East Salem teachers' salaries were less than those in the surrounding districts. However, it also pointed out that the length of their school day was briefer, their school year 5 days shorter, and several of their fringe benefits considerably more generous. When these things were factored in, the pamphlet argued, East Salem's pedagogues were not so badly off.

Moreover, the brochure put considerable stress on the fact that, whatever their salaries relative to colleagues in neighboring districts, compared to the community's residents East Salem's teachers were living high. The average annual income for teachers was almost $36,000, fully $10,000 greater than the average for other residents—and they earned that sum for 10 months' work, not 12. Why, the brochure asked, should teachers live so well at the expense of those who were struggling to stay off welfare? Sam had to admit that regardless of the merits of this comparison, it was likely to have a powerful effect on voters.

The brochure also scoffed at the idea that every student should become computer literate. It pointed out that as computers became common in the workplace, less skill was required by most jobs, not more. It said that by far the most common use of these machines was in supermarkets, where checkout clerks dragged purchases over optical scanners. Today, store clerks didn't even have to know how to operate a cash register, much less program a computer. Computer literacy was just the latest educational fad, and an expensive one to boot. The brochure went on to cite some educational research to the effect that already thousands of computers were gathering dust in school districts around the country. Were East Salem's residents to pay for a similar distinction? Sam wasn't sure, but he suspected that the brochure's writer just might have his or her facts right about all of this.

But Sam was very sure that at least in a few places the facts were wrong. The brochure claimed, for example, that a district administrator had taken a trip (paid for by taxpayers) that had been primarily for pleasure. It also said that one reason that school costs were so high was because the district had allowed teacher-pupil ratios to get much smaller than was standard elsewhere in the state. Finally, it asserted that the school system had lost almost $15,000 in state funds in the previous year because the superintendent had failed to meet a state deadline. Sam knew that he could show that these claims were simply wrong.

Finally, the brochure closed with a ringing call to arms. All taxpayers were invited to attend an open meeting in the high school auditorium to share their concerns, organize to oppose the coming budget vote, and elect a regular slate of officers. (That's real chutzpah, Sam thought; they want to use school facilities to help them oppose good education!)

Whether or not all of the pamphlet's facts were correct, however, Sam knew that printing and mailing it would have a disastrous effect on the upcoming budget vote. It would certainly sway many to vote "no." And given the probable closeness of the vote, it would only have to sway a few. Perhaps worse, publishing it would certainly help make his board member's worst fears come true. The district would have helped establish and legitimize a permanent, organized, and powerful opposition to good education in East Salem. In the future, getting any budget approved, regardless of its merit and austerity, was going to be harder. Sam wasn't at all sure that he had to be a party to that.

Perhaps the best thing to do was to tell Mr. Foster "thanks, but no thanks." The East Salem Taxpayers' Association would have to take care of its own publicity.

Some Questions

1. We have said that in a free society people have a right to express their opinions. Does that entail an obligation on the part of public officials to help them do so? Is Sam Turner obligated to use school funds to help the East Salem Taxpayers' Association?

2. It is often said that the school must remain neutral when political interests are at stake. That is, if it provides one side of an argument, it should also provide the other. Must it also remain neutral when the political interests at stake are educational in nature?
3. Would Dr. Turner be within his rights to demand that the factual errors in the brochure be corrected if he were to consent to publish it? Wouldn't that amount to censorship?
4. Can the right to express an opinion be curtailed when the opinion will harm others? Is that the case here? Suppose for the moment that East Salem will be unable to attract good teachers unless salaries are raised and that as a consequence children will in fact be harmed. Is that fact sufficient grounds for refusing to publish the brochure?
5. What would you do if you were Sam? How would you justify your decision? Is your argument a consequentialist or a nonconsequentialist one?

Two Black Swans

Susan Rossmiller had been taken aback by Steve's question. Steve was one of the brightest kids in her ninth-grade health class, and he often asked penetrating questions. But he had outdone himself on this one. She would have to think carefully about her reply.

The class was studying human sexuality. That was often a touchy subject, and it was especially so in Corinth. The people in the community held fairly conservative views about many subjects, and sex was one of them. Indeed, the introduction of the unit into the health curriculum had raised a small furor: Wasn't it a subject better left to parents? Would it encourage teenage experimentation? In the end, however, the board was convinced that the unit was needed. Figuring importantly in the decision was the fact that the board had a great deal of respect for Miss Rossmiller. She was smart, professional, and sensitive to parents' concerns. She could be counted on to handle the material in an appropriate manner.

Anyway, on this particular morning the subject of sexual abuse had come up. Pupil interest was undoubtedly piqued because of a notorious incident that was even then being tried in the local court as well as the local paper. A good citizen of Corinth stood accused of molesting an 11-year-old girl, and the town was in an uproar. That sort of thing had never occurred in Corinth before. Or at least people didn't talk about it, if it had.

Miss Rossmiller had welcomed the introduction of the topic. She viewed it as presenting an opportunity to educate her students about the subject, to warn them, and to encourage them to report any incidents that they might encounter.

The lesson had been proceeding smoothly when Steve asked his first question: "Is it true, Miss Rossmiller, that sexual relations with children are always bad?"

She hadn't hesitated before replying. "Of course it is. Experts who have studied the problem are unanimous that it is, Steve. Such sex is very often accompanied by assault of the most horrific kind. It's only recently that the problem has been recognized for what it is, a particularly offensive form of child abuse. I think . . ."

Steve interrupted. "I'm sorry, you misunderstood my question. I didn't mean abusive sex, where physical harm occurs. Of course children are hurt by that. Adults are too for that matter. I meant a gentle, loving sex. Isn't it possible that an adult and a young person could fall in love? I mean physical love. And couldn't they have a sexual relationship without the young person being harmed? I'm not talking about very young children. Baby girls. But what about older kids—say 10 or so? And suppose that the young person is a boy? Would that always be bad?"

The usual studious notetaking in Health 9 came to an abrupt halt. Steve had the undivided attention of the entire class. Some were looking at him in a speculative manner. A couple of the pupils tittered, and one boy asked if Steve had anyone in particular in mind. Indeed, Miss Rossmiller made a mental note to speak privately with him. Perhaps his questions weren't entirely academic in origin. This time she hesitated before responding.

"Well," she said, "perhaps such things might be possible. There might be no actual physical harm as a result. But as I said earlier, physical harm is only a part of the story. The psychological harm that results can be devastating to a young person. It often scars them for life and prevents them from entering into a really loving adult relationship with their husband or wife."

"Yes, I can see how that's possible," said Steve. "But again, that wasn't quite what I asked. I asked whether or not sex with a child is always bad. The reading we did and your discussion convinced me that it is most of the time. But is it always?"

This time Miss Rossmiller hesitated even longer. "Well, I don't know if it's always bad. I'm not even sure that you could find out. What would you do? Run a survey of everyone in the world who's ever experienced it? But, as I've said, all the experts agree that it's very harmful, and it's especially harmful to the personal growth and psychological development of children."

"No, of course you couldn't run a survey," Steve responded. "That's silly. You don't have to do that. If you think that something is always true, there's a simpler way to find out if you're wrong. You go out and search for an instance when it isn't true. If you find one, just one, then you know you've been wrong. I remember hearing a teacher in science say that once long ago a person had said that all swans are white. Then another person showed that there was such a thing as black swans. They live in Australia, I think. Anyway, the second person showed that the first was wrong, and he did it by finding one black swan."

Miss Rossmiller leapt at the opportunity. She wanted to end this conversation and get back to the lesson at hand. "That's a very good point, Steve. In fact, that's how scientists often approach their work. They set up a statement—they call it a hypothesis—and then they deliberately go out and try to design an experiment that'll show their hypothesis is wrong. If, after repeated tries, they still can't show the hypothesis is wrong, then they conclude that it must be right. But obviously you can't do that with child abu . . . I mean sex with children. Maybe we should get back to the lesson now."

But Steve wasn't ready to do that. "Well, I don't think that's quite right. I mean about the scientists. I think that if they keep trying to falsify—'falsify,' that's the right word, isn't it?—if they keep trying to falsify a hypothesis and they can't, they can only conclude that the hypothesis probably isn't wrong. They can't conclude that it's right. At least that's what I learned in science. Anyway, that's beside the point. Isn't it true, that if you could find just one case of a child having sex with an adult where no harm resulted, then you could conclude that sex with children isn't always bad?"

By now Miss Rossmiller had the uncomfortable feeling that she was being backed into a corner. Nevertheless, she was a good teacher, and she recognized that it would be undesirable to use her authority to close down the discussion and get back to the lesson she had planned. So with some trepidation she plunged ahead.

"OK, Steve, I'll grant your point. If we could find one such case, then my 'hypothesis' would be shown to be false. But to the best of my knowledge, there are no such cases. So can't we say that I'm probably not wrong? Again, none of the experts in this area have suggested otherwise."

"Well, that sort of depends on what you mean by 'expert,' doesn't it," Steve said. "I remember reading once about some of the Greek philosophers. Aristotle, and those guys. They were pretty smart. I guess you could call them experts. They were also big on morals. They thought everyone should behave according to some very high principles. Some of them were supposed to be really great teachers. Just like you, Miss Rossmiller. Anyway, the point is that a lot of those guys had sex with the young boys who were their students. I don't think they'd have done that if it was always bad for the kids, seeing as how they were such great teachers with such great morals, right?"

"Look, Steve, I don't know much about Greek philosophers, and maybe they did have sex with their students. But that was a long time ago and in a different culture. Maybe the Greeks of those days thought it was okay. But in our culture, today, it's not okay. We think it's harmful."

"But that's my point, Miss Rossmiller. If something is harmful in one culture and not in another, then it's not always harmful. That's one black swan, isn't it?"

"Well, maybe, Steve. But we don't really know what effects those sexual relationships had on those kids. And besides, perhaps the Greeks had a different idea about what counts as harm. They seem to have had peculiar ideas about a lot of things. And now can we get back to . . . "

"That's a good point, Miss Rossmiller. We can't really know if those kids were harmed. It happened so long ago and everything. But I'm not really sure that it's always harmful to children today and by our own standards.

"You know, Miss Rossmiller," Steve went on before she could interrupt, "I've always been impressed by the way you use outside materials, novels and stuff, to help us learn about health. I've often heard you speak of your love of literature. How we can learn more about human nature and human behavior from great writers than we can from psychologists. I remember your talking about how—what's his name, Vonnegut?—could teach us a lot about right and wrong and good and bad. That's right, isn't it? Novelists can teach us about lots of things, even health?"

"Yes, Steve," said Miss Rossmiller, sounding resigned.

"Well, I haven't read any of the really great writers like Vonnegut, Miss Rossmiller, but I did read a novel by a guy named Nabokov. He's supposed to be pretty good, too. The book's called *Lolita*. It was really funny. Anyway, in the book this old guy falls in love with a young girl. Maybe she was 10 or 12. And he has sex with her. Or at least he does when she lets him, which isn't nearly often enough to suit the old codger. And she doesn't suffer any 'psychological damage' But he sure does. He spends all of his time following her around like a sick puppy. Talk about psychological damage! She turns him into a basket case. So, there's a second black swan, one from our own times. Maybe sex with children isn't always bad—or at least it isn't always bad for the children. But then, maybe Nabokov wasn't as good a writer as Vonnegut.

"So anyway, I was thinking, Miss Rossmiller. If having sex with children isn't always harmful, maybe sometimes it's helpful. Maybe some kids would actually benefit from it. If we could find one case where . . ."

That's when the bell rang and Health 9 came to an end. In the general bedlam that characterized the changing of classes at Corinth High, Miss Rossmiller had time to wonder what her class had learned today. And she realized that she might have time, if she hurried, to get a copy of *Lolita* from the library before her students got them all.

Some Questions

1. Miss Rossmiller should wonder. Suppose that many of her students left the room firmly convinced that, at least sometimes, it's not harmful for children to have sex with adults. Is that a permissible outcome for a sex education class? If not, why not?
2. Consider a stronger supposition. Suppose that some students left having learned that children can sometimes exert a powerful control over adults, and not be harmed in the process, by granting them sexual favors. Is that a permissible outcome? If not, how could Miss Rossmiller have prevented it without trampling on Steve's right to express himself and on the free flow of opinions in the marketplace of ideas?
3. We have mentioned John Stuart Mill. Mill advocated the free and critical exchange of ideas as the best route to the truth regarding any matter, an exchange much like the one between Steve and Miss Rossmiller. But Mill certainly wasn't thinking of high school health classes. Are there any restrictions that you would consider appropriate on the free expression of ideas in a classroom? If so, what are they?
4. A truly free marketplace of ideas would be one in which the participants are all equally equipped to evaluate the evidence. Can there be such a marketplace? In particular, can a classroom be one? Was Miss Rossmiller's such a marketplace? What problems may arise if some participants in the marketplace are better equipped than others?
5. If you were an administrator, and a parent complained to you about Miss Rossmiller's handling of this class, what would you do?

The Last Straw?

Bill Flemming was in the second year of his probationary period, with one more to go before a tenure decision would have to be made. Gail Bestor, the principal of Westfield High School, had been wrestling with the decision of whether to extend his contract for that year. Until a couple of days ago, she had been leaning toward doing so, but had not really made up her mind. Then "Mr. O" had settled the matter this morning.

Bestor had thought long and hard about Flemming's renewal. In some ways he was an entirely competent, even excellent, teacher. He certainly had admirable rapport with some kids. Just the day before she had overheard a group in the cafeteria discussing him, and several had argued that he was the best teacher at WHS. What they seemed to like most was his ability to challenge their ideas, to make them think deeply about important social issues, and to see others' points of view. Those were certainly important attributes in a social studies teacher. In addition, he obviously was willing to spend a great deal of time with students. Evelyn Whiting, this year's valedictorian, had told Mrs. Bestor that "Bill" took hours of his own time to talk with her about the merits of various colleges, to explain the intricacies of scholarship applications, and even to visit her home to convince her parents that she should be permitted to go to Harvard, thousands of miles away, instead of the local community college, which they had originally favored. "Bill's been infinitely more helpful than our guidance counselors," she had said.

The problem was that most students at WHS weren't in the same league as Evelyn. At best, the majority managed to get through the school and graduate; by every objective standard, academic matters were not their forte. And Mr. Flemming seemed to have little time or interest in working with anyone who didn't have an IQ over 120. He was clearly at his best with highly talented pupils—ones who could follow the intricacies of his arguments and who were able "to think deeply about important social issues," a goal he had often stressed in conversations with Mrs. Bestor.

It wasn't that he was intolerant of average or poor students. They just seemed to fall by the wayside. Gail Bestor reflected that if WHS were made up of Evelyn Whitings, she would rehire Flemming without a moment's hesitation. But it wasn't. Besides, Flemming had another annoying proclivity. He was quick to see injustices, even where none were intended or existed. He was a champion of students' rights and had had several altercations with his colleagues and the administration over incidents in which he thought a student was being treated unfairly. That, in itself, was fine as far as Gail Bestor was concerned. As principal, she sought to be fair, and if she had not been, she appreciated being told about it—privately, and in a professional manner. It was Flemming's style, however, to be confrontational. This tendency and this morning's incident put the last straw on Mrs. Bestor's indecision.

The incident had its roots in a situation that had begun months ago when Mrs. Bestor had appointed a committee of students and faculty (including Mr. Flemming) to draw up a new Code of Student Conduct. When the committee had brought a draft of the document to her three weeks ago, she had insisted on several changes, over the strenuous objection of Flemming and the student members. Basically, Gail had wanted more administrative discretion in student discipline cases, without having a judicial-like proceeding over relatively minor infractions. Flemming and the students seemed to want something approaching a trial before the state's supreme court before a decision could be made or a punishment meted out. In the discussion over these issues, Flemming's confrontational approach had come to the fore, and he had led the student members into something very close to a challenge of her authority. He had also been inflammatory: At one point he had referred to "dictatorial administrators," among whom he seemed to include Mrs. Bestor. When the meeting had broken up, the only agreement that had been reached was to meet again. Gail thought it best to overlook this outbreak on Flemming's part as she tried to reach a balanced and fair decision about his reappointment.

The next time Mrs. Bestor heard about "dictatorial administrators" was over the airwaves as she had driven to work this morning. "Mr. O.," a disc jockey who catered to the musical tastes and doings of the local adolescents, broadcast his lengthy and very slanted view of WHS's new Code of Conduct and its principal. The story included a brief interview with Flemming, in which he forcefully presented his opinions on the matter.

When Mrs. Bestor arrived at work, she immediately called in the teacher to find out where the announcer had gotten his story. To Flemming's credit, he freely admitted that while enlisting the support of "Mr. O." had been the students' idea, he had encouraged them. He said he wanted to illustrate for the students how public opinion could be mobilized on one side of a political issue. When the disc jockey had called him later to verify the students' story, Flemming also consented to a taped interview, the juicer excerpts of which "Mr. O." had aired this morning.

And that was the last straw. Mrs. Bestor decided then and there that she could do without the services of Bill Flemming next year.

Some Questions

1. Are there any limits on Bill Flemming's right to free speech regarding issues in the Westfield School District as a consequence of his being a teacher in that system? If so, what are they?
2. Some people would argue that Flemming's right to express himself is limited by the requirement that WHS be operated in an orderly and effective manner and that the notoriety resulting from the disk jockey's broadcast is detrimental to meeting that requirement. Is that so? How is it detrimental?
3. Flemming's comments during the committee's meeting with Mrs. Bestor might be said to constitute unprofessional conduct. Just what, if anything, is *unprofessional* about publicly criticizing another educator and, at least implicitly, impugning his or her motives?
4. Does it make any difference to the morality of Mrs. Bestor's decision not to rehire Flemming that she had serious doubts about his teaching competence prior to the "Mr. O." incident? How?
5. What would your decision have been if you were the principal? How would you justify it? How might others argue against it? Is there a right decision in this case?

CHAPTER 3

Individual Freedom and the Public Interest

A CASE

Sam Endicott choked and very nearly dropped the glass of beer into his lap. The young woman on the stage bore a remarkable resemblance to Susan Loring, the ninth-grade English teacher at Dennison Junior High School. The gut-slamming music and disorienting strobe lights must surely be affecting his senses, he thought. The woman was not exactly dressed in Miss Loring's usual, rather severe, English-teacher tweeds. In fact, she was not exactly dressed—unless wearing only a sequined G-string counted as being dressed.

Endicott stared at the undulating dancer. The resemblance was striking, but it just could not be. Miss Loring was by far the best teacher he had ever had in his years as principal of Dennison. Everyone on the staff respected her. She was idolized by her students, especially the girls, who, Sam reflected, were beginning unconsciously to ape her speech and dress—to the immense improvement of their own. While she was certainly beautiful—the entire class of ninth-grade boys had fallen instantly in love with her—she was also the consummate professional. Indeed, she had skillfully turned their adulation to educationally constructive purposes. Her obvious love of the Romantic English poets had proven infectious, and Endicott had recently heard some of the toughest boys in his school quoting Keats. The idea that she could be the star dancer in a topless bar was ludicrous.

Nevertheless, he did recall Susan's telling him that she was finding it impossible to care for her seriously ill mother on her teacher's salary and that she was moonlighting on weekends to supplement her income. He had responded that as long as her outside work did not interfere with her responsibilities at Dennison, he had no objection. Since then, he had noted no evidence of any diminution of her teaching competence. If anything, she had gotten better. Perhaps because the strain of trying to make ends meet had been alleviated, she was now even more involved in her profession.

It was at this point in his musings that the music ended and the dancer disappeared behind a curtain as the lights went up. Whoever the woman was, Sam had to admit, she was talented. Instead of the mindless bump-and-grind routine one might expect in such places, her dance had evidenced a sensuous beauty, a lithe grace that approached artfulness.

Sam glanced around at the other patrons—all unfamiliar men. He was uncomfortably aware that community opinion would not be terribly supportive if word got around that the school principal had been seen in a topless bar. He was glad that he was in Belleville, a neighboring town to Spencertown, his own school district. Spencertown would be outraged if such a bar opened within its own borders. Even so, Sam was sorry he had stopped for a beer on his way home from a countywide administrators' meeting. While he firmly believed that his own and his staff's personal, out-of-school lives were no concern of others, he also recognized that his position as a public school administrator might lead some to think that he should hold a different view.

Endicott sighed, put down his glass, and was preparing to leave when he felt a hand on his shoulder and an unmistakable voice say, "Hi, Mr. Endicott! How did you like my routine?"

He swung around to stare into the smiling face of Susan Loring, still in her costume. His embarrassment was bone-deep. He was embarrassed for her, for himself for being seen there, and most of all for his wretched eyes that refused to remain fixed on Susan's face.

DISPUTE

A: Teachers are special. Like it or not, they serve as role models for impressionable young people, and so they have a special obligation to be good that even doctors and lawyers don't have.

B: What do you mean, "good"?

A: Why, morally good, of course! If a teacher lied to the principal when he or she visited the class, or if a teacher stole supplies from the class next door, the students might think stealing and lying were okay. Teachers have to set a good example.

B: Would being a prostitute be setting a good example?

A: Of course not!

B: But what if a teacher was an amateur prostitute only on weekends and traveled to the city to ply his or her trade and no one in the school district knew about it? You can't set an example if the students don't know what you are doing.

A: It is just a matter of time. Someone would find out and then the students would know. It just isn't right. Such a teacher should be dismissed.

B: But don't teachers, or anybody else for that matter, have a right to
       choose the kind of life they want to lead? What they choose to do
       on their own free time, as long as it doesn't harm anybody, should be
       their own business, not anybody else's—not the principal's, not the
       superintendent's, not the school board's, not the parents'.

A: In public schools, the administration and the board have a respon-
       sibility to the community and to the students. What teachers do on
       or off duty is the administration's business if it might have a negative
       effect on the students.

B: What do you mean, "might have"? Who is to decide that? And what's
       negative? Years ago such things as teachers marrying, going to dances,
       or drinking in public were frowned upon by some communities and
       were even cause for dismissal. Teachers have lives, too. They can't be
       put up on pedestals and hermetically seated off from the adult world
       they also live in. That wouldn't be fair.

A: But nobody forced them to be teachers, and being a teacher requires
       being a very special person, because, like it or not, you are a role
       model for your students.

B: I don't like it! Sure, in the classroom, I would uphold and radiate
       community standards, but what I do with my own private life would
       be my own business.

A: No, as a teacher, it is ultimately the public's business. That's just the
       way it has to be.

CONCEPT: PERSONAL LIBERTY

Is there anything wrong with Miss Loring's working as a topless dancer?
Does her doing so somehow make her unfit to teach? In addressing these
questions, we will focus on the nature of personal liberty, but there are
other issues involved. One of them is gender equity. Because Mr. Endicott
is the principal of Dennison, he has authority over Miss Loring, and he
can focus the question on her behavior. Yet he has discovered her second
profession because he is patronizing a topless bar. As he is uncomfortably
aware, the people of his district might be as unhappy about the fact that he
was patronizing this bar as they would be about Susan Loring performing
in it. Are they right?

   One response to this question is that if is wrong for Miss Loring to
perform in a topless bar, then it is just as wrong for Mr. Endicott to patronize it. Whatever standard is applied to Miss Loring should be applied
to Mr. Endicott as well.

   There are some considerations that might count against this judgment. One might argue that Mr. Endicott should be judged more harshly

than Miss Loring. Like many sex workers, she is a victim, forced to submit to the exploitation of men because she is unable to earn an adequate living in any other way. That teachers may be underpaid because teaching is a female-dominated profession might add to this sense of her exploitation. Sam Endicott, however, is not exploited. He is participating in the exploitation. On the other hand, one might argue that there is a considerable difference in degree of involvement between being an occasional patron of a topless bar and being a topless dancer. Or one might argue that there is a relevant difference between being a teacher and being a principal. This might cut either way. Perhaps principals, because their position is more responsible, should be held to a higher standard. Perhaps teachers, because they have direct contact with students, should be held to a higher standard. Notice the underlying principle. It is the principle of equity we will develop further in the next chapter. People who are similarly situated should be treated in a similar way. This suggests that whatever standard is applied to Susan Loring must also be used to judge Sam Endicott. Yet we have suggested some reasons to ask whether they are similarly situated.

We hope that as you discuss the matter of individual liberty you will also consider the gender-equity questions that are raised. Our primary concern in this chapter, however, is with personal liberty. Does Susan Loring have a right to her second profession, and does Sam Endicott have a right to patronize a topless bar? How shall we think about the question of personal liberty?

First, consider some of the potentially relevant features of the case. It appears that Miss Loring's effectiveness in the classroom is not being impaired. Her students like her and learn from her. Moreover, so far as Mr. Endicott can tell, she does not bring her second profession to school. There is nothing in her dealings with her students that is the least suggestive of sexual permissiveness. It is doubtful that she is influencing the values of her students in a manner that any would consider objectionable. Finally, there is nothing illegal about Miss Loring's second profession.

On the other hand, there is no doubt that her second profession would be regarded as immoral by the majority of the citizens of the Spencerville school district. Most would be shocked by her behavior and would be reluctant to have their children taught by her. Don't their views about the moral character of the people who teach their children count for something? Moreover, it seems quite possible that sooner or later the parents and students of Spencerville will find out about how Miss Loring spends her evenings. While she has been discreet enough to find work outside of the district, someone will surely find his way to the bar in Belleville. On this point Mr. Endicott is exhibit A.

What effect would Miss Loring's second profession have on her students once they knew about it? She is, after all, widely respected by them.

Wouldn't this make her a poor influence? Also, it seems likely, should the news leak out, that visits to her place of employment would be high on some students' agenda. Of course, minors are not permitted in the place, but Mr. Endicott had few illusions about their ability to triumph over this trivial obstacle. Then what? After today's performance, Mr. Endicott would certainly view Miss Loring in an entirely different perspective. He wondered what her students would be thinking about while she taught. He was sure that it would go beyond Keats. How are these facts relevant?

Perhaps we might start with the case for Miss Loring. We could argue that Miss Loring's life after school is her own private affair. She should be responsible to the school only for the proper performance of her job. What she does on her own time is none of the school's business. She is accountable to the school only for how well she teaches English to her students. Otherwise the school should have no interest in how she lives her private life.

One of the key features of this argument is the distinction between the *private* and the *public* sides of Miss Loring's life. Perhaps a moral principle of the following sort is being appealed to justify her privacy. *People can hold accountable by others only for those actions that harm others. They cannot be denied the freedom to perform those actions that affect only their own welfare.* John Stuart Mill has put the argument in its classic form:

> . . . the sole end for which mankind are warranted, individually or collectively, in interfering with the liberty of action of any of their members is self-protection. That the only purpose for which power can be rightfully exercised over any member of a civilized community, against his will, is to prevent harm to others. His own good, either physical or moral, is not a sufficient warrant. . . . The only part of the conduct of anyone for which he is amenable to society is that which concerns others. In the part which merely concerns himself, his independence is, of right, absolute. (Mill, 1859/1956, p. 14)

We might, then, define private behavior as behavior that affects the welfare only of those who engage in it. Public behavior, by contrast, affects the welfare of others. Democratic governments may take an interest in public behavior defined this way, but a person's private behavior and private welfare are his or her own business.

It might, then, be argued that the reason Miss Loring's second profession should not be the business of her first employer is that it is a private matter. The point is not, of course, that she does it in private. Obviously the point of her job is to be visible. Rather, the idea is that she and her audience are performing actions of their free choice and not interfering with each other. No one is forced to watch. Everyone is there voluntarily. Since everyone involved is a willing participant, there are no grounds to

subject to control by the school even if it might influence students in a way that community sentiment considered undesirable.

Where does this leave us? We would like to draw two conclusions relevant to thinking about professional ethics. First, it seems reasonable to us to hold that the role of a teacher should be construed broadly enough to include moral education. We would argue that a teacher's influence on the character and moral convictions of his or her students cannot be discounted as unrelated to the teacher's job. Second, however, the area of the teacher's life that should be treated as private and not under the school's control must be determined by balancing the importance of the particular right or interest under consideration against the possible effect of the teacher on students. There are some areas of people's lives, such as religion and politics, where there are strong reasons for respecting privacy unless extremely undesirable consequences are involved.

Other areas are of less importance. If a teacher's preference for garlic for lunch interferes with his afternoon teaching, the school may take a legitimate interest in his diet. It is unlikely that great violence would be done to an individual's freedom of conscience or basic political rights by restricting his garlic consumption. Deciding what is public and what is private is not, therefore, simply a matter of deciding whether an action has an effect on an important interest of the school or of deciding if it might do some harm. It is, instead, a matter of weighing the importance of the kind of privacy involved against the public interest threatened.

ANALYSIS: THE NATURE OF MORAL JUDGMENTS

One set of ideas that is important to the discussion of many moral issues (including this one) is the difference between what we shall call facts, moral principles, and preferences. Consider an example of a statement exemplifying each:

1. The grass is green.
2. We should always tell the truth.
3. Pickles are better than olives.

The first statement expresses a fact. Factual statements describe. They say something about the world. They are true if the world is the way they say it is. Otherwise they are false.

The second statement expresses a moral principle. It does not claim to describe any state of affairs about the world. Instead, it says something about how the world ought to be. A certain kind of action is obligatory. Moral principles involve concepts such as right and wrong and express duties and obligations. Unlike facts, they are not refuted if they do not describe the real world. "The grass is green" is not true unless the grass is green. But "we should always tell the truth" is not refuted if people lie.

The third statement expresses a preference or a value. Preference or value statements assert that some things are good or that some things are better than others.

These different kinds of statements appear to be true (or false) in different ways. Factual statements are true when they describe the world the way the world is. This does not seem to be true of statements of moral principles or of value statements, however. This is not to say that facts are irrelevant to the validity of moral arguments. If, for example, we believe that it is wrong to cause needless suffering, the fact that ridiculing some-one causes needless suffering is relevant to establishing the moral judg-ment that we ought not to ridicule that person. This does not, however, turn the moral judgment into a description of the world. Nor is it true because it correctly describes the world. Likewise, statements of moral principles such as "one should always tell the truth" or "slavery is wrong" may contain facts relevant to their justification or "truth," but they are not descriptions; they are prescriptions and proscriptions.

On the other hand, it is not clear that statements of preference are true in any way at all. We know of no way, in general, to decide if pickles are really better than olives. Indeed, we have identified statements of value with preferences partly because we believe that they often are only expres-sions of individual taste or personal preference and that they do not fulfill general truth conditions. (On the other hand, it does seem possible to have a meaningful discussion about whether Bach is better than rock music.) However, it is our purpose neither to argue about the possible objectivity of some kinds of value judgments nor to deal with the concept of ethical relativity. (We will discuss this issue later.) What is important is to realize that moral judgments and value judgments are different. This is important because the confusion of moral judgments with value judgments is often the source of bad arguments about ethics.

One common mistake is to start from the idea that value judgments have no truth conditions and move, via the confusion of moral judgments with value judgments, to the conclusion that moral judgments have no truth conditions. Statements such as "pickles are better than olives" are treated as though they are identical with statements such as "you should always tell the truth" Both are seen as matters of preference. Neither is true or false. They simply express what we like or how we feel.

This conflation is incorrect. Moral judgments have a different type of content from statements of personal preference. They state that some kinds of behavior are obligatory, not just for oneself but also for others. Moreover, it often seems possible to give reasons for or against them in a way that does not seem possible for statements of preference. If I believe that it is okay to lie whenever I feel like it, it is possible for someone to point out to me reasons why I should not believe this. If I happen to like olives better than pickles, it is not clear how it is possible for anyone to show me that I am in error.

Thus the confusion of moral judgments with preferential value judgments is one reason (a bad reason) for skepticism about the objectivity of moral judgments.

A second problem also results from the confusion between value judgments and moral ones. Generally it is wrong for one person to impose his or her values on another. If I decide to like pickles or skiing or canoeing, no one has a right to tell me that I must prefer olives or pole vaulting or marathon running. My preferences are a matter of my free choice. But it is a mistake to apply a similar logic with respect to moral principles. On one hand, it is to be desired that people will come to accept their moral obligations freely because they understand that the reasons for them are persuasive. On the other hand, it is often perfectly reasonable to coerce individuals who do not freely accept their moral obligations. The fact that a particular individual is not persuaded of an obligation to abstain from theft or murder is not a reason for permitting him or her to engage in such behavior. Moral principles express obligations to other people. It is often reasonable to enforce them. The injunction not to impose one's values on others is misplaced if it means that we can never enforce moral obligations.

These observations give us another approach to thinking about the distinction between public and private matters and the scope of individual liberty. We might conclude, given the above argument, that values are private matters, but moral principles are not. Values express our choices as to our own good. We have a right to choose our own values and to pursue them. No one has a right to impose their values on us. Moral principles are, however, a matter of public concern. While it is desirable that people come to their moral principles voluntarily, moral principles express duties and obligations to other people. They may, therefore, be enforced.

Consider how this might be applied to the case of Miss Loring. It might be argued that Miss Loring's behavior and that of those who come to see her involve no moral issues at all. The matter merely has to do with different preferences or values. Miss Loring may enjoy her second profession just as she does her first. That she enjoys it is a reason why she should be free to choose to engage in it if she so chooses. Others enjoy watching. That, too, is their choice. They are merely expressing their preferences.

Of course some may find Miss Loring's performance objectionable. Terms such as *indecent, lewd,* or *offensive* are often used to characterize topless dancing. But are these not also expressions of taste or, more accurately, distaste? It is surely true that many individuals in our society would find

Miss Loring's performance distasteful. But that, in itself, is not a reason for attempting to suppress it. For if tastes are different from moral principles and if tastes are private matters, to find something distasteful is not necessarily to find it immoral.

If we follow the logic of this argument, we will be led to the conclusion that there are no grounds for Mr. Endicott to object to Miss Loring's second profession. Many of the parents of the Spencerville school district may find her performance offensive. But it is simply a confusion to find it immoral. No issue of morality has yet been identified. Moreover, people have the right to choose their own preferences. In our society part of being a free person is having the right to determine one's own conception of one's good. Others have no right to impose their values on us. But for Mr. Endicott to attempt to get Miss Loring to quit her second job, or to threaten her with termination if she is unwilling to do so, would be to do precisely that. It would be to impose the preferences of the citizens of Spencerville on Miss Loring and her audience. If no moral issue is involved, if what is at stake is a mere difference in preferences, it is difficult to see what justification there is for interfering with these choices.

This argument would be decisive were it not for one further consideration. While generally we believe that people do have a right to their own choices about their own good and that it is improper to interfere with such choices, this principle may not apply when the selection of preferences is inconsistent with some moral principle. Consider an example. Some Americans enjoy baseball. Others do not. It would certainly be unreasonable for those who do not like baseball to attempt to prevent baseball lovers from attending games. Not too many years ago, however, many Americans expressed their preference not only for baseball, but for baseball played only by white people. Can we treat this preference as merely a matter of taste and conclude that no moral issue is involved? Could we argue that those who objected to the segregated leagues had no right to do so and merely were attempting to impose their preferences on others?

We doubt that many of our readers will be willing to accept this line of argument. Why not? The reason seems obvious enough. Some preferences can conflict with moral principles and thereby lead to conduct that is unjust. Thus while it generally may be the case that preferences are private matters, that is not always true. Preferences can be constrained by moral principles.

To complete this discussion, then, we should ask whether the preferences expressed in Miss Loring's case are inconsistent with any moral principles. Many believe that the preferences expressed by those who watch Miss Loring's second profession are inconsistent with the dignity of women. They find that such preferences lead to the treatment of women as objects and enforce attitudes of male exploitation and dominance. Such arguments seem to be plausible and worthy of further attention. If they are found on further examination to be persuasive, Mr. Endicott possibly will have found a reason to interfere with Miss Loring's second profession.

Our discussion to this point, then, suggests that distinguishing between those aspects of life that are to be left to the decision of the individual from those in which interference may be justified is a complex affair requiring the consideration of a variety of factors. To demonstrate some of this complexity, let us look at arguments for individual liberty as they might be put forth by consequentialists (appealing primarily to the principle of benefit maximization) and nonconsequentialists (appealing to respect for persons).

One type of consequentialism is utilitarianism. It holds that happiness is the ultimate good and that the best acts are those which produce the greatest good for the greatest number. How might a utilitarian reason about individual liberty? Obviously what is required is an argument that shows that not interfering with people in the private sphere of their lives produces better consequences (more happiness) for more people than does interfering. Why believe this? One argument is that individuals are their own best judges of what makes them happy. If I attempt to make decisions about your happiness, I am likely to choose for you that which I value. I may be mistaken about your wants and needs. You are in a better position than anyone else to know what you like. A second argument holds that it is the freedom to decide itself that makes people happy. Freedom is a part of happiness. Therefore, give more people freedom and more people will be happy. A third argument is that freedom provides for experimentation in diverse ways of living, a kind of grand experiment in diverse lifestyles that permits human beings to discover new and valuable ways of living, thereby increasing their own happiness. It also permits society to grow. This, too, promotes the general happiness.

Nonconsequentialists, on the other hand, will appeal to the central notion of respect for persons as moral agents and the conditions necessary for moral agency. Consider three such arguments:

First, respect for moral agency requires respect for free choice. If I am to regard you as a moral agent capable of free choice, I must respect your choice simply because it is your free choice. That you have freely chosen some good as your own requires me and other moral agents to honor that choice. That is a part of what it means to respect moral agency.

Second, granting people freedom to make their own choices is a necessary condition of moral responsibility. We cannot hold people responsible for their choices while, at the same time, interfering with their right to choose. To view people as responsible for themselves is to grant them the right to decide for themselves.

Third, if we object to or interfere with others' choice of their good to further our own interests, we treat them as though they were obstacles to our ends without considering their rights to determine their own ends. If we are to regard other people as moral agents like ourselves, we must show their choices the same degree of respect that we expect them to show ours. To fail to do so is to treat them as means to our ends.

None of these arguments for personal liberty lead to the conclusion that people should be free to do whatever they want simply because they have chosen to do so. All of them require that we find a reasonable way to distinguish between the private sphere and the public sphere. As we have seen, however, this is not an easy distinction to draw. And while we have considered many plausible arguments, we have not solved Mr. Endicott's problem. Nonetheless, we may have learned something about ethics and moral reasoning in the process. Let us consider that possibility.

We began the section on analysis in this chapter by distinguishing between facts, preferences, and moral principles. One reason for doing so was the belief that people are often misled into a position of moral skepticism by bad arguments that seem to turn on labeling preferences and moral principles as values. It is then held that values are matters of taste and that we have a right to our own free choices concerning them. People who claim that it is possible to reason about moral principles are then accused of the dual crimes of seeking to reason about a matter that is merely a matter of taste and of seeking to impose their values on others.

Both of these claims are weakened by distinguishing between preferences and moral principles. The case for treating preferences as matters of taste seems intuitively more plausible than the case for treating moral principles as matters of taste. It is difficult to know how to argue that pickles are better than olives. Even if we can argue that some preferences are better than others, for example, that Bach is better than rock, it does not follow that we can impose our views on others. On the other hand, it is not so hard to argue that murder and racism are wrong or that honesty and keeping one's promises are obligatory.

Also, it makes more sense to apply the principle of noninterference to preferences than to moral principles. We have provided a variety of arguments to show that (other things being equal) people have a right to freely choose their own conception of their good. However, moral principles assert duties and obligations, hence we can, in many cases, legitimately interfere with those who breach them. It is the point of moral principles to regulate the interactions among human beings.

These arguments seek to dispose of a common confusion about values and moral principles. They do not, however, show that objective moral reasoning is possible. Indeed, the distinction between facts and moral principles has often been used in an argument to show that moral reasoning cannot be objective.

The essential claim is that moral principles cannot be derived simply from facts. The Scottish philosopher David Hume (1888/1967, pp. 469–

470) provided one such argument. Hume noted that one of the properties of a valid argument is that all of the terms that occur in its conclusions are also contained in its premises. Consider:

All men are mortal.
Socrates is a man.
Therefore, Socrates is mortal.

If the argument was slightly changed, we would see a conclusion that did not follow from the premises in the argument (even though it might be true). Consider:

All men are mortal.
Socrates is mortal.
Therefore, Socrates' dog is mortal.

We cannot reach a valid conclusion about Socrates' dog unless the dog is referred to in the premises of the argument. Valid arguments, after all, tell us what follows from our premises. Noting this, Hume then pointed out that it is impossible for any argument containing only factual premises to lead validly to a conclusion about what we ought to do. For any such argument has a new idea in the conclusion that was not in the premises—the idea of obligation. "Ought" conclusions cannot follow from "is" premises.

Do we have a response to this argument? First, it is important to be clear about what follows from Hume's argument. It does not show that moral knowledge or moral argumentation is impossible. If it is correct, it shows only that moral claims cannot be derived solely from facts. Second, syllogistic argument may not be the form moral reasoning takes. We want again to commend our strategy concerning how to develop a view about moral reasoning by engaging in moral arguments and seeing how we construct them.

CONCLUSION

We began with a problematic case. In order to deal with it, we decided that we needed to distinguish between public and private actions. We borrowed one from John Stuart Mill: People are entitled to complete freedom in the private sphere, but they might be accountable to others in the public sphere. Mill's way of making the distinction was tested in two ways. First, we tested it by applying it to other cases. We found some instances where its application seemed to produce objectionable consequences. That seemed to be a reason for modifying it. Second, we attempted to illuminate the concept of individual liberty by seeing how it might be argued for in terms of two abstract moral views that we had sketched earlier, the principle of benefit maximization and the principle of equal respect for persons.

Has this process of moral reasoning that we have engaged in been helpful? It is fair to say that it has not been entirely successful. We and Mr. Endicott still seem to be unsure about what to do in Miss Loring's case. Moreover, we have linked the still-unclear distinction between public and private actions and the complex idea of individual liberty to two different general moral theories, consequentialism and nonconsequentialism, which have quite different views about what is fundamentally at stake. In short, we have made the issue more complicated without resolving it.

On the other hand, we believe that we have made two kinds of progress in our quest to understand the process of ethical reasoning. First, we have learned to use our own moral experiences as evidence for the adequacy of our formulations of moral principles. For example, we rejected some formulations of the public/private distinction because they led to morally counterintuitive conclusions when applied to some cases. We thus offer as one noteworthy feature of moral reasoning the claim that our moral experience, our sense of what is right and wrong in a given case, counts initially as evidence for our moral theories. This is a theme we shall develop later.

Second, even if we have not resolved many of the issues we have raised, we have come to understand what is at stake in them in a more fundamental way. That, in itself, may lead to more responsible moral decisions. But it is also an optimistic sign about moral reasoning. Ethics, like other kinds of thinking, can be a difficult and complex process. That it does not always lead immediately to clear and obvious decisions is not a sign that ethical reflection is impossible. Indeed, that we can come to understand the issues better is a sign that ethical thinking can produce some results.

ADDITIONAL CASES

Tiger! Tiger! Burning Bright

Sharon Athis was obviously troubled. She had come into Smith's office shortly after the semester began and requested an appointment with a counselor. As head of the counseling service at Entwood Community College, Smith was responsible for conducting entrance interviews with new clients. The purpose of these interviews was to ascertain the nature of students' problems and to assign them to the appropriate counselor, if that was warranted. In Sharon Athis's case, it surely was.

Sharon was a somewhat overweight and plain young woman, shy, afflicted with a rather severe case of acne, and very anxiety ridden. In their 30-minute interview she became increasingly distraught. At first she discussed only her weight and skin problems, and Smith suggested that she see a physician at the Entwood Health Service. Sharon greeted this suggestion with silence. When she began to speak again, it became clear that these problems were not what was troubling her. As nearly as Smith could determine, her anxiety had to do with her boyfriend, someone named Blake. However, she obviously could not bring herself to discuss it with Smith. The psychologist guessed that it was a difficulty he often saw in freshman women—a developing sexual relationship that provoked rather severe, but temporary, anxiety symptoms. He suggested that Sharon make an appointment with Dr. Cleis, one of his staff psychologists.

Bernice Cleis was an extremely competent and professionally self-assured person. While she had been on Smith's staff for only three years, having come to Entwood immediately after earning a Ph.D. in counseling psychology, she had quickly established herself as one of the more accomplished members of his team. She was particularly successful with anxiety cases of the sort that Sharon Athis seemed to represent. After Athis left, Smith pressed the switch on his intercom and spoke to Cleis. He described his initial interview and said that Athis would be calling for an appointment.

Several months passed, and Smith thought little more of Sharon Athis. Her case had come up once in a staff meeting, when Dr. Cleis had discussed several therapeutic techniques she had been using successfully with cases of sexual anxiety. In reviewing his staff's appointment schedules, Smith did notice that Dr. Cleis was seeing Athis more often than was usual. He supposed that Sharon's problem was more severe than he had originally thought.

In the spring two events occurred that, taken jointly, worried Smith considerably. First, late one evening after emerging from a movie in a neighboring town, he had seen Dr. Cleis and Miss Athis together. They were laughing and obviously engrossed with each other as they walked arm in arm down the darkened street. Neither saw him. Smith was generally of the opinion that personal relationships between a psychologist and patient were unwise. He made a mental note to discuss the matter with Cleis at an early opportunity.

Even more distressing was a note he received from Dean Lamb the following week. Attached to the note was a letter to the dean from Mr. Athis, Sharon's father, asking Lamb to speak with his daughter. Mr. Athis was very worried. He said that Sharon had become extremely morose and given to crying much of the time while she was at home for visits. Last weekend she had spent the entire time in her room, barely speaking to either of her parents.

Further, Mr. Athis had found a disturbing poem on Sharon's dresser not written in her hand and signed "B," which he enclosed. It read:

Abstinence sows sand all over
The ruddy limbs and flaming hair,
But Desire Gratified
Plants fruits of life and beauty there.
B.

Though Mr. Athis was upset, he seemed to be a reasonable man. His letter went on to say that he realized his daughter was no longer a child and that she was likely to have become romantically involved with some young man. However, Sharon's romance with "B" did not seem to him to be usual. "B" was clearly causing his daughter immense anguish. He and Mrs. Athis were seriously worried about her mental health. He also said that Sharon absolutely refused to discuss her boyfriend with either him or his wife. He closed his letter by apologizing for making an unusual request. He was frightened for his daughter, and he asked that Dean Lamb please talk with her and, if possible, do what he could to help her through a sadly atypical first love affair.

Lamb's note accompanying this letter asked Smith to please call Sharon in and to do what he could for her.

Smith wondered if either the dean or Mr. Athis suspected just how atypical this first love affair might be. While the author of the poem was certainly a male, he was less sure of its plagiarist.

That night Smith stayed late in his office clearing up the day's paperwork. About 9 P.M., in what he thought was an empty building, he was startled to hear a door close and the sound of a woman sobbing. After a moment he realized that his intercom was on and that he was hearing someone in another office. He was reaching over to turn off the device, when he clearly heard Bernice Cleis say, "Sharon, I told you not to go home. I knew it wouldn't help, and I've missed you."

Smith hesitated, his finger on the intercom switch.

Some Questions

1. Would Smith be violating Cleis's right to privacy if he left the intercom on? Does a professional psychologist have a right to privacy in his or her relations with a client?
2. If you answered "yes" to the above questions, distinguish privacy from confidentiality and secrecy. Which of these, if any, does Cleis have a right to as a practicing psychologist? Does it make any difference that Cleis is an employee of a school and not in private practice?

3. What obligations, if any, does Smith have to Sharon Athis?
4. Suppose this case had taken place a few months earlier, that is, when Sharon Athis was a senior in high school. Would that change your analysis? Why?
5. If you were the president of Entwood, would you expect Smith to come to you with the story? If he did, what would you do and how would you justify your decision?

Pregnant

It was the end of the school year, and Helen Nelson was, as usual, very busy. Perhaps that was why she had not noticed Rebecca's pregnancy. Rebecca had called in sick several times during the last couple of months, but Helen really had not thought much about it. Now she would have to think very hard about it.

Helen was the principal of Southwest High School, a large center-city institution in one of the more economically depressed areas of Worcester, a city that was itself economically depressed. The school had a reputation for being "tough," and Helen had to struggle each year to recruit new teachers.

Given a choice, most novices headed for the more affluent suburbs that surrounded Worcester, where teaching was supposedly easier. Further, many of the more experienced members of her own staff transferred to other, better, schools within the district if an opportunity arose. Helen had been working on this problem for a couple of years, but so far she had met with little success. In any case, every spring Helen spent a very large part of her time trying to staff her building for the following September. Since March she had been occupied almost entirely in lining up new faculty to replace the inevitable turnover. Finally, that morning, on the very last day of school, she had filled the single remaining vacancy for the next year. Or so she had thought, until Rebecca walked in.

Rebecca Tomlinson's appointment was at the close of the day. Tomlinson was a valued member of Southwest's math department. Indeed, with seven years' experience, she was very nearly its senior member. She was obviously nervous when she entered the office and sat down. After the usual chitchat about summer plans, Rebecca got to the point. She was expecting a baby in early November. "You probably don't know," she said, "but my husband and I have been trying to have a family for several years. So we're pretty happy."

Helen offered her congratulations, though inwardly her heart sank. Now she was going to have to find a math teacher for September, and that was going to be hard. They were in very short supply, and she wasn't sure she would have any luck getting a reasonably competent person. The really good ones would have already signed contracts.

She also began doing a little math herself. If Rebecca was expecting in early November, presumably she had known for at least a couple of months.

Helen was more than a little exasperated that Rebecca had not told her before today. But the worst was yet to come. "Anyway," Rebecca continued, "I've decided to work as long as I can, probably till the end of October, assuming the doctor continues to say it's okay. Then I'll take the rest of the year off and be back in the classroom a year from September."

"Do you really think that's wise, Rebecca?" Helen said as calmly as she could. "After all, you'll only get in a couple of months of work next fall, and then have to quit. Wouldn't it be better to just stop now and take it easy until the baby comes? Your job will be waiting for you the following year."

"Ben and I have talked about that possibility, Mrs. Nelson, but frankly, it's out of the question. Ben's been laid off, and we simply need the money, especially with a baby on the way."

Helen leaned forward across her desk. "Look, Rebecca. I don't think you realize what sorts of problems this causes. You know that good math teachers are scarce. I'll be doing well to get a certified person in your classroom by September. If I can't offer a job to anyone until November, I may as well forget about it. At best I'll have to take a substitute who's likely to babysit your class for an entire year. You know what kinds of people I've had to get to sub for you. They couldn't teach geometry or trig. I don't think that last guy we got to cover for you could teach fourth-grade arithmetic! It's not fair to the students to stick a sub in there for almost the entire year. These kids have enough problems as it is. Your first obligation is to your students."

"No, Mrs. Nelson, my first obligation isn't to my students. It's to my family," Rebecca snapped back. "I'm sorry if this creates a problem for you and for the kids. If I had a choice about the timing of my pregnancy, or when I take my leave, I would have arranged it to be less inconvenient. But I don't have any choices. So I'm going to be at my desk and ready to teach in September. You'll just have to do the best you can. Besides, district policy is quite clear about this. I'm entitled to a year's maternity leave, and it can begin whenever I want it to, as long as I'm physically capable of doing my job. And Dr. Fischer said he didn't foresee any problems. He thought I could probably work right into my last month."

I'll bet he didn't foresee any problems, Helen thought. What do physicians know about recruiting math teachers?

Some Questions

1. We have tried to draw a distinction between public and private acts. But what sense does it make to think of a pregnancy as a public or

private act? Does the public/private distinction help Helen Nelson think about her problem? How?

2.   We have said that "others may not interfere with our preferences unless those preferences themselves conflict with some moral principle. That we find someone's preferences distasteful (or inconvenient) is not a reason for interfering with them." Is there any moral principle involved in this case such that Helen Nelson could rightly interfere with Rebecca's plans for her maternity leave? If you respond that students' needs for a competent math teacher are justification for interference, just what moral principle is that?

3.   If you think that there is a moral principle embedded in students' needs, what about the clause in the teachers' contract regarding maternity leave? Isn't that a moral principle? Surely honoring a contract is one. How should these two be balanced?

4.   How can school districts avoid this sort of problem—that is, last-minute resignations—besides simply relying on the professional commitment of teachers? Try your hand at drafting a policy for Worcester that will balance the rights of teachers and those of the district.

The Aryan Brotherhood

Sarah Katz disdained *The Publican*, so she had missed the article. But after the third phone call in an hour, she went out to buy a copy of the newspaper. She was not particularly perturbed. Even if her callers had correctly reported the contents of the story, she did not put much stock in the whole business. She knew *The Publican*, and she knew Fred Mueller. The former was a first-rate scandal sheet; the second a first-rate physics teacher. When she returned to her apartment with the paper, she set her answering machine to intercept calls, fixed herself a drink, and settled down to read the article.

In essence her callers seemed to have gotten the story right. Apparently *The Publican* had been doing a weekly series on radical fringe groups of one sort or another located in and around Camden. The star of this week's installment was a little beauty calling itself "The Aryan Brotherhood," and Fred Mueller was identified as a member of the group.

According to the reporter (who had posed as a recruit in order to get the story), the Brotherhood was a paramilitary organization whose members spent much of their spare time running about in the woods dressed in camouflage, carrying simulated weapons, and getting ready to defend their homes and families after the imminent collapse of U.S. society. The tenets of the organization included absolute white supremacy, the intellectual inferiority of everyone else, the existence of a Jewish-communist conspiracy, a denial that the Holocaust had ever happened, and the belief that every (white) citizen had a God-given right to own a heavy machine gun.

Sarah would have dismissed the article and the Aryan Brotherhood without a second thought were it not for the prominent place it gave to Fred Mueller, "a long-time member of the faculty of Camden High School." According to *The Publican's* reporter, Fred was a lieutenant in the organization and its designated "intellectual leader" The reporter wondered "how Mr. Mueller managed to teach physics to Camden High's minority and Jewish students, when he holds the racial and ethnic prejudices he does."

If the facts were correct, Sarah would wonder, too. But she knew that he did manage to teach physics to blacks and Jews as well as "Aryans." As principal of Camden, she had had ample opportunity to observe Fred, to read his department chairman's evaluations, and to talk to his students. While Mueller probably wasn't the best teacher in the school, he was certainly better than most. More importantly, as far as she knew there had never been the slightest hint of bigotry in anything he said or did in the classroom. Indeed, only a week ago Susan McIsaac, an African American senior, had made it a point to praise Mueller to Sarah for the extra time he had spent with her to help her with a particularly difficult unit in the advanced placement physics course. And Susan was not the first black student to make such remarks to the principal.

Before Sarah retired for the night she made a note to herself to talk to Fred in the morning. She was uneasy about even broaching the subject with him. After all, even if *The Publican's* story was completely accurate, she was not sure that Fred's political beliefs, no matter how bizarre, were any business of hers.

As it happened, she didn't need to make an appointment to see Fred. By the time she had finished a couple of routine chores, the first period had ended and Fred Mueller was in her outer office with a gaggle of noisy students in tow, Susan McIsaac among them.

When Sarah had quieted them down, it became obvious what had happened. Many of the students had read the article and had begun questioning Mueller about it as soon as class began. Fred had refused to talk about the story and instead had tried to teach his planned lesson. When they had persisted, some to the point of shouting, Fred had become angry. "My political beliefs and affiliations are none of your damn business," he had said. It was at that point that the period had ended and the whole irate group had trooped down to Sarah's office.

In the office most of the students merely repeated the newspaper's accusations and demanded that Mueller respond. For his part, Fred took the same tack he had taken in the classroom; he didn't have to explain himself to students. Susan McIsaac, however, put the matter in a different light.

"Look, Miss Katz, Mr. Mueller's never said anything in class that's out of line or derogatory. But it isn't true that his political and racial beliefs are only his business. From now on, every time he looks at me, or I have to ask him a question, I'll be worried that he'll be thinking I'm another dumb black. I can't learn from a person who I think doesn't respect me."

After Sarah dismissed the students, she sat down to talk with her physics teacher. "You know that I agree with you," she said, "but Susan has a point, Fred. Perhaps you'd like to tell me about *The Publican* story."

Mueller paused a long time before responding. "No, she doesn't, and no, I wouldn't, Miss Katz. Susan doesn't have a point, she has a problem. And it's her problem, not mine. She's reacting to something she's read in a yellow rag. Last week she told me I was a good teacher. I'm the same person I was last week. I haven't changed. I'm still a good teacher. What's changed is Susan's perception and attitude. That's her problem. Second, I wouldn't like to discuss the story with you either. I may be a physics teacher, but at least I know about the Fifth Amendment and my right to privacy—even if you and these high school seniors seem to be entirely ignorant of them. I've said all I'm going to say about this. My political beliefs and affiliations are my own business, as long as I don't try to foist them on my students. And no one can accuse me of doing that."

Some Questions

1. Suppose you are Sarah Katz. What position would you take regarding Mueller's claims? Why?
2. Suppose that the facts in *The Publican* story are absolutely correct. Consider the following line of argument. If Mueller is a history teacher, believing the Holocaust never happened is demonstrable evidence of incompetence in his field. That isn't true, of course, if he's a physics teacher. In the former case then, wouldn't Katz be justified in trying to get Mueller removed from his job, but not in the latter case? Would Mueller's views be more "dangerous" if he taught history?
3. Still supposing that the facts in the story are correct, does it make any difference to your decision in the role of Sarah Katz that these facts were gathered through a subterfuge and that Mueller didn't wittingly and publicly announce his Nazi-like beliefs?
4. Compare this case to the case concerning Susan Loring's second profession. Does the school have a duty to promote racial tolerance? Does this distinguish this case from the one concerning Susan Loring? Does the fact that this case involves the right of freedom of association distinguish them?

CHAPTER 4

Equal Educational Opportunity

A CASE

Mr. Bergen had known the politics of this one would be tough. He was now getting an education in how tough. The newly organized Citizens for Excellence was on his case. This was not the year to be against excellence in the Applegate School District. He needed to explain to the board why his decision against putting more money into a program for the gifted and talented was not being against excellence.

Mr. Bergen's district had a unique population mix. For years it had been a farming community. That was still substantially the case. But for the last few years, the district had undergone considerable gentrification. Affluent people from the nearby metropolis had discovered the charm of the rolling hills and pleasant countryside of Applegate. Many of the farmers had succumbed to the lure of the real estate developer's dollars and sold their dairy farms and orchards to the newcomers.

The third portion of the population consisted of migrant workers, most of whom were Spanish speaking. While this portion of the population was fairly small and was dwindling as the farms in the area declined, still about 7% of the children in the Applegate schools were Spanish speaking.

They were a difficult population to work with. The most obvious problem was their poor command of English. Moreover, he suspected that many of the families were illegal aliens. At least they were quite shy of public officials, including him. These problems were compounded by the fact that they were a transitory population. Families would arrive for the fall picking in the orchards. The majority, for whom the working season was over after the fruit was picked, would crowd into trailers to await spring. Their children would start school late and leave early. They might be gone for weeks if their parents found work out of the district. Few of the children would return to the Applegate schools the following year.

Mr. Bergen felt a compelling obligation to help these children. While they were in his district, he felt it his duty to see to it that they got the best education that he knew how to contrive for them. He had badgered the board into hiring a consultant to develop a program. The consultant had produced one that Mr. Bergen thought was first rate. It offered some hope to these children. It was expensive.

Mr. Bergen nevertheless believed that he had a reasonable chance at selling the program to the board. One of the nice things about the newer residents of his districts was that they built expensive homes and had few children. Applegate's coffers had the wherewithal for a new program.

Unhappily, Citizens for Excellence had come up with their own version of a new program. It was an extensive set of new offerings for the district's gifted and talented children. All of the district's new landed gentry seemed to come equipped with at least one child who was thought to be gifted and talented. Some of them really were. This program, too, was expensive. It was clear that there would be only one new program. The only question was which one.

Mr. Bergen favored the program for the Hispanic children. Gifted and talented children had a way of taking care of themselves in this world, especially when their parents were wealthy. The Hispanic children, on the other hand, were in desperate need of a decent education. This seemed decisive to him.

It did not seem decisive to the members of the Citizens for Excellence. They were full of talk about our society's desperate need for mathematicians and scientists, and about how the schools had failed to develop the technological leadership for the next generation. It was of utmost importance to them that we keep ahead of our economic competitors. Fading to accept their program was positively un-American.

Mr. Bergen was not against scientists, although he was less sure that his primary duty as an educator was to win some contest with our economic competitors. But he also knew where the power in his district resided. The new residents paid the majority of the taxes. They and the farmers were a substantial majority of the voters of the district. Neither group was overconcerned with the welfare of the Hispanic population. The newer residents thought the Hispanics' crowded trailers and noisy children degraded the neighborhood. The farmers did not believe that people needed to know much to pick fruit. The migrants did not vote.

As Mr. Bergen entered the board building, he knew that if the program for the Hispanic children was to get off the ground he would have to be persuasive tonight.

DISPUTE

A: In this country, we believe in the importance of equality and especially equality of opportunity. Our schools are one of society's most
important institutions for teaching the young about equality and for
actually providing it. Thus we have special programs for the disadvantaged, those who need a leg up.

B: I agree about equality being a good thing. But something sounds
funny here. Doesn't equality mean equal treatment? If you give
more resources to one group of students, aren't you treating others
unequally?

A: Yes, in a way, but what you are ultimately doing is ensuring that
those who were unequal to begin with will have a chance to be more
equal educationally with those who are lucky enough to get a good
start in life. Equality of opportunity means giving everyone a real
chance to succeed and not just giving them equal resources. Besides,
these are society's resources, and investing them in the disadvantaged will bring about such social benefits as less crime and more
productive workers.

B: Yes, they are society's resources, and just think how much more social
benefit might come from investing our resources in the best and the
brightest, in our future scientists, doctors, researchers, and inventors!
If you are going to provide opportunity, then these are the most important opportunities to provide. To be fair about it, all you have to
do is give each person an equal chance to display his or her talent.
Then nurture it wherever you find it, even if that means putting more
money into programs for the talented few.

A: But that would be giving even more advantage to the already advantaged. Equality and fairness demand that we treat people *differently*.
. . . Did I say that? I think I am getting confused.

B: If you think you are confused, what about the students in our schools?
We teach them about the importance of equality as a basic value in
our democracy, and then proceed to treat them unequally by giving
some groupings of students more of our finite resources than others!

CONCEPT: EQUALITY

Mr. Bergen has a problem about equal opportunity. He believes that fairness requires him to provide additional resources for a program for the
disadvantaged students in his district rather than for the district's gifted and
talented students. Does fairness actually demand this? If the school board
votes the money for a gifted and talented program, will that be unjust?

Consider how each side in the dispute might argue for their view. Mr. Bergen seems to believe that the main reason the Hispanic children in his district should have the additional resources is that they need them more. He has appealed to the criterion of need in justifying his choice. Those who have supported the program for the gifted and talented have implicitly argued that the children in this program should receive the additional resources because they can put them to the best use. It is they who will make the larger contributions to the national welfare. Here the assumption seems to be that the criterion for dispensing educational resources should be ability. We should expend disproportionate resources on those who are the most academically able, because it is they who will do the most with them to the benefit of all.

To begin thinking about this choice, consider an additional principle. We will call it the *principle of equal treatment*. It says: *In any given circumstances, people who are the same in those respects relevant to how they are treated in those circumstances should receive the same treatment.* A corollary of this principle is that people who are relevantly different should be treated differently.

What does this principle mean? Suppose we are deciding about admitting two students, Smith and Jones, to a select university. Smith and Jones have received the same score on the admissions test. Should we admit or reject Smith and/or Jones? The principle of equal treatment does not say. All that it says is that whatever treatment we accord to Smith, we must also give to Jones, because Smith and Jones are the same in the relevant respects. The principle also requires that we should have reasons for how we treat people (Peters, 1970). If, for example, we were to argue that Smith should be admitted to the university, we might do so by giving as our reason that the score that he achieved on the test indicated that he had the ability to do the work. This argument logically connects a characteristic of Smith, his test score, to a treatment, university admission. The crucial thing is that any argument that succeeds for Smith must also succeed for Jones insofar as Smith and Jones are the same on the relevant criterion. We cannot, therefore, reasonably argue that we ought to admit Smith but not Jones.

How do we get from the principle of equal treatment to the idea of equal educational opportunity? Often the most important issues regarding equal opportunity concern what we will treat as irrelevant criteria for purposes of access to educational programs. There is a strong presumption that such characteristics as race, sex, religion, and ethnicity are irrelevant to most legitimate educational purposes. Thus if we find that someone is providing different treatment to two individuals in ways having to do with these characteristics, that is compelling evidence that an injustice is taking place. It is not altogether decisive, however. Presumably it is permissible to use race as a criterion in identifying those who are to benefit from a program designed to remedy racial discrimination. And it is legitimate to use religion as a criterion for admission to a theological seminary. Nevertheless, given that race, sex, religion, and ethnicity are irrelevant to almost all legitimate educational purposes, a strong presumption exists that their use as a criterion for the allocation of educational resources is illegitimate.

This analysis suggests that any argument about equality of opportunity will involve three sorts of claims.

1. Moral claims that equality consists in treating equals equally and unequals unequally.
2. Relevancy claims that certain factors are relevant to how people are to be treated and others are irrelevant.
3. Efficacy claims that particular kinds of treatments produce desirable results.

A full consideration of equality of educational opportunity, then, requires that we specify the full range of educationally relevant factors and the treatments that are appropriate. It is this that Mr. Bergen is not yet able to do. He has two groups of individuals who are very different. Presumably both ability and need are educationally relevant factors. But Mr. Bergen needs to know how they connect to different kinds of treatments. He needs to know what counts as fair treatment in this case.

We might approach his dilemma by asking how we can think about it from both the perspective of the principle of benefit maximization and from the perspective of the principle of equal respect.

The principle of benefit maximization requires that we look at the problem in terms of the maximization of some good. Let us assume that what we wish to maximize is a rather vague commodity that we shall simply call "human welfare." We might also assume that, while human welfare is not identical with how productive a given society is, a society's productivity is a fair measure of how well off people are. From the perspective of the principle of benefit maximization, then, the principle of equal treatment is justified by arguing that making decisions about people on the basis of relevant rather than irrelevant criteria is the most efficient use of resources and opportunities. If we fail to treat equals equally and unequals unequally, we will end up using our resources and opportunities less effectively than we might and thus not maximize human welfare.

For example, why is it objectionable to take race into account in hiring? From the perspective of the principle of benefit maximization, the reason is that it is inefficient. If we consider race in hiring, that means that sometimes we will not hire the best person for the job because that person is a member of a certain race. Thus we will get a less efficient worker for our money because we have used an irrelevant characteristic in deciding whom to hire. The same argument can be made for educational opportunities. If we are to put our educational resources to the most effective use, then we will not use such characteristics as race in deciding who is to receive what opportunity.

We can also appeal to the principle of benefit maximization in deciding what is to count as a relevant criterion. If we want to know what characteristics we should look for in a good employee, the answer is that we want those characteristics that will make that person the most productive. If we are looking for basketball players, height will be a relevant criterion. If we are looking for accountants, mathematical ability counts. Likewise, if we wish to know about the characteristics that we should look for in allocating educational resources, the question is what characteristics permit people to make the most efficient use of resources.

This argument appears to be the one appealed to by those who are arguing for the program for the gifted and talented. In effect, they have claimed that the reason the district should put its money into a program for the gifted and talented is that that is the most efficient use of the resource. These children are the society's future leaders and scientists. If we spend the money on them, we will be putting our money to its most productive use.

Can Mr. Bergen appeal to the principle of benefit maximization on behalf of the disadvantaged Hispanic students, or can it only be used to justify the spending of our educational resources on those who are the most academically talented? Think about it. It may not be true that spending our educational resources on the most academically able is always the most efficient way to spend them. For example, it is possible that putting extra resources into the education of the most able students will produce little extra benefit. It may be that we would end up spending money to teach these children what they would otherwise learn by themselves. Or it may be that we have reached the point of diminishing returns with these children. Whatever additional learning we purchase for them by creating a new program will be small in relation to the costs involved. Moreover, the benefits for society in a program for the Hispanic children of Mr. Bergen's district may be considerable. These are children who, if their educational needs are not attended to, may be economically marginal for the rest of their lives. If they fail to achieve at least minimal competence while they have a chance to be in school, they may face lives of unemployment. They will become a constant drain on society's resources. But if Mr. Bergen's program succeeds, these same children will have a chance to become useful and productive members of society. Thus it is entirely possible that Mr. Bergen's program for the Hispanic children of his district will have benefits for society that exceed those of the program for the gifted and talented. If Mr. Bergen wishes to persuade his board to invest in a program for the Hispanic children using the principle of benefit maximization, he will have to persuade the board that meeting their needs is the most productive use of the money.

Looking at the idea of equal opportunity from the perspective of the principle of equal respect gives us a different way of seeing the issues, even though there will be many areas of agreement. Those who argue from the perspective of the principle of equal respect for persons, for example, will still wish to distinguish between relevant and irrelevant characteristics. They, too, will insist that treating equals equally and unequals unequally is a moral obligation. Moreover, relevant and irrelevant characteristics will be distinguished in much the same way that they were under the principle of benefit maximization. Relevant characteristics will be those that are relevant to legitimate purposes. In hiring, those purposes will be getting the job done. In education, they will be learning. Nothing about the principle of equal respect for persons requires us to hire people who cannot do the job or to expend educational resources on those who cannot profit from them.

There are, however, some important ways in which the principle of equal respect for persons gives us a different picture of equality. One difference is that equality of opportunity will be argued for in a different way. Consider how we might object to the use of race in hiring from the perspective of the principle of equal respect. Let us suppose that Jones refuses to hire Smith as a carpenter. If Jones's reason is that Smith is not as good a carpenter as some other, Jones has not denied Smith's fundamental worth as a person in refusing to hire him. Jones may continue to regard Smith as a person deserving respect and may consistently continue to think of him as his equal as a human being. He need only believe that there are better carpenters available. But if Jones refuses to hire Smith because of his race, he has rejected Smith's fundamental worth as a human being. When we deny someone an opportunity for some irrelevant reason, we, in effect, say that we are rejecting him because we believe that he is less than a full-fledged human being. We do not want to associate with him for some reason that is fundamental to who he is. Jones could not refuse to hire Smith because of his race and continue to see Smith as a worthy and deserving person, as someone who is his equal as a person and who deserves fair treatment. To deny any benefit or opportunity to a person on the basis of irrelevant characteristics is, therefore, to deny that person's equal worth and to refuse to accord that person equal respect.

A second difference between the principle of equal respect and the principle of benefit maximization is that the principle of equal respect need not require us, in all cases, to select the most efficient use of resources. That use of resources that best expresses equal respect for persons need not be the one that maximizes some outcome.

For example, assume that we know that the program for the Hispanic children would be of some benefit to them. It would allow many of them to achieve some degree of economic stability. But let us also assume (for the sake of the argument) that the overall economic impact of the program for the gifted and talented would be greater. Given these assumptions, the principle of benefit maximization produces an obvious choice. We should choose the program for the gifted and talented. Is that the only defensible choice? Mr. Bergen might respond that it is not. Despite the assumption that the program for the gifted and talented has a larger overall impact, the program for the Hispanic children is more crucial for them as persons. It will make the difference for them between economic marginality and stable and productive lives. Even if the overall impact of the program for the gifted and talented would be greater, the need of the Hispanic children overrules it. It is unfair to deny them this chance for a better life. There are times when meeting the need of some is more important than maximizing the average welfare of all.

Mr. Bergen's claim also might be argued for by appealing to the principle of equal respect. If human beings are of equal value, then their interests and their welfare are of equal value. But the principle of benefit maximization does not always respect each person's interests and welfare equally. Sometimes it seems to tell us that we may trade the welfare of some for the welfare of others. Indeed, we may do this whenever the average welfare increases. But to do this is to treat some people as though they were merely means to the welfare of others. It is to fail to treat their interests and welfare as of equal worth with that of others. It is to fail to respect them as persons.

Thus, the principle of benefit maximization can conflict with the principle of equal respect when it requires that we trade the welfare of some for the welfare of others. There are times when this seems unfair. Can we ever justify unequal treatment? What might be an alternative? Suppose we held that we were only permitted to have an unequal distribution of some resource when those who received the lesser share benefited as a consequence, a perspective given in-depth examination by John Rawls (1971). We will call this the *maximin principle*. It requires us to maximize the welfare of those who receive the minimum share. In the case at hand, this would mean that we should prefer the program for the Hispanic students so long as this program produced greater benefits for them than those that would result for them from spending the money on the gifted and talented. We would do this even if spending the money for the gifted and talented produced higher average benefits.

The maximin principle has three features of note. First, while it does not require that all benefits be distributed equally, it does require that inequalities (departures from an equal distribution) are to be permitted only when everyone benefits as a result. Inequalities may only be justified by showing that those who receive the lesser share are nevertheless better off than they would be under an equal distribution. What is forbidden is inequalities that trade the welfare of some for the welfare of others.

Second, this principle is especially attentive to the needs of society's most disadvantaged. It requires, in effect, that we may only distribute resources in such a way as to result in their benefit. We may not distribute resources so as to promote the average welfare if the disadvantaged are made worse off as a result. The welfare of the least advantaged, not the average welfare, is made the touchstone of social justice.

Third, this principle seems to respect everyone equally. While it does not require that everyone be equally well off, it does prevent some from being well off at the expense of others. Inequality in the distribution of resources is permitted only if all benefit.

Does this help Mr. Bergen? Very likely it does. It gives him a way of thinking about his choices that supports his feeling that justice requires paying special attention to the needs of his district's disadvantaged students.

ANALYSIS: MORAL EXPERIENCE

In the preceding discussion we introduced a new moral principle, the principle of equal treatment. This principle requires us to treat people who are similarly situated in some relevant way the same and people who are differently situated differently. We found that we could argue for this principle by appealing either to the principle of benefit maximization or to the principle of equal respect. Both appeared to require it, but for different reasons. It also turned out, however, when we looked at a specific case concerning the gifted and the disadvantaged and how resources were to be divided between these two quite different groups, that the principle of equal treatment was insufficient to decide the matter. We had to return to the basic principles of benefit maximization and equal respect. However, this produced conflicting results. It appears, then, that we should begin to ask whether there are any reasons why we should prefer one of these basic principles to the other? Let us consider some arguments.

One objection to the principle of benefit maximization is that, on occasion it appears to justify results that seem intuitively unfair. In our case it seemed as though it might justify denial of an important educational program to children with a desperate need. There is a stronger case than this that can be made against the principle of benefit maximization, however.

It is important to recognize that the principle of benefit maximization will justify any exchange between the welfare of one group and the welfare of others so long as the average welfare increases. What the principle demands is that the average welfare be as high as possible. Suppose, then, that at some historical moment slavery was the most productive economic system. Does the principle of benefit maximization justify slavery? It appears that if it is, in fact, true that people are on the average better off in a society where some individuals are owned by others, then the principle of benefit maximization would justify slavery. But surely any moral principle that can justify something as morally offensive as slavery must be suspect.

Moreover, slavery is not the only morally problematic potential consequence of the principle of benefit maximization. It appears that any human right might be threatened if its denial leads to an increase in the average welfare. In chapter 2 we appealed to the principle of benefit maximization to justify intellectual freedom. We argued that individual freedom was efficient in producing the cumulative happiness of all. But suppose there were cases in which the consequences were otherwise. Perhaps there are circumstances where freedom is not conducive to the overall happiness. Ms. Fitzgerald's superintendent, Dr. Higgins, believes this about her case. Does it follow that we must suspend freedom in such cases? It appears that the principle of benefit maximization would require it.

It seems, then, that the principle of benefit maximization is a potential threat to basic rights. Not only does it permit us to trade the welfare of some for the welfare of others, it also allows us to trade the fundamental human rights of some for the welfare of others. All that matters is that the average welfare increase. This counts heavily against the principle. The principle of equal respect, however, has no such consequences. Its central requirement is that we respect the rights of others and not trade rights for welfare.

This suggests that consequentialist theories generally have a kind of liability that nonconsequentialist theories do not. They justify basic human rights only when and if the consequences of these rights are desirable on the average. Otherwise, consequentialist theories can lead to trading the rights of some for the welfare of others. Is this decisive? Before we bury the principle of benefit maximization and consequentialist ethical theories generally, we should attempt some defense of them. Consider two arguments.

First, consequentialists often argue that the imagined undesirable consequences of an application of the principle of benefit maximization are just that, imaginary. Take the case of slavery. If enslaving some people increases the average welfare of a society, then the principle of benefit maximization justifies slavery. But are there any real circumstances in which slavery would make society better off as a result? Consequentialists are likely to argue that when we look at the full range of slavery's consequences in any society, the answer must be "no." Perhaps some economic efficiencies might result from slavery in some cases, but consider other consequences. A slave-holding society must put much of its resources into means of oppression. It must have numerous police, soldiers, and overseers. Besides the fact that these individuals are unproductive, they can become threats to the liberty of the owner as well as the slave. Moreover, slavery has undesirable consequences for people other than the slave. The owner must live in fear of the slave. In these ways, the institution of slavery generally weakens the fabric of society. A slave-holding society must be fractious and unstable. Therefore, no actual slave-holding society can satisfy the principle of benefit maximization. That, after all, is why slavery is unjust. In real cases, consequentialists argue, the principle turns out to lead to an affirmation of human rights, not to their denial.

Second, nonconsequentialist views can also have troublesome results. In the previous section of this chapter, we argued that the maximin principle gave best expression to the principle of equal respect for persons. Inequalities are permissible only if they benefit everyone, especially those who receive the lesser share. But this might, under some circumstances, require us to forgo very substantial gains for almost everyone if only a few were benefited thereby. Suppose that a private school received a very substantial facilities gift, enough to build a needed modern library and to add a gym or swimming pool to their nonexistent physical education facilities. However, their rich benefactor made the gift with the stipulation that it be used in accord with a maximin principle. Therefore, the headmaster decided to spend all of the money to accommodate one paraplegic student with very expensive special equipment and substantial building alterations, including elevators, which, of course, all students could use to their benefit when they were not being used by the most disadvantaged student. Is that fair? Is it not sometimes morally appropriate to trade the welfare of one or the few for the welfare of the many? Are the many to be held hostage to the few? Thus, there is something to be said for consequentialist views and the principle of benefit maximization.

Are these considerations helpful? Obviously, we have not decided the issue. But we have learned something about the structure of the arguments for and against two general views of morality. It appears that when the principle of benefit maximization clashes with the principle of equal respect, the central concern is the extent to which we are willing to allow certain kinds of trades. When, if at all, are we willing to trade the welfare or the rights of some for the welfare of others? Are basic human rights negotiable? Can we suspend them if the general welfare requires it? If we have not resolved the dispute, at least we have achieved greater clarity about its nature. We also have a better idea of what is at stake when we make moral choices, even if it is more complex than we might like it to be.

Have we learned anything about moral reasoning? Here, as in the previous chapters, we have tested the moral principles that seem basic to our moral theories by deriving their consequences and by testing these consequences against our moral sensitivities in specific situations. For example, we generated some doubts about the adequacy of the principle of benefit maximization by noting that under some circumstances it appears to have morally abhorrent consequences. We tested the maximin principle in a similar way. This play between situations, principles, and intuitions is a characteristic feature of moral reasoning.

We appear to be engaging in a general process of encountering a situation in which some moral choice is required and to which we have a certain intuitive moral reaction. Mr. Bergen, for example, felt that it was unfair for the available resources to go for a program for the gifted and talented when there were other students who were far more needy. He was not, however, clearly able to say why. One way to help achieve clarity about our moral intuitions is to attempt to state a moral principle or principles that might serve to justify them. When we are able to formulate a principle that underlies our feelings, we then proceed to test that principle against other cases. We ask what the consequences of applying this principle might be in different situations. If we find that these results are also consistent with our moral experience, then that is a reason for accepting the principle. If, however, the principle seems to have morally objectionable results when applied to other kinds of cases, that counts against it. We thus test our moral theories against our moral feelings, much as we test scientific theories against data.

We also can achieve a higher degree of clarity about what is at stake in our moral choices by developing our moral theories. Linking issues about freedom and equality to principles such as the principle of benefit maximization or the principle of equal respect has helped us to develop our moral theory by appealing to moral ideas that apply to a broad range of cases. We can thus test our moral ideas against a broader and more adequate range of possibilities. Moral reasoning, then, seems in some respects like other forms of reasoning. It is logical and objective, considering all possibilities and legitimate criticisms. It involves both constructing theory and testing the consequences of theories against experience.

CONCLUSION

Note also that while we have not resolved the tension between the two major moral theories with which we have been dealing, we have made some progress. We have shown, for example, that some important ethical ideas have considerable justification. For example, the principle of equal treatment has been tested successfully against our moral experience. Moreover, it seems theoretically consistent with the principles of both benefit maximization and equal respect. That counts strongly in its favor. That we have not solved every problem we have raised should not be too discouraging. We have, after all, tried to raise the difficult problems. And we have at least achieved some clarity about them. That seems reason for optimism about the possibility of objective moral reasoning.

ADDITIONAL CASES

Can Mathematicians Reason?

Gauss Function, the head of the mathematics department at Boston Scholar High School, had agonized over his decision for too long already. He would have to write his letter of recommendation today, if it was to reach the Integral Institute before the fellowship deadline. He would have to decide among Elizabeth Fitzgerald, Charles Miller, and Ramon Ortega.

Each year 10 Integral Summer Fellowships were awarded to high school juniors who were going on to study mathematics in college. Fellows spent their summer at the Integral Institute in California working with some of the nation's top mathematicians. The competition for these awards was intensely keen. The best students in the entire nation would be competing. Winning an Integral Fellowship virtually guaranteed admission to the best universities in the country.

The primary criterion to be considered, according to the fellowship form, was "creative promise," the candidate's potential to do original mathematical research. Obviously this criterion required a highly subjective judgment from referees. While high school grades and test scores would be considered, the form stressed that they would not be determinative. The application also stressed that the Integral Institute was especially interested in promising minority and women students.

Function knew that his nominee would be accepted. Don Von Neumann, the head of Integral, would place commanding weight on any recommendation he submitted. Function and Von Neumann were old friends. They had earned their Ph.D.'s together at Yale, and they had kept in touch over the years. While Von Neumann had gone on to a distinguished career in mathematical research, Function had dropped out of what he termed "the academic rat-race" to take up high school teaching, because, as he said, he wanted the chance to help develop young minds and introduce them to the beauty of mathematics. Despite his career choice, Function continued to do scholarly work in mathematics and to contribute to research journals. Von Neumann often said that he admired his old friend's ability to teach in a high school and simultaneously be a practicing mathematician.

Whenever Von Neumann came to Boston he always looked up his friend, Gauss Function. On one of these occasions he had talked of the Integral Fellowships. He had said that, in choosing fellows, he rarely looked at grades or test scores. "Mathematical creativity isn't measured by such trivial aspects of academic culture," he had said. "Give me the considered assessments of people whose judgments I can trust."

Function knew that he was one of the people Von Neumann trusted. He also knew that he was in essential agreement with his friend; only creative mathematicians were qualified to recognize creativity in their students. However, Function was also acutely aware that the practical result of this was to create what some people would refer to as an "old-boy network." Hence, Function was always especially attentive to affirmative action considerations. He believed that in the past women and minorities had been unfairly discriminated against in mathematics, and he vowed to do his bit to overcome this legacy whenever the opportunity presented itself. In the present case he wasn't sure if one had.

On the one hand, if GPAs and test scores had been critical, Function's task would be simple: Elizabeth Fitzgerald would win his support hands down. The young woman had a 4.0 GPA and 800s on the SAT. By objective measures she was a gifted student. He was less sure of the originality of her mind, however. He had glimpsed only flashes of the creativity that separates gifted researchers from pedestrian ones. He was sure Fitzgerald would be a competent mathematician; whether she would be an outstanding one was problematic.

On the other hand, Charles Miller seemed to have the greatest potential for creative research. In class the young man was often brilliant and raised startlingly perceptive questions. The problem was that he wasn't always around to ask questions. He skipped many of his classes; he was disdainful of subjects that didn't interest him; he was an unbridled egotist. Partly as a consequence of these qualities, his grades were abominable. Mostly, however, his dismal record was a result of his simple refusal to do work that, he claimed, "bored" him. While Miller said he was going on to do mathematics in college, Function doubted whether any good department would accept him. He certainly wouldn't get in without an Integral Fellowship.

But Miller's personal characteristics made Function wary of recommending him. Function suspected that if Miller found the Integral Institute "boring," he would spend the summer on a California beach surfing and smoking dope. Frankly, Function didn't like risking his standing as a judge of talent by recommending Miller. If the young man "bombed out," Function suspected that his future nominees to Integral would no longer be assured of acceptance.

On the third hand there was Ramon Ortega. On paper Ortega's record was far superior to Miller's but nowhere near Fitzgerald's. He was a straight A student in math, but only an average one in his other subjects, with good but not outstanding SATs. He rarely spoke in class, and Function had no clear idea of how gifted he was. The department head suspected that much of Ortega's trouble stemmed from a manifestly poor elementary education, but he was unsure of this. Thus, on the major criterion of creativity, Function considered Fitzgerald and Ortega essentially equal (and relatively unknown) quantities. Miller, he was sure, had more potential.

It was when he considered affirmative action criteria that he found himself in a real quandary. Fitzgerald was as close to being a genuine aristocrat as U.S. society could produce. She was the scion of an old Boston Brahmin family. The Fitzgeralds (and their money) had been around almost as long as Boston had. With her academic record and her family's wealth, prestige, and political clout, she was certain to gain admission to any university in the country. She certainly did not need a fellowship. Nevertheless, she was a woman, and women were badly underrepresented in mathematics. A fellowship would certainly give her career a boost. On the fourth hand, then, Function wondered whether Fitzgerald's sex was really relevant to his decision. Could being a female ever be a real handicap to anyone who came from the Boston Fitzgeralds?

But if Fitzaerald's sex was relevant, despite her magnificently endowed background, what about Ortega's ethnicity? Function was as troubled by Ortega's status as a Hispanic as he was by Fitzgerald's sex. It turned out that Ortega had not been born in Puerto Rico, but in Boston, as had his mother (whose maiden name was Smith, Function discovered). Mr. Ortega was from Puerto Rico, but he had been in Boston since early childhood and was now the proprietor of a successful construction firm. While hardly from the same social stratum as the Fitzgeralds, the Ortega family was solidly bourgeois. On the fifth hand, then, should Ramon really be considered disadvantaged or Hispanic for affirmative action purposes?

Finally, on the last hand of this n-dimensional space, there was Miller. He was the quintessential WASP. Born and bred in a Boston suburb, the sole son of middle-class professionals, he had nothing to recommend him for affirmative action purposes. Indeed, he represented precisely the sort of person whose ubiquity affirmative action was designed to curtail. Should Miller's WASPness count against him?

Gauss Function considered these things as he sat down to write his old friend Von Neumann.

Some Questions

1. Affirmative action is a national policy designed to right past wrongs done to minorities and women. Does righting those wrongs necessar-

ily require the commission of another wrong against nonminorities and men?

2. How might affirmative action be carried out so as to avoid such wrongs? Be specific. That is, write a policy for the Integral Institute that will increase the representation of women and minority members in mathematics, while avoiding an injustice to other groups.

3. How does your suggested policy for the Integral Institute stack up against the principle of equal treatment we discussed under "Concept: Equality" earlier in this chapter?

4. If your policy violates the principle, can you justify the violation without recourse to an argument resting on righting injustices done in the past to women and minorities?

5. Suppose that our description of Miller's abrasive personality and unwillingness to do "boring" work had been omitted from the case, but all else remained the same. Would your choice of who should receive the fellowship change? If so, why do sex and minority status only count when weighed against personality quirks?

Bigotry?

Normally the meetings of the New Athens Administrative Cabinet were prosaic affairs. Indeed, Sarah Brownell, the superintendent, sometimes had difficulty keeping her principals awake. The details of budgets and personnel policies often had a soporific effect when they followed hard on the heels of a school cafeteria lunch. But today the meeting had grown increasingly tense. The longer Fred Katz spoke, the more restive everyone had become.

Fred was the principal of New Athens High. Its head for over 20 years, he was a quiet, thoughtful man whose forte was the meticulous analysis of problems followed by carefully considered action. Changes were not instituted frequently at NAHS, but when they were, they were usually appropriate ones. He also had a reputation for being plainspoken and not taking kindly to criticisms of his school if he thought they were unjustified.

As Fred spoke, Sarah had noticed that several of her principals were glancing surreptitiously at Jim Crawford, wondering how he was reacting to Katz's statements. Jim was staring very hard at Fred, but he was not saying a word. Finally, the tension had become palpable, and Sarah had interrupted to say something to the effect that nothing could be decided today anyway and that they had to get back to the agenda if they were to finish at a reasonable time. But even after an hour spent on the intricacies of the bus schedules, the air was still charged when everyone left. Everyone except Jim Crawford, that is, who stood waiting in the hallway. "Can I talk with you for a few minutes, Sarah?" he asked.

Jim was New Athens's only black principal. Sarah herself had appointed him to head Jefferson Elementary School shortly after she had become superintendent two years ago. She was committed to school integration, including the integration of the district's professional staff. She thought such an appointment was especially important because the community's black population had grown substantially in recent years. She was pleased with her choice. Jim was a good educator and a dynamic leader; already she was beginning to see the effects of that leadership at Jefferson. Staff morale was high, pupil achievement was increasing, and a number of parents, both white and black, had spoken highly of him. In fact, it was Jim's initiative that had provoked his remarks to Fred Katz during the meeting.

Jefferson Elementary, Jim's school, was a feeder to New Athens High, and he had become interested in the educational careers of Jefferson's graduates when they entered the secondary phase of their educations. In following up on that interest he had interviewed some former pupils, talked to the guidance counselors at NAHS, and collected some statistics. During the "new business" part of the meeting, Jim had presented the results of his work.

He began by describing the tracking system at the high school. Its curricula, like those of many U.S. secondary schools, were divided into college, general, and vocational tracks. Most of the students in the first track went on to the state university. A substantial number of those in the general track either went to the local community college or took white-collar jobs in the numerous electronics firms in the area. But according to Jim's figures, most of the students in the vocational areas took blue-collar jobs, entered military service, or were currently unemployed.

Also like most tracked secondary schools, NAHS's tracks were closely associated with race, Jim said. Fifty percent of the students in the vocational curriculum, 30% of those in the general track, and only 20% of the college-bound group were black.

Jim saw these figures as indications of inequality of opportunity in NAHS. "What's happening over at your shop, Fred?" he asked the high school principal. "Most of those black kids are coming out of my school, and I think they've been adequately prepared. Why are they being shunted into the bottom track?"

The question caught everyone's attention. Fred, as was typical, took the time to scrape the dottle out of his pipe before replying.

"You know, Jim, I wondered about the same thing a few years back, and I took the time to study the matter carefully." (Sarah smiled inwardly. In a single sentence Katz had managed to suggest that he was way ahead of Jim in recognizing a problem and that Jim hadn't given it adequate thought.) "I don't recall the details of my investigation, but the gist of it was as follows:

"I remember being concerned about possible racial bias in my staff. But the fact that a number of black kids were in the college track at least suggested that if the staff were biased, they were being selective about it. They couldn't have been prejudiced against black students per se. Then I interviewed almost half of the kids in the vocational track. It wasn't anything formal, you know, just casual conversations in the halls and so forth. Nearly all of them told me that they were in the vocational track because it's where they wanted to be. They don't want to go to college. They like it. They like taking auto mechanics, cosmetology, or the food service program.

"And those are good programs. Just a week ago, in fact, I was speaking to Ruth Higgins, a woman who runs a beauty shop over on the west side of town. Most of her customers are black, you know. Anyway, she'd just hired one of our girls, and she was telling me how well she's doing. Said the girl had obviously learned a lot in the cosmetology program.

"Now it happens that I know the kid she was talking about. She'd been a hell of a problem for her first couple of years in high school. Mother's the only one at home, a raft of kids, drunk half the time, a series of boyfriends streaming through, welfare—the whole bit. And the daughter looked like she was heading for the same sort of life. Instead, the kid got interested in cosmetology, started getting passing grades for the first time in her life, hung in there, and graduated. If we'd stuck her in the high track studying American literature and algebra she'd have been in over her head. She'd probably have dropped out and be on welfare today. Instead she's got a job and a decent start in life. What's wrong with that?

"I also talked to some of the parents. Most of them aren't interested in sending their kids to college. Kids aren't just stuck in the vocational programs, you know. We look at their test scores. We consider the recommendations of their elementary teachers. But most of all, we talk to the students and to their parents. They participate in the choice of curriculum, when the decision is made in the ninth grade. We explain the advantages of each of our programs. And then the parents, the students, and the guidance counselors decide together. But the parents and the students always have the final say. We'd never put a kid in any track if they wanted another. If the kid looks like he or she can handle the academics, we encourage them to enter the college program. But many don't want it. What are we supposed to do? Put them in a program against their wishes because it looks better for us to have racially balanced tracks? Or maybe we're supposed to abolish the tracks altogether, so everyone has to study Shakespeare, trigonometry, and French, whether they're able to master those things or not and whether they're going to college or not.

"Finally, don't take what I'm going to say wrong, but let's face facts, even when they're unpleasant ones. Every piece of evidence I've ever seen points to the possibility that black kids, on average, aren't as academically talented as whites. Maybe it's because of 'socialization,' whatever the hell that means. Maybe it's because their peer culture doesn't value academic success as much. Maybe it's because of the disintegration of the black family. Maybe it's because of America's history of racism. And maybe, just maybe, it's because black people aren't as intelligent as whites. I don't know, you don't know, and neither does anyone else know. Anyone who says they do is either a fool or a liar. If . . . "

It was then that Sarah Brownell interrupted and called the meeting back to its agenda.

When Sarah and Jim entered her office after the meeting, Jim had exploded. "Look, Sarah, Katz has got to go," he began. "I couldn't believe that a man as intelligent as he would mouth the racist crap that he did. The black kids in this town have got to have a chance at a better life. I don't have to recite the statistics on black poverty, unemployment, and youth crime in New Athens. You know them. And schooling is their chance. Maybe their only chance. Funneling them into cosmetology and food service occupations is a bad joke. That's no chance at all.

"When I started looking into this problem, I knew what I'd find at NAHS—that most of the black students were in the lower track. That's true in most schools. What I didn't expect to find was a principal who thought that that's where they belong. 'Maybe it's this. Maybe it's that. And maybe, just maybe, it's because black people aren't very smart.' Jesus! Well, there's another 'maybe' he left out. Maybe it's because our high school principal is a bigot.

"Katz is smart, I give him that. But racism is a disease that infects smart people, too. I'd hoped that when I discussed this problem with Fred he'd put his intelligence to work to help solve it. But he's not part of the solution, he's part of the problem. Nothing will happen at that school while he's the principal.

"Get rid of him. If you have to, 'promote' him to some harmless job in the central office, while you still have the chance. Once this gets out there'll be hell to pay. And it will get out—there were 12 people in that room today besides you and me. The black community in this town won't tolerate those sorts of attitudes anymore."

Sarah told him that she needed some time to think over the whole incident. But she knew she wouldn't have too much time. She recognized the thinly disguised threat in Jim's last remarks.

Some Questions

1. Fred Katz's comments to his colleagues are a mixture of facts and opinions. Which are which?

2. Assume for the purposes of discussion that the facts regarding how NAHS students get placed in tracks are correct—for example, that parents and pupils have the final say, that they are presented with an unbiased description of the advantages and disadvantages of each track, and so forth. In those circumstances, do Katz's opinions make any difference? How?
3. We have said that people have a broad right to express any opinions they wish, without fear of governmental interference or punishment. If Sarah gets rid of Katz, will he have been punished for expressing an unpopular opinion?
4. Are there any special restrictions that should be applied to educators' opinions regarding race that should not be applied to any other citizen? If so, what are they?
5. Suppose it is true that pupils at NAHS are placed in the track that they and their parents want. On what grounds does the school have an obligation to try to convince them that they are wanting the wrong thing? Is racial balance one of those grounds?
6. Does Katz have any right to expect that opinions expressed to colleagues in a private, professional meeting will be treated as confidential communications? If someone "leaks" Katz's comments to the public, would that person have acted unprofessionally?

Little School, Big Problem

In Fred Hastings's professional opinion, the North Creek School District was simply too small. Perhaps the time had come for him to act on that judgment and annex the district to Esterville.

Hastings was the commissioner of education for the state of Columbia. As commissioner, he was responsible to the state board of education for the effective and efficient operation of all of the schools in the state. He considered the North Creek School District to be neither effective nor efficient.

The school system had a total K–12 enrollment of only 254 pupils. Last year its graduating class had consisted of 15 students. Further, its enrollment had been declining for a decade. If present trends continued, it could be below 200 in five years. With those kinds of numbers, it simply could not offer an adequate educational program—at least not without levying astronomical taxes on its residents. And the people of North Creek could barely afford their current modest school taxes, much less astronomical ones.

Esterville, on the other hand, was a moderate-sized town only 15 miles to the west of North Creek. Esterville School District enrolled something over 3,000 students and offered, as nearly as Hastings could tell, an entirely adequate education to its pupils. Further, Esterville's school-aged population had also been in decline, and so it had plenty of room in its elementary and secondary schools to absorb North Creek's students. In fact, the Esterville Board of Education had recently indicated its willingness to annex its Lilliputian neighbor. The road connecting the two districts was a good one, so it would be easy to bus North Creek's pupils into the larger town for their education.

There were a lot of very good reasons to do just that. Because North Creek was so small, it was unable to offer many of the courses that were routinely offered to pupils in other districts in Columbia. For example, French was the only foreign language that the school system offered, and it provided only two years of that. Last year two of its second-year French students had requested another year of that language. Obviously the district couldn't afford to pay a teacher to instruct a class of only two students, and so the students went without. However, Esterville offered four years of French (and four of German). If North Creek were annexed to Esterville, students who wanted advanced levels of a foreign language would be able to take them. The same situation obtained in most of the other academic and vocational subjects—calculus, computer programming, and farm mechanics were just a few of the courses that would be available to North Creek students if they were bused to the neighboring district.

Nor was a deficient curriculum the only problem faced by the district. For example, because there were so few teachers, each one had to cover all aspects of his or her subject. Thus, North Creek's two science teachers taught general science, earth science, biology, chemistry, and physics. Needless to say, they were not well qualified in all of these.

Perhaps because of these sorts of problems, the district's students scored relatively poorly on standardized tests designed to measure advanced levels of subject-matter knowledge. However, if they weren't exactly the best physics and foreign language students in the state, they certainly weren't the worst. More importantly perhaps, they were well above the state means on tests of basic skills.

Scheduling problems were severe in the high school. This was because many courses could only be offered every other year. If students missed taking a course in the normal year, or if they failed a course and had to take it over, the chances were very good that they would have to wait two years and that it wouldn't fit into their program.

High-quality faculty were hard to recruit and retain in North Creek. Many teachers were unwilling to live and work in the "boonies." This recruiting problem was made worse by the relative poverty of the district; its salaries were among the lowest in Columbia.

These problems, and many others, would be substantially alleviated if North Creek was annexed to Esterville, making a single larger district. It was within Hastings's authority, as commissioner of education, to force such a consolidation if, in his judgment as a professional educator, such an action was the appropriate remedy for the district's deficiencies.

The problem was that neither the students nor the residents of North Creek thought that their schools were particularly deficient. More precisely, while they admitted to many of the problems just noted, they claimed that little schools such as theirs had many virtues, and that these virtues offset their deficiencies. For example, they pointed out that because their schools were so small, virtually all students participated in numerous extracurricular activities. These activities gave them a chance to develop new skills and leadership abilities. Everyone who wanted to play basketball made North Creek's team, and everyone who wanted to write had a place on the school's paper and yearbook. If forced to go to Esterville, many of those opportunities would disappear.

Further, because North Creek's classes were small, teachers got to know students well and could better meet individual needs. Individualization was further abetted by the fact that teachers, parents, and students met each other frequently outside of school in stores, churches, and social events. North Creek students did not suffer from the anomie so prevalent among their counterparts in larger schools. Serious discipline problems were almost nonexistent.

Finally, North Creek School was the center of the community. It served as a site for social and athletic events and was a source of community pride. Indeed, just the year before the district's marching band had won the state championship in its division and come home to the village's equivalent of a ticker-tape parade. This sort of unity of school and community would vanish if students were bused to Esterville. Residents were very possessive of their school. They were adamantly opposed to any attempt to merge it with its larger neighbor.

Hastings recognized that small size had certain advantages and that these might be lost if North Creek was merged with Esterville. But the fact remained that because of the inevitable curricular deficiencies of small schools, North Creek's students were getting a lower-quality education than other students in the state. It was Hastings's job to insure that equality of educational opportunity existed in Columbia. And whatever else that phrase might mean, it certainly meant that some children in the state ought not to receive a substandard education merely because they happened to have been born in a small rural village—or merely because they and their parents happened to be satisfied with the school there.

Some Questions

1. Assume the facts of the case are correct, in particular that North Creek students are unable to take many courses that students else-

where in Columbia can take. Is that a denial of equality of educational opportunity? Why?

2. If you answered "yes" to question 1, consider the following: Suppose there is a very wealthy district in the state of Columbia that offers its students seven different foreign languages, including Urdu. Are the other students in Columbia denied equality of opportunity because they cannot take Urdu?

3. In part, the impending conflict between Commissioner Hastings and the people of North Creek has to do with differing conceptions of student need. The commissioner thinks that students need the better teachers and richer course offerings that would be available to them in Esterville. The people, on the other hand, think that students need the more intimate surroundings of a small school. Who is entitled to decide such questions?

4. Consider the "principle of equal treatment" discussed under "Concept: Equality" earlier in this chapter. How are the students of North Creek and Esterville alike, such that the former should receive the same high school courses as the latter? Is that a question for professionals such as Hastings to decide?

CHAPTER 5

Educational Evaluation

A CASE

"He'll resign for how much?" Paula Carlton could hardly believe her ears. John Corrales, the attorney for Frank Banner, had just proposed that she could have Banner's resignation for the price of a good recommendation to be approved by Corrales and a buyout of Banner's contract for a mere $100,000. "One hundred thousand," Corrales repeated. "You know that if we go to court over this it will cost you more than that. Besides, if you go to court with the case you've got you are going to lose. You'll have spent the money and Frank will still be here."

Paula Carlton's first thought was to throw Corrales out of her office on some appropriate part of his anatomy. The idea that she had to bribe a clearly incompetent teacher to resign and had to favorably recommend him to some other unsuspecting school district to boot was hard to accept. However, she was constrained from depositing Corrales on his posterior in the hall by the fact that he was probably right. The case she had for dismissing Banner was not sound. Moreover, if the district pursued the matter in court, it would be expensive. Quite possibly Corrales's proposal was a good deal for the district.

Frank Banner was one of two tenured teachers at West High whom Paula Carlton considered incompetent. He was also the worst and potentially the most dangerous. From almost the first day she had been on the job as superintendent of the New Delaware School District, she had started to get parental complaints about Banner, who was one of three chemistry teachers at West High. Parents claimed that Banner taught their children nothing, that he knew little about chemistry, and that discipline was nonexistent. By the time she had received her fifth parental complaint, she decided to look into the matter.

She had first called Ben Belnap, West High's principal. He had been distinctly unhelpful. He reported that Banner was not West's best teacher, but that he was certainly not incompetent. As for parents, "they complain about everything." Her next step was to pull Banner's personnel file. Three things stood out. First, Banner's students scored markedly lower on the state's standardized achievement test in chemistry than did the students taught by other teachers at West High. Since the chemistry classes were untracked and used the same curriculum, she could see little that would account for this difference except the quality of instruction.

Second, although Belnap's yearly evaluations of Banner had been unenthusiastic, they were hardly indicative of incompetence. Belnap was required to evaluate each teacher at West on several factors, using a five-point scale on which 5 was excellent and 1 was unsatisfactory. He had given Banner a 2 on discipline and a 2 on classroom management. Other categories such as lesson plans and lesson preparation had rated scores of 3 or 4. At the bottom of the evaluation form in the section for comments he had written, "Some areas of performance could use improvement." Looking farther back into the file, she found that Banner had received similar ratings for several years.

The third thing that came to her attention was that the file contained several letters from irate parents, one of which was signed only "a concerned parent." All of these letters accused Banner of gross incompetence. Several also accused him of heavy drinking, although there was no suggestion that he was drinking on the job. Unfortunately, there was no indication that Belnap had taken any steps to check out the substance of the complaints. Nor was there any indication that Belnap had acquainted Banner with the existence of these letters. They had simply gone into Banner's personnel file.

Paula Carlton's next step was to discuss the file and the complaints with Banner. His defense was that he had a different teaching philosophy from the other chemistry teachers at West High. He believed in a nondirective approach to teaching. Moreover, he believed in teaching students to think, not just to regurgitate facts. Of course his students did not do well on the state's tests, but they were excellent critical thinkers. He pointedly noted that the district had no policy specifying any particular teaching strategy, and it had prided itself in leaving such decisions to the professional judgment of teachers.

This discussion had left Paula Carlton uncertain about what was going on. She decided to pay a surprise visit to Banner's chemistry class. Nothing in the parental complaints or Belnap's evaluations prepared her for what she saw. Banner spent the period apparently teaching chemistry to his desk and the chalk board. It was hard to judge the content of the lesson because it was largely inaudible. She did note that two of the three equations written on the board were incorrect. She was pleased that she remembered some of her college chemistry.

Students in the class ranged from inattentive to positively disruptive. Most were engaged in private conversations. Several others were doing homework for other classes. Most alarmingly, three students were heating a beaker over a bunsen burner, dumping into it spoonfuls of chemicals that were taken, seemingly at random, from jars removed from an unlocked cabinet. Mr. Banner seemed oblivious to this. Paula Carlton wondered if she should check out the school's liability insurance. But the experience was sufficient to convince her that Banner had to go. No student was about to learn chemistry from Banner. They would be lucky to get through the year without blowing themselves up. Banner seemed the teacher the state legislature had in mind when it wrote the law on dismissal for incompetence.

Nevertheless, it was not clear that he could be dismissed for incompetence. His record did not indicate incompetence. Could he be dismissed as a result of one observation and unsubstantiated parental complaints? That was doubtful. Neither could he be left in the class until a defensible case was developed. Could she trust Belnap, the principal, to build a case? He did not seem to take teacher evaluation seriously. Moreover, she was reluctant to leave Banner in the class for that long. He was not only inept; his lack of supervision was dangerous. Perhaps the $100,000 was a small price to pay.

DISPUTE

A: A person is innocent until proven guilty.

B: Sure, that's true in a court of law, but what if you see someone who is obviously incompetent? As an administrator, you have an obligation to protect students from incompetent teachers. Each day lost in a classroom is a precious commodity that can never be reclaimed. You have to be courageous and get rid of incompetence as soon as possible. That's what your job is really about.

A: I'm not against courage or for students losing valuable learning time, but there have to be procedures to protect teachers against arbitrary and unfair administrators, don't there? Without set procedures, administrators could just fire teachers on a whim or because they don't like them or something like that. And that wouldn't be fair.

B: You sound like a union representative! What about being fair to students? Is it fair to put them into a room with a teacher you know can't teach? I know we have procedures for bringing charges of incompetence against teachers, but I am arguing that they are too complicated and time-consuming. They protect the teacher, not the students. We ought to get rid of such procedures and let the administrators do their job. Trust us and give us the power to run good schools, and we'll do it, by God, or you can fire us, too!

A: If you were to be fired, wouldn't you want to know why and on what basis you were being fired?

B: Well, yes.

A: And wouldn't you want to have a chance to defend yourself if any of the negative claims being made about you weren't true?

B: Yes.

A: And if you were told you were incompetent and you thought you were quite competent, wouldn't you demand to compare your evidence of your competence to their evidence of your incompetence?

B: Yes.

A: Then you want to be considered innocent until proven guilty.

B: I sure do!

A: Well??

CONCEPT: DUE PROCESS

The issues in this case concern due process. Paula Carlton has reason to believe that Banner is incompetent. It is less clear, however, that she has evidence that could be defended in court. Nor is it clear that Mr. Banner has been treated fairly. Most of the questions about the adequacy of Paula Carlton's case against Mr. Banner and the fairness of his treatment are issues of due process. Due process is, of course, an important legal concept. But it is also an ethical concept. Here we will be concerned with its moral content.

What is due process? Generally, issues of due process concern the nature of fair procedures for making decisions. The question is: What counts as fairness in making decisions about matters that affect others' lives? Questions of due process are not usually directly concerned with the fairness of the decision itself, but with the fairness of the process used to reach it. It is too much to demand of administrators or of any human being that every decision reached be correct. But we can expect decision makers to take proper care in how they reach their decisions. Due process tells us what counts as taking proper care.

At the core of the concept of due process is the idea of rationality. Rationality requires that equal regard be given to all sides in a case and that all appropriate evidence be brought to bear. What is to be desired in any decision is that it be justified by available evidence, that it be reasonable. Due process defines the kinds of rationally required procedures that will yield reasonable and justified decisions. Conversely, failure to follow due process procedures is usually to fail to take due regard for evidence or for other reasonable requirements for procedural fairness. Rationality is not all that there is to due process, but it is its central element.

Consider some of the features of due process.

One aspect of due process is the idea of notice. If people are to be judged according to the quality of their performances, it is reasonable to claim that they have a right to know the standards according to which they are to be judged. It is unreasonable and unfair to hold people responsible for meeting expectations of which they are ignorant.

This aspect of due process requires that people be judged according to standards that are both known in advance and sufficiently clear that people can know what counts as meeting them. Arguably, this aspect of due process has been violated in Mr. Banner's case. He has been evaluated annually, but these evaluations have given him no reason to believe that his work was unsatisfactory. If the district is now to attempt to dismiss him for doing the same quality of work that he has been doing all along, it is reasonable to accuse the district of lacking consistent public standards for evaluating teachers. Moreover, the district has no policies concerning acceptable teaching methods. They have left such matters up to teachers. Thus Mr. Banner has a reasonable case that he has not been given fair notice of district expectations and a chance to comply with them.

A second aspect of due process is the rational requirement that standards must be consistently applied. Two students who do the same quality of work ought to receive the same grade. Likewise, a teacher whose performance is consistent from year to year ought to receive the same evaluation. Thus, if the district should claim to have some known standard for evaluating teachers, Mr. Banner can claim that this standard was not applied consistently to him. The fact that he received radically different evaluations from Mr. Belnap and from Ms. Carlton indicates that such standards as the district has are capriciously applied.

A third component of due process is that decisions should be made on the basis of reasonable evidence and that procedures should be followed that make such evidence available on a systematic basis. There are a number of things in this case that suggest procedural problems in the collection of evidence. For one, Paula Carlton has based her decision to attempt to dismiss Banner on a single personal visit. But visits from the superintendent are not normally a part of the procedures for evaluating teachers. Nor is one visit sufficient for such a judgment. Moreover, the visit was unannounced. Paula Carlton has not given Mr. Banner a chance to prepare for his evaluation. Arguably, of course, it is more important to discover what teachers normally do than it is to discover what they can do. Nevertheless, unannounced visits are often inconsistent with common practice in teacher evaluation and may be a violation of due process.

Paula Carlton has also relied on standardized test scores to evaluate Mr. Banner. If such test scores are to be fairly used, it must be the case that teachers whose teaching is compared are teaching similar students and are attempting to accomplish similar goals. Paula Carlton has some evidence to believe the former. Students are not tracked into the three sections of chemistry. Yet the quirks of high school scheduling can often generate sections of students of differing ability without a conscious effort at tracking.

Perhaps one section of chemistry conflicts with orchestra or with an advanced placement math class. Such things can introduce a selection effect into test scores. Due process requires that if test scores are to be used in evaluating teachers, one must be able to show that differences in scores are due to differences in teaching ability, not to differences in student ability. Moreover, Paula Carlton has reason to believe that the goals of the different chemistry teachers are not identical. If this is true, it may well be the case that the standardized test is less appropriate for Mr. Banner's class.

Finally, the fact that Mr. Belnap has introduced unverified and, in one case, anonymous letters into Mr. Banner's file raises an issue of due process. Unless further steps are taken to verify the parents' complaints, they have the status of hearsay evidence. They are simply unsubstantiated rumor. One of the rules for collecting and judging evidence is that hearsay is not acceptable evidence. Thus complaints about Mr. Banner's teaching should not be part of his file. Especially, they should not be used in making any judgment about his fitness to teach unless they are independently established.

A final feature of the concept of due process is that such standards as are used in judging individuals or their work have to have a rational connection to a legitimate purpose. Paula Carlton has apparently not based her case against Banner on the charge that he is a heavy drinker. Were she to do so she would very likely violate this standard of due process unless she was also able to show that his drinking affected his job performance. Otherwise, the fact that Banner drank, even the fact that he was a heavy drinker, would lack a rational connection to any legitimate purpose of the school.

We observed at the beginning of this discussion that at the core of the idea of due process is the notion of rationality. We have seen in general how this is so and seen that due process has to do primarily with ensuring that reasonable decisions are made about other people in a rationally justified way using adequate evidence. Let us now consider more directly how these various aspects of due process connect to rationality and the adequacy and reliability of evidence.

Often due process standards are simply procedures for collecting and evaluating evidence. The notion that hearsay evidence is an unacceptable basis for making a decision about a person, for example, is based on the view that rumors, opinions expressed by people who are not expert about some matter, or testimony by people who are biased or not known to be reliable observers are suspect as evidence. Rationality demands that evidence from such sources should be disregarded or independently checked. The evidence provided by parents in this case should be regarded as hearsay. The point is not that parents are somehow particularly stupid or dishonest. Possibly much of what they have said will check out. At the same time, they have not been in a position to observe Mr. Banner's class, they are not expert about chemistry or teaching, and they must also rely for much of their information on their children. Moreover, since their children are not doing well in Mr. Banner's class, they may be biased. There is thus much reason to be cautious about the reliability of their views.

Many other features of due process are also designed to generate reliable evidence. In proceedings in which a suspension or termination is possible, administrators are required to provide a hearing in which evidence is checked and witnesses are cross-examined. The point of such a hearing is to provide an opportunity to check the reliability of the evidence on which a decision is based. When the decision is particularly important, elaborate procedures may be required. Again, the point is not to make the decision more complex or to harbor incompetents. It is to ensure that important matters are decided on the basis of reliable evidence.

The emphasis on judging people according to known and clear standards has a similar connection to rationality. Reasonable judgments require some standard of judgment. For example, an administrator who lacks a clear view of what counts as good teaching cannot make a reasoned decision about whether a particular instance of teaching is good. Nor can teachers make a reasonable attempt to follow the standard if it is unknown or is so unclear that it is impossible to know what counts as meeting it. Moreover, a rational judgment of a teacher's ability cannot be made if the teacher does not know what is expected. Rational decision making is thus impossible in the absence of clear standards.

Finally, the demand that standards be consistently applied expresses a demand for rational decision making. Here the argument is identical to that made in the previous chapter for the claim that equals must be treated equally. If two teachers, Jones and Smith, perform identically on the appropriate, standard, any argument for giving Jones a certain benefit contingent on that performance will also be an argument for giving the same benefit to Smith. A procedure that assigns different benefits to teachers who have performed similarly is, therefore, not only unjust, but irrational.

In essence, then, due process requires administrators to make reasonable decisions by following rational procedures that generate reliable evidence and consistent judgments. Generally, the extensiveness of the effort required to generate reliable evidence should be proportional to the seriousness of the interest affected.

ANALYSIS: RESPECT FOR PERSONS

In previous chapters we have tried to show how the concepts we have dealt with can be interpreted within the context of different ethical theories. We have looked at consequentialist theories, for which the principle of benefit maximization is primary, and nonconsequentialist theories, for which the principle of respect for persons is primary. We have tried to be evenhanded in our presentation, although the astute reader may have detected a higher level of enthusiasm for nonconsequentialist views. Here we want to argue for the primacy of the value of respect for persons. The point of our argument is not that the principle of benefit maximization has no role in ethical thought. It is, rather, that it should be subordinate to the principle of equal respect. It will be convenient to argue this here because the principles of due process seem to fit most comfortably into a nonconsequentialist framework.

Why give people due process? Given the discussion above, the question is tantamount to asking why people should be treated reasonably. For someone for whom the principle of benefit maximization is primary, the answer must be that the consequences of treating people reasonably are better than those of treating people unreasonably. If teachers are evaluated capriciously, for example, they may be denied some benefit, such as tenure or a merit-pay raise, causing them to become discouraged and not try to perform better. Reasonable treatment, it would seem, produces better consequences than unreasonable treatment.

No doubt this is true. Yet we can reasonably ask if it is really necessary, in order to show that we should treat people reasonably, to prove that some type of benefit would be maximized. What about cases in which no benefit is achieved in treating someone reasonably? Isn't it possible to argue that we simply should treat people reasonably because it is our moral responsibility to do so? Isn't treating others reasonably a part of our making morally responsible decisions and a part of respecting the value of others? Suppose that we could point to some situations in which unreasonable treatment did no harm and reasonable treatment produced no good. Should unreasonable treatment be condoned? Consider, for example, another area that often raises issues of due process: grading. Suppose that a teacher capriciously assigned a particular grade to a student in a high school class. But suppose also that nothing turned on the grade. Perhaps the student had already been admitted to college, thus rendering the capricious grade harmless. Would it then be morally acceptable to assign the grade on an entirely arbitrary basis? Could we toss a term paper down the stairs and assign a grade on the basis of which step the paper landed on? No harm—no foul?

One response to this question is that some harm inevitably results. The student who has been graded capriciously will inevitably feel wronged. He or she may resent the teacher or become alienated from the subject matter or education generally. Thus there is harm done. But such a response is, at its heart, a nonconsequentialist one. If no benefit is at stake, why should the student feel wronged by being graded capriciously? In fact, from the consequentialist point of view, if no benefit is at stake, the student has not been wronged. Or if he or she has been wronged, the wrong consists in the fact that arbitrary treatment denies the student equal respect. If the student *justifiably* feels wronged, it is because the capricious treatment is an affront to the student's dignity and worth, not because he or she has lost some benefit. The other harms result from the initial feelings of having been treated unfairly. They are only harms if this initial reaction about being unjustly treated is warranted. It appears, then, that the principle of equal respect is central to the notion of due process in a way that the principle of benefit maximization is not.

Moreover, approaching issues of due process through the principle of benefit maximization often produces odd results. Consider the matter of discipline and punishment. One important moral concept about punishment is that the punishment should fit the crime. Generally, the idea seems to be that people who have done something morally wrong deserve to suffer in proportion to the evil they have done. Too much punishment or too little is inappropriate. This conception of punishment makes sense from the nonconsequentialist point of view, because it recognizes that people are morally responsible for their choices and that they can do evil. It recognizes that people are sometimes guilty. And it provides a way to absolve guilt through punishment. One justly suffers proportionately to the wrong one has done.

Consequentialists have considerable difficulty in explaining why punishment should fit the crime. For the consequentialist, punishment, if it is appropriate at all, must be justified by its consequences. Deterrence of further misbehavior is typical of the desirable consequences thought to result from punishment. But how much punishment is enough if the point of punishment is to deter? The answer, of course, is that the punishment required is that which is enough to discourage people from misbehaving. But there is no special reason to assume that such punishment as is sufficient to deter will also fit the crime.

Chewing gum is a common school "crime." Its punishment is normally a modest reprimand or a brief detention: trivial punishments for a trivial infraction. It is obvious to any teacher that these punishments do not deter. Students continue to chew gum. We propose that if gum chewers were to be hung from the school flagpole, gum chewing would quickly cease. Indeed, once the policy was announced (assuming it was believed), we suspect that gum chewing would cease immediately, relieving the administrator of the unpleasant duty of executing any bubble-gum malefactors. Nevertheless, the suggestion seems highly offensive. Presumably that is because the punishment is radically inappropriate to the offense. It is, however, difficult for the nonconsequentialist to explain why the solution is inappropriate if it works.

Nonconsequentialist views also provide more plausible accounts of due process. We are obligated to treat people reasonably because they are people. Treating people reasonably respects them as persons. Capricious treatment denies the worth of the person maltreated.

It is important here to return to the concept of persons as moral agents. Persons are free and rational moral agents who are responsible for their choices and who have the duty to choose wisely. Presumably part of what we mean by the idea of responsible and wise choice is that decisions will be made reasonably on the basis of evidence. Respect not only for persons, but also for reasoned decisions, thus seems central to the non-consequentialist view. To treat others capriciously seems not only to fail to show them equal respect, but is to act in a way that is inconsistent with one's own status as a free and rational moral agent.

We want to offer two additional arguments for a nonconsequentialist viewpoint. First, it seems that the principle of benefit maximization may presuppose something very like the principle of equal respect. Most human beings value their own happiness and their own welfare. But why should they value the happiness and welfare of others? Note that the principle of benefit maximization requires people to value the welfare of others equally with their own. It requires of us, not that we act so as to maximize our own welfare, but that we act so as to maximize the average welfare. Indeed, the principle of benefit maximization can require an individual to act against his or her own welfare because the average welfare requires it. According to the principle of benefit maximization, everyone's happiness or everyone's welfare counts equally. But why should this be so? Why should we be concerned about anyone else's welfare? Or why should we care more about the welfare of human beings than cows? Here, while other answers are possible, it is very tempting to appeal to the idea of respect for persons. We should care about the happiness or welfare of others as well as our own because they, like us, are persons. Their interests and their welfare are equally as important as our own. Such a response is surely attractive and plausible, but to give it is to make the principle of benefit maximization subordinate to the principle of equal respect. In short, it is to grant the point that we are arguing. The principle of equal respect for persons is morally basic. Other principles are justified in its terms and are subordinate to it.

A final argument has to do with the concepts of happiness and growth. It is one that should be particularly appealing to educators. Consider that a nonconsequentialist view places a premium on the capacity for reflective, rational choice. Recognizing that people are free moral agents, its central concern is that this capacity for rational choice should be exercised responsibly. However, neither the capacity for free choice nor the skills and attitudes for its responsible exercise are present at birth. Infants do not choose, they respond to stimuli. The growth of the capacity for free and responsible choice is a difficult and complex topic. It would be possible to engage in a long discussion of how or even if it is possible. We make two assumptions. First, growth as a moral agent is possible, and the process of becoming a moral agent involves learning and education. Second, educators are in the business of creating responsible moral agents. Indeed, we believe that it is their central task.

Suppose, however, that happiness was possible apart from moral growth. Consider a rather imaginative but, we hope, forceful example. Imagine that in some future time a group of scientists announced that they had discovered a way to make all of humanity infinitely and permanently happy. All that was necessary was for people to turn themselves in to a hospital where they would have electrodes implanted in their brains that would stimulate their pleasure centers at appropriate intervals. Since they would be blissfully unaware of anything except their own pleasure, they would be fed intravenously and would be confined to the hospital bed for the rest of their days. People need not be concerned about this, however, because the advance of robotics and automation have made the economy self-sufficient, self-regulating, and foolproof. Human beings need be concerned about nothing beyond their own happiness. Indeed, once they were wired in, they would need to be concerned about nothing. Concern itself would be a thing of the past. The mind would be given over entirely to the experience of happiness.

This thought experiment proposes a trade. It asks whether we would be willing to exchange the use and development of our faculties, those faculties of reflection and choice that mark us as persons, for a life of guaranteed and unending happiness. Our moral sensitivities rebel against such a proposal. We expect most readers will agree. But what is the basis of such a response? Here it is easy for a nonconsequentialist to respond. The proposal requires us to abandon everything that is morally central to a responsible human life. It is not an acceptable exchange. It is not clear what a consequentialist (at least one for whom the good to be maximized is happiness) could say. The thought experiment stipulates that happiness is maximized. What else counts?

CONCLUSION

Socrates is recorded as saying that the unexamined life is not worth living. Why not? In our view, the point of this maxim is that to fail to reflect on how one lives is to fail to recognize one's status as a moral agent. It is to refuse to be responsible for one's self. In a fundamental way, it is to refuse to be a person. We have been unhappy with consequentialism because for consequentialists it is happiness or human welfare, not growth as persons, that is central. Growth for the consequentialist is a contingent value. It is a matter of interest only when it leads to happiness.

In our view, growth as a moral agent, as someone who cares about others and is willing and able to accept responsibility for one's self, is the compelling matter. Promoting this kind of development is what teachers and administrators ought to be fundamentally about, whatever else it is that they are about. As educators, we are first and foremost in the business of creating persons.

ADDITIONAL CASES

A Letter of Recommendation

September 23, 1986

Mr. John Sitallsky
Superintendent, York School District
1301 West Avenue
York, New Hampshire 90814

Dear John:

Your letter arrived yesterday, and it was good to hear from you. I hope things are settling down. From your description, York sounds like a damned difficult district. A superintendency is a tough job under any conditions. When it's your first one, and you've got a board the likes of York's, it can be awful. Hang in there. You remember my first year at Westville, when you were principal out at Hammond School. That was my first job as a chief school officer, and I thought I'd never make it through the year. I've always appreciated the support you gave me in that difficult period.

Anyway, you asked about Carol Miller. I'll tell you what I can, but my memory may be a little hazy on some of the details. It's been almost five years, and since I'm no longer in Westville, her records aren't available to me. Be sure to get them from the personnel folks there, so that you can check on my recollections of her performance.

Mrs. Miller came to the district in the Spring of 1977 to fill in for my regular home economics teacher, who went on maternity leave. As I recall, she was highly recommended by her professors at State. Initially, I'd planned to keep her only until the end of the school year, because I expected Mrs. Woodwall (the regular home ec teacher) to return to the classroom in September. When Woodwall decided at the last minute to stay home and raise her kid, I was stuck, so I kept Miller on.

All in all, it was a good choice. I don't recall exactly how many times I observed her classroom, probably two or three, but I do remember that she always struck me as being well prepared and as taking an interest in her work. I very definitely recall her capacity to motivate her students, especially the boys—most of whom didn't want to be in a home economics course. She was, I think, a damned good home ec teacher. Certainly better than Woodwall.

I also remember appointing Miller to head up a curriculum revision committee during her third year at Westville. I had occasion to work with her directly then, and I remember that she impressed me as being thoroughly trained in her field. As far as subject matter competence goes, she's probably as good as you're going to get.

On the downside, there's the matter of her attendance. At least while I was running Westville, I could count on her to use every sick day, personal day, and professional day she had coming. I could also count on her to cash them in on Mondays. Every administrator knows that teachers tend to get sick on Fridays and Mondays, but Miller must've set a record in that regard. Be sure and check on this matter with whoever's personnel director in Westville these days.

A pattern of absences is important to recognize, but it's more important to know why it occurs. Maybe Miller just happens to catch colds on Mondays. I don't believe that for a minute, but it's possible. Perhaps, like most of the others who pull this stunt, she just wanted more long weekend vacations than the school calendar offers. I'd give that explanation a "definite maybe." What makes me doubt it is that she only missed work on Mondays, not Fridays and Mondays (which, you'll soon discover, is the usual pattern of the long weekenders on your faculty).

What I heard was that she and her husband hit the bottle pretty hard on weekends, and they needed Mondays to sober up. Now, I don't know that for a fact, of course. But I met her husband's boss once at a Kiwanis meeting, and he (the boss) complained of the same pattern of absence in Miller's spouse. He said that he knew the Millers very well socially and that they were both "a couple of lushes." His words. He claimed that their drinking was the reason neither one could make it to work on Mondays.

I'd try to clear this up, if I were you. I think Mrs. Miller's a pretty good teacher. I'd hire her, if it weren't for the absenteeism. Even with it, I might employ her, if I could be sure that she just likes to take her vacations in three-day chunks. (I'd certainly sit down with her beforehand and have a little heart-to-heart about where I expected her to be on Mondays. But I'd probably hire her.) However, if she's into the sauce so heavily that she needs to take a day off every couple of weeks to recover, I wouldn't touch her with the proverbial ten-foot pole. There's too much at stake. We can't risk having an alkie running a classroom, especially a home ec classroom, where there's always the risk of a serious accident. The teacher really has to be alert in those situations, not hung over.

Well, that's about all I can tell you about Carol Miller. Best of luck in the new job, and give my regards to Helen and the kids.

Sincerely,

Charles L. Kaufmann,
Superintendent
Polk County School District

Some Questions

1. Has Kaufmann behaved unethically? That is, does reporting hearsay evidence in a letter of recommendation count as behaving unethically?
2. If you answered "yes" to the previous question, how could Kaufmann fulfill his responsibility to provide an accurate recommendation and alert his colleague to what is potentially a very serious problem? Sketch out such a letter.
3. Presumably the heavy use of alcohol or other drugs by a teacher is relevant information for judging that teacher's fitness for the classroom. Also presumably, most teachers who abuse alcohol or drugs will not volunteer that fact to prospective or current employers. How then are school administrators to gain such information without violating a teacher's rights to privacy and due process?
4. We have said in this chapter's opening case study that to consider heavy drinking in a performance evaluation would be a violation of a teacher's due process rights unless it is also shown that the drinking affects his or her job performance. Short of the teacher's being "falling-down drunk" in the classroom or something equally obvious, isn't such a matter impossible to prove? If you think it is possible, describe how you would do it.
5. Administrators sometimes argue that it is okay to "cut corners" on matters such as a teacher's due process rights if the purpose is to benefit the school. Is it okay? Would a consequentialist and a nonconsequentialist answer this question differently?

A Matter of Standards

Charles Brick was troubled. As principal of Eastview High School, it was his responsibility to make recommendations regarding the appointment and tenure of his faculty to the district's superintendent. He was not sure what he should recommend regarding the reappointment of Lillian Wilson. More to the point, he was not sure how he could reasonably decide what to recommend.

Lillian was in her third year as an American history teacher at Eastview. As a consequence, she would either be awarded tenure or released at the end of the current term. In deciding which of these two courses of action to take, the principal always relied heavily on his department chair's judgment. Brick realized that as an ex-physical education teacher, he was not as good a judge of the subject-matter competence as the department head in that subject.

The problem was that Chesterton School District required that probationary teachers be evaluated by two department chairpersons during their first three years. On the surface, this policy made sense. It was supposed to insure that another perspective was brought to bear in the evaluation process and thereby insure that beginners' careers were not dependent on the perceptions of a single person. Thus Wilson had been evaluated by Charlie Tomkins, the head of the social studies department, three times during her probationary period at Eastview. But she had also been evaluated by Rita Morales, the social studies chairperson at Roosevelt High School, an equal number of times during the same period. And these evaluations, in accordance with district policy, had been carried out quite independently of each other.

The district's teacher evaluation form provided a series of scales for observers to use in judging a teacher's competence. Various instructional criteria were to be rated on a five-point scale, from "outstanding" to "below average." For example, the observation instrument required observers to rate the following items:

> *Discipline:* Does the teacher maintain control of the class at all times? Are disciplinary procedures fair? Describe.
> *Individual Differences:* Does the teacher adapt his or her instruction to take account of individual differences among pupils? Give examples.
> *Lesson Objectives:* Were lesson objectives made clear to pupils? Describe.

The problem arose because Morales's and Tomkins's evaluations were in nearly total disagreement. Morales had given Wilson "outstanding" on several of the rating scales and "above average" on all of the remainder. She had strongly recommended Wilson's reappointment. On the other hand, the highest rating given to Wilson by Tomkins was "average" He had rated her "below average" on several of the criteria, and he had recommended against tenure. It was hard for Brick to imagine a more disparate set of evaluations.

What was even more astonishing was that Morales and Tomkins had apparently observed much the same behavior on Wilson's part. For example, under the item concerning individual differences, Morales had written:

> Excellent. Teacher had collected a variety of books on the same topic that required different levels of reading skill. These books were readily at hand during the lesson, and they were assigned to students according to their reading competence. I also noted that she varied the complexity of the explanations she gave according to student ability.

On the other hand, Tomkins had written in response to the same question:

> Below average. Teacher relies heavily on books to individualize instruction, but the same basic lesson was taught to the entire class.

While attempts were seemingly made to vary the level of discourse in the classroom, these must be faulted because attempts to simplify explanations often resulted in oversimplified, even incorrect, remarks.

In an attempt to reach some sort of justified conclusion regarding Wilson's competence, Brick had called Morales and Tomkins into his office to discuss their evaluations. That had not helped at all. In fact, all it seemed to accomplish was to make the two department heads distrustful of each other's competence. The two had ended up arguing over vague and (to Brick's mind) largely irrelevant aspects of educational philosophy.

Brick was unsure how to proceed, and his recommendation to the superintendent was due in less than a week.

Some Questions

1. We have said that due process requires that standards be sufficiently clear that people can know what counts as meeting them. Consider the standards involved in this case—namely, those for discipline, individual differences, and lesson objectives. Do these meet the clarity standard required for due process? Why or why not?
2. If you answered "no" to the previous question, can you write suitably clear standards for these matters? Write one for classroom discipline. If you have difficulty doing so, what does this say—in principle— about meeting due process standards in teacher evaluation?
3. Why not bring in a "tie-breaker"? That is, what would be ethically dubious about getting another social studies chairperson to come in to observe Wilson and make a recommendation to Brick?
4. Most school districts do not have the double evaluation system described in this case—that is, with department heads from two schools carrying out evaluations of probationary teachers. Is having two separate evaluators a good idea? Consider this policy in the light of the consistency standard of due process.
5. In education, one standard approach to the problem of vague criteria is to break down global requirements into highly specific ones. Writing "behavioral objectives" for student evaluations is an example. What might be wrong, from a due process perspective, with this approach to teacher evaluation?

A Problem of Grades

The meeting with the parents of the students in Mrs. Milner's high-track junior English class had gone smoothly enough. No individuals had lost their composure. There had been no overt belligerence. Still, Janet Mc-

Donald, the principal of Washington High, had no clear idea of what she would do about the matter.

The complaints were about Mrs. Milner's grading. She seemed to view the teaching of American literature roughly in the way a drill sergeant viewed recruits' initiation into the Marine Corps. A mixture of toughness and capriciousness was seen as a virtue. Mrs. Milner was young. In fact, it was her first year. She would learn that excellence and maintaining standards were not synonymous with mindless discipline and vicious grading. But that would be too late for this year's students. Janet McDonald hoped that the students' willingness to read good literature would recover from their experience. She was more concerned about miseducation than misgrading.

Parents had raised four issues. First, the average in Mrs. Milner's college preparatory class was substantially lower than those in the other sections taught by other teachers. Yet these other sections had the same curriculum and students of similar ability. The average in Mrs. Milner's class was a feeble C-, while that of other classes was B. Parents pointed out that English grades were crucial in college admissions. Many of the students wanted to enter highly selective schools. Poor grades in junior English could make a substantial difference, not only because a C- did not look good on a transcript, but because it unfairly lowered a student's rank in class compared to pupils in other sections who were doing the same quality of work.

Second, Mrs. Milner used what the parents called a "fudge factor" in her grading. A fourth of the grade was based on what she called "class performance." Most students seemed to think that class performance was equivalent to bootlicking. Students who stayed after class and expressed their undying love of *Moby Dick* and *The Scarlet Letter* inevitably did well in this aspect of their grades.

Third, Mrs. Milner used grades for discipline. She had a system of "errors." Students got an error for such things as being late for class, chewing gum, and talking. Parents thought that these things were unrelated to students' performance in English.

Finally, Mrs. Milner's grading of essays seemed highly subjective, if not downright capricious. Parents had brought in some copies of exams and essays. Janet McDonald had to admit that she was often unsure what Mrs. Milner's questions asked. Further, comments and grades on the essays seemed capricious. The teacher seemed able to overlook a glaring ineptitude in sentence construction while objecting to a plausible interpretation of literary material. Janet McDonald wondered if Mrs. Milner wasn't punishing students for not accepting her views on a story or novel.

The principal largely agreed with the parents' complaints. Moreover, she wanted to do something. In her experience, capricious grading was a major source of parent grievances and student alienation. But what to do? It was difficult to confront Mrs. Milner with the matter. Principals were supposed to support their teachers, at least publicly, against parents, weren't they? Moreover, Janet McDonald couldn't introduce the problem into Mrs. Milner's regular teacher evaluation. That would be to evaluate her on the basis of hearsay evidence. She could not personally verify much of what parents had told her. Finally, it was difficult to deal with the matter by means of a school policy on grading. Washington High did not have such a policy, because in its principal's experience such policies were either so vague as to be unenforceable or so rigid as to cause more problems than they solved. Perhaps getting the faculty to consider such a policy might help to sensitize them to the inadequacy of their current practices. But for this year that wouldn't help rescue junior English students from Mrs. Milner's clutches.

Some Questions

1. Clearly, it will be a relatively simple matter for McDonald to call in Milner and clear up the matter of grading before the next year's crop of students enroll in junior English. What is she to do, however, about the grades Milner has already awarded?
2. We have said that school grading policies are often "either so vague as to be unenforceable or so rigid as to cause more problems than they solved." Why should that be the case?
3. As an exercise in policy making, try your hand at writing a grading policy for a high school. What would be desirable attributes for such a policy?
4. We have said earlier that standards for judging individuals or their work should "have a rational connection to a legitimate purpose." In this case parents object to using grades as disciplinary tools, arguing that they should only reflect mastery of English. Argue the opposite view, that is, that lowering or raising a student's grade because of classroom behavior is a legitimate act and not inherently a violation of due process.
5. Do you think that a student's effort should be considered when a grade is awarded? That is, if a student tries very hard but does poor work, do you think the student should be given a passing grade? (Perhaps a low one, but passing nonetheless.) If so, how is this different from considering classroom behavior when awarding grades?
6. What purposes do grades serve? How might different answers to this question affect your view of fair procedures for assigning grades?

CHAPTER 6

Educational Authority and Accountability: Community, Democracy, and Professionalism

A CASE

Fred Canter believed in accountability. He really did. He worked for the citizens of his district. The money he spent wasn't his. The children he educated weren't his, either. He had them on loan (so to speak) from their parents, and he didn't think he was entitled to the sole say about how they were educated.

That at least was something everyone agreed on. That Fred Canter was the principle of South Elementary didn't make him education tsar. He was to be held accountable. On the other hand, it did not seem that there was much agreement about to whom he was accountable or for what. His school had lots of stakeholders (whatever they were). Of late the term *stakeholder* reminded of the story of Dracula. People held stakes to be driven through the heart. "Hyperbole" he thought. "Let's not get too paranoid."

It was all those state assessments. Every year his students got tested in math, reading, and writing. Many of them got tested several times. The state mandated some tests because the feds insisted, and they required others because—well, they wanted them for some reason. His kids got tested a lot. And the superintendent and the school board wanted the district's schools to do well on these tests. After all, the results got published. There was an annual ritual of public shaming of those who didn't measure up. And there were annual demands that poorly performing schools be reconstituted or that teachers' pay be determined by the scores of their kids. Fred sometimes wondered if people ever noticed how closely test scores in most schools correlated with the percentage of the children on reduced or free lunches. Heretofore, he had not worried too much about these tests. His school did well on them without paying much attention to them. He had a dedicated, collegial, and competent teaching staff of which he was justly proud. He had worked hard to shape them into a learning community.

The trouble really began with the school board. Or maybe it began with the fact that the state's tests weren't very good. Word had gotten around that the scores on these test responded well to a lot of test preparation. "Drill and kill?" Perhaps that was uncharitable. Drill was better than no teaching at all, and some people argued that teaching to a good test was a good thing. But Fred wasn't too much interested in arguing testing theory right now. His school board had mandated that his curriculum be focused on (they said "aligned with") the tests. Moreover, two weeks before the tests were given, teachers were required to spend almost all of their time working on practice tests.

Fred was not enthusiastic about this. His school was doing fine. They had a good curriculum and a good strategy for teaching it. When a student wasn't doing well, that student got help. Parental participation was encouraged. Parents were involved in the school and listened to by the teachers.

Fred had called a meeting of the teachers and explained to them what they were required to do. They were most unhappy. They had called a meeting to which he was not invited and a minor miracle had occurred. All of his teachers agreed on something. They had produced a letter that they had all signed. It read:

Dear Dr. Canter,

We have considered the board's new policy on testing and what we are expected to do to implement it. We cannot in good conscience comply. Our current curriculum is one that has been developed by experts and is supported by research. We have met frequently to discuss the implementation of this curriculum and the teaching strategies it requires. We have consulted with parents and listened to their views. We have become what you have urged us to become— a learning community. We want the best for our children, and we work hard and collectively to assure ourselves that all our children are learning. We leave no child behind. Our children succeed. They succeed in our classes, they do well on state tests, and they achieve these results without our teaching to the test and without distortion of our curriculum.

Now you are asking us to truncate and distort our excellent program so that we can engage in endless test preparation. You have preached to us that modern societies depended on lifelong learners capable of creativity and critical thinking. Yet you demand that we depart from sound teaching methods and substitute a "drill and kill" approach because a group of ignorant and self-serving politicians have chosen an educational strategy more notable for its catchy sound bites than for its educational wisdom.

We refuse. Our professional judgment and our consciences will not permit us to comply. We demand that you present our case for exemption from these policies to the school board and, if they are unwilling to agree, that you help us to work around and subvert their demands.

"Well," Fred thought, "I imagine I'll take a request to the school board about this. I doubt I'll show them this letter. I hope the teachers will be discreet about it." They were not discreet, however. A few days later, Fred received another letter, this time from the parents of the South Elementary PTA. They had met and decided to support the teachers in their rebellion. Their letter read:

Dear Dr. Canter,

We have read the letter that the teachers of South Elementary have sent to you regarding the new board policies. We are agreed that these policies will be harmful to the education of our children. We are not opposed either to accountability or to testing. At the same time, we are concerned that the amount of testing has gotten out of hand. The time our children spend taking tests is time taken away from teaching them. Some of us have argued that we should boycott these tests, but we have not done so because of our respect for you and the fine job you have done. We do not wish to place you in a difficult position with the board of education.

However, the new board policies are unacceptable. The teachers of your school have worked with us in planning our curriculum. We believe in it. We work with our children to further its goals. We help them with their homework, and we volunteer at the school. We feel that we are an integral part of the school community and its work. Now we must defend what we have collectively achieved. The school board proposes that we throw these achievements away so that we can emphasize test preparation in order to succeed on tests on which we are already succeeding. There may be schools in the district that would be improved by these policies, but South Elementary is not one of them.

In addition to the points made in the teachers' letter, we would add that these children are our children. That we send them to you does not mean that you have our permission to do whatever you want with them. You educate them with our approval and as our agents. You do not have our permission to adopt educational practices that are harmful to them. This is a free country. Its people are citizens, not subjects. We insist that you resist the school board's ill-considered policies. We will assist you in this in any way we can. If you are not able to do this, we will have to consider keeping our children home on testing days.

Fred noted that the parents group had copied their letter to the superintendent and the board. No doubt he would soon hear from them. Well, the letter might do some good. Board members were elected, and the superintendent served at their pleasure. The threat of a public boycott would certainly get their attention. However, this was a large district, and it had a number of poorly performing schools. The board and the superintendent were focused on improving the performance of these schools, and they were under a great deal of pressure to do so. Rightfully so. Fred did not believe that the rebellion that was developing at South Elementary was likely to be widespread. Indeed, the views of his teachers and parents might easily be represented as those of a small elite resisting progressive policies in order to promote the welfare of their children at the expense of all of the children of this district. Fred thought this was unfair but not implausible. So he was on the hot seat. His school community wanted an exemption from the board policies. They wanted him to get it. He doubted he could succeed. He wondered if he should try and what he would do if he failed. He recalled the final words of the *Declaration of Independence*. The signers pledged their lives, their fortunes, and their sacred honor to independence. Well, most of his teachers had tenure, and the parents didn't work for the school district. They had pledged his livelihood, his fortune, and his sacred honor to *their* declaration of independence. "Thanks a lot," thought Fred.

DISPUTE

A: When it comes to how to teach and what to teach in a school, teachers should have the right to choose what's best for their students. After all, they are professionals.

B: But what about the state or federal mandates or even a board of education specifying a particular text or curriculum? The teachers are legally bound to follow the mandates of those who are legally responsible for the schools.

C: Wait a minute! What about parents? Shouldn't they have a say in their children's education?

B: Sure, but parents are also citizens in our democracy. And so they can elect the people they have faith in to do what's best for their children on federal, state, and local levels. But after that, they have the responsibility to obey the laws and mandates that their duly elected representatives put forth.

A: Well, teachers are democratic citizens, too, but they also are professionals, and if the school board mandates a procedure or curriculum that the teachers collectively and professionally agree is potentially harmful and/or probably will produce negative educational effects, they have a professional obligation to either refuse to do so or at least to try to find ways to get around such directives.

B: If they do that, it's tantamount to breaking the law. They should be arrested!

C: But suppose the teachers are right? As parents, we would want our teachers to protect our kids from potentially miseducative experiences. They know more about educating kids than politicians. We would trust their professional judgment.

B: You parents and teachers just don't understand. It's the way a democratic society works. Once you've voted in your representatives, you don't have a choice no matter what you think.

CONCEPTS: ACCOUNTABILITY, DEMOCRACY, COMMUNITY, AND PROFESSIONALISM

Accountability

Fred Canter has a lot of people who want him to do different things. He has his "orders" from the school board, demands from his teachers, and a "request" from the PTA. He might respond to the issue with a "grease the squeaky wheel" approach, but he might instead consider some of the principles at stake and assess their implications for his action. Both the teachers and the parents who have placed demands on him have appealed to certain "legitimation" principles. Both groups have claimed their decisions carry force because they have been democratically achieved. The teachers have also appealed to the idea of professionalism. They are the professionals. They have professional knowledge on their side. If Fred is to behave professionally, he will do what they want. The teachers and the parents have also appealed to the idea of community. Their voices express the will of the school community of which Fred is both member and leader. If Fred is to be loyal to the community, he should do what they want. The school board also has some principles to appeal to. It is a duly elected legislature. In democratic societies, the legislature is sovereign. Everyone agrees that Fred should be accountable—to them—and that he can show his willingness to be accountable by doing what they want.

All of the principles—democracy, professionalism, community—to which our parties appeal should have some standing in our ethical universe. The task Fred faces is not to decide which principles are right and which wrong. It is to find a way to integrate or balance these otherwise laudable principles when they conflict. As we will suggest in the next section, he needs to find a reflective equilibrium.

Let's begin by considering some different answers to the question, "Accountable to whom?" Everyone agrees that Fred and his school should be accountable to someone for something. Right now, in our society accountability has come to mean something fairly narrow. Being accountable means to accept certain standards of achievement as defining success in one's task. Standards are assertions about the educational goals to be achieved. They say "what students are to know and be able to do." They should be measurable and measured—usually by some form of standardized test mandated by the state government and increasingly under the direction of the national government. As of this writing the No Child Left Behind Act is the paradigm of what accountability means.

We need to take a broader view. Here are several answers to the question, "To whom should educators be accountable?"

1. *To the legislature*: In modern liberal democratic societies, the central political principle is the sovereignty of elected legislatures. Congress, state legislatures, and (typically) school boards are elected legislatures. Fred is employed by a legislature, a school board; he is bound by a contract in which he has agreed to accept employment in exchange for obeying the directives of his employer, which, as an elected legislature, expresses the will of the people. Here Fred faces a dilemma that is common in democratic societies: What do principled people do when they believe that the legislature has erred?

2. *To the "consumer"*: We are not merely a liberal democratic society, we are a capitalist society with a market economy. The form of accountability appropriate to a market economy is consumer sovereignty. People should be able to choose among competing vendors of goods and services. These vendors must satisfy their customers' needs and wants or face the loss of their business. The power consumers have over vendors is the power to take their business elsewhere. The assumption is that, other things being equal (which is often not the case), competition among vendors will produce the best goods at the lowest price for the consumer. Since Fred Canter's school is a public school (and thus part of a public monopoly), this picture of accountability is not at issue here. We note it in passing because it is a part of the modern debate about accountability.

3. *To parents*: While schools in our society are largely government financed and government operated, our society does not view the authority of schools over the education of the children who attend them as total or as fully superseding the rights of parents. While there are numerous views as to how this shared authority

over children is to be understood, it is clear that parents or legal guardians retain some rights to control the education of their children and that the school must answer to them for how their children are treated and educated. The letter from the parents appeals to this idea when it says, "These are our children." Note, however, that these parents do not assert their right as individuals or as citizens to a say about the education of their children. Instead they claim that the fact that these children are theirs makes them a part of the school community in a way that other people who live within the district and who vote to elect the school board are not. Hence their voice has a special claim to be heard, they are a kind of mini-political community, and Fred has a special obligation to attend to their views.

4.   *To professional standards*: The teachers have appealed both to their standing as special members of the community and to democracy. However, the core of their argument is an appeal to professionalism. Their claim is that they know what is best for children, that their actions are guided by their concern for the welfare of children, and that their judgment should be respected. Moreover, the knowledge of what's best is not a matter of personal opinion, but of collective expertise achieved by research and refined to fit the local situation by their deliberations on their own professional experience.

The school board, the state, the parents of the children in South Elementary, and the teachers all want Fred to be accountable to them. In making their arguments, they appeal to different legitimacy principles or different interpretations of the same principles. We can consider their views by addressing three sets of questions:

1.   What is a democracy? What form of democratic authority should characterize schools?
2.   What is a community? Who are its members? Which community should dominate in decisions about schooling?
3.   What does it mean for teachers and school leaders to be professionals? What authority over education should be ceded to professionals?

Democracy

We view democracy as a way of decision making that respects the political equality of all citizens of a political community (or a polity) over matters that are appropriately decided by that community. Democratic government, as Lincoln said, is of the people, by the people, and for the people. It rests on the consent of the governed. We might view the idea that democracies respect political equality as captured by two criteria for determining if a decision is democratically made. A decision is made democratically if

1. The interests of each member of the polity are fairly considered.
2. Each member of the polity has a fair opportunity to influence the decision.

Both parts are required. A benevolent monarchy might meet the first criterion, but not the second. It would fail to be a democracy because it denied its citizens their right to a voice in decision making. However, the first criterion is also required. Suppose a society elected its leaders and respected the idea of majority rule. Nevertheless, the majority might treat a minority tyrannically, refusing to take their interests into account in decision making. Such a society would also be undemocratic. Neither society would have the consent of the governed.

Americans tend to identify democracy with voting and electing people who represent them in legislatures. They view these institutions as expressing their consent. This is appropriate because voting for elected representatives may satisfy both criteria. Electing representatives to a legislature is not, however, essential to democracy. Democratic decisions might be made by informal discussions among citizens who act when a consensus is reached among them. Conversely, electing a legislature does not ensure democracy. Some citizens may be excluded from participation in elections, or, once elected, legislators might look after their own interests or the interests of their group rather than the interests of all.

The arguments for representative democracy generally appeal to practical considerations. It is difficult to make decisions by discussion and consensus among citizens when the polity has grown large and the issues it faces complex. Representative democracy, however, may exact a cost in citizen participation. As the number of citizens grows larger, the voice of each counts for less, the opportunity to discuss decisions with fellow citizens may decline, and participation may be reduced to voting. Some writers on democracy have wanted to distinguish two types of democracy, representative democracy and participatory democracy. Advocates of participatory democracy often argue that democratic decisions should, as much as is possible, be made at the local level because, they claim, this facilitates citizen participation, and, in doing so, also creates better citizens. Moreover, local decision making permits decisions to better reflect the needs and wishes of local communities.

One liability of a high degree of localism in democratic institutions is that it permits individuals in one community to make decisions that affect the welfare of citizens of others without their consent. Education is a good example of this problem. We live in a mobile and interconnected society. Students educated in one district are unlikely to work and live in this district their entire lives. The success or failure of the schools in one area can affect the welfare of people in many other jurisdictions. To the degree that this is so, it suggests that larger jurisdictions (such as states) should have authority over the smaller jurisdictions within them. Conversely, to the degree that it is not so, local decision making should prevail. Democratic societies, thus, must not only make decisions democratically, they must also locate the appropriate "polity" to make the decision.

This need to find the right "polity" to make educational decisions is solved in the United States by multiple political jurisdictions and "nested" legislatures. The U.S. Congress makes some kinds of educational policies concerning issues where the national interest is thought to predominate (such as issues concerned with equal opportunity). State governments make others. School boards (or other local legislatures) make still others. This system is complex and often messy, but it does reflect some attempt to locate decisions where they belong and can be best made.

An argument that Fred Canter should primarily be accountable to the state and to the school board might go like this: Our society is committed to the democratic governance of education. It expresses this commitment by recognizing the sovereignty of elected legislatures over education. Different legislatures are involved in making different educational decisions. There is a division of labor among them that depends to a considerable degree on judgments about where local decision making is most appropriate and where state governments should hold sway. In the current case, the state legislature, following some federal guidelines, has developed educational standards and tests that are at the heart of the idea of accountability in the state. Some details of implementation have been left to local school districts who are themselves responsible to the state. Fred Canter is an employee of the school district. His primary duty is to carry out the policies they develop, not just because he is their employee, but because following district policy is the only way to respect the will of a sovereign and democratically elected legislature. Fred is fundamentally accountable to the board of education.

Community

Appeals to the authority of a community occur in two ways in this case. First, both the parents and the teachers claim to be a community and that this entitles them to a say about educational programs in South Elementary. Second, both the parents and the teachers claim that community is something to be valued and enhanced. We will look at the arguments of the parents in this section and the arguments of the teachers in the next.

We might attribute to the parents an argument like this: These children are our children. Our families are the people on whom educational decisions at South Elementary most directly impact. Hence, we are the heart of the community of South Elementary; we are those citizens who should be regarded as the primary decision makers. When we come together to express a democratically achieved view about the education South Elementary provides for our children, our views should carry the largest weight. We should be viewed as a local "polity" whose decisions are sovereign for this school. You, Fred Canter, are fundamentally accountable to us.

The conception of democracy we have sketched above provides some support for the parents' view. These parents have achieved a collective voice about the education of their children in which all had an opportunity to be heard and in which the interests of all were fairly considered. Moreover, while other people may be affected by the decisions made about the education of their children, it is certainly true that their children are those who are primarily affected. Parents have a special responsibility to care for their children. They cannot exercise this responsibility unless they also have the authority to direct the education of their children. Hence even if education is viewed as a governmental responsibility, the authority of government over education cannot be absolute. Parents have a right to some say. When they are able to express this authority collectively as the parents of South Elementary have done, their claims might be viewed as having especially strong force.

However, the view that the voice of parents should dominate is problematic. It does not take into account the interests of other citizens. Other citizens are asked to pay for schools and are affected by the success of schools. Also, the political traditions of the United States have given very little weight to the rights of parents *as a collectivity* to govern public education. Parental rights have been viewed as rights individual parents have over their own children. Constitutionally, education has been viewed as the responsibility of states, but traditionally educational authority has been vested largely in local legislatures—school boards. Education has been viewed as the responsibility of local communities expressed through local political institutions. This was partly owing to the fact that local communities were expected to pay for their schools. While authority over education might have been delegated to school councils or boards of governors consisting largely of parents, this has not been done, or where it has been done these groups have had little real authority. In fact, in recent years authority over education has tended to move upwards so that state legislatures and Congress have become more active in educational policy making. These traditions of political authority cannot be set aside whenever local groups of parents feel that their interests are not well served by them.

The parents of South Elementary have claimed that they are members of a community in a different sense. Perhaps we should not view them as a political community, but as part of the school community whose views need to be respected in order to affirm the values of community. Let us explore this idea.

It has become popular to say that schools should be communities. Communities are often formed around commonalities. People may be members of a shared ethnic group, a common race, or a shared religion. Sometimes when we appeal to the authority of a community, what we are saying is that there are certain traditions, practices, customs, or values that have authority for members of a community because the community is their community.

Educational communities may be of this sort. People of a common religion or ethnicity may come together in a school in order to explore and express their common traditions. Generally, however, public schools are not communities of this type. Indeed, we usually hope that public schools will form a community of people from diverse religions, ethnicities, and traditions.

Another kind of community results from people coming together to pursue a common project. In South Elementary Fred Canter has been successful in getting parents and teachers to work together for the sake of the education of their children. This community appears to have met two important and related conditions for creating school community. First, the members of the community not only agree that the education of their children is important, they agree on a shared conception of the education they wish to provide. Second, they have worked together to achieve this shared conception, and they continue to work together to provide it. They view their school as a shared project. The parents and teachers of South Elementary are a community because they cooperate to pursue ends they have collectively chosen.

In the case of South Elementary this shared conception of education has been created by extensive participation involving the teachers, Fred Canter, and the parents of the children in the school. To see why participation is important, consider two other ways in which a consensus about the basic aspirations of the school might have been achieved. The conception of the education to be provided might have been entirely the creation of the school's staff and rooted in the professional judgment of the staff. But when this happens, parents are more likely to see themselves as the clients of the school than as members of a community. While that may not be a bad thing, the relations among professionals and their clients has a different character than the relationships between communities and their members. The essential difference is an inequality in power that results from a different level of expertise.

The conception of the school's educational project might also be something that reflects the antecedently held values of those who created the school, and the school community might be created by virtue of parents choosing a school the values of which they share. Here religious schools would be an example. These schools might become communities because parents share the school's fundamental commitments and because parents are invited to participate in the activities and operation of the school. Religious schools and other private schools are often characterized by a sense of community. At the same time, it is rare (although not unknown) for public schools to be chosen in this way. When public schools are neighborhood schools, a shared conception of the school's educational project must be forged among those who happen to be in the neighborhood. This is likely to require extensive participation by the members of the community.

Communities promote certain values that are intrinsic to the nature of community. People see themselves as belonging to the community or as members of the community. They are likely to have a sense of ownership of the community. Cooperation in working towards shared goals and the knowledge that goals are shared may help create loyalty and trust. These are all likely to be considerable assets in the effectiveness of the school and may lead to learning that is more self-motivated and less alienated as children come to feel themselves to be members of a community and internalize its commitments. (At the same time we should also consider the potential for communities to stifle dissent and marginalize those who do not share the communities' core values.)

If a school has become a community in a way that creates some of these "goods" of community, does this give the community authority over educational decisions? The parents and teachers of South Elementary feel themselves to be members of a community. They feel that this sense of community is an asset in the education of their children. They also believe that this sense of community is threatened when the school board or the state legislature overrides the consensus that they have achieved and insists that things be done its way regardless of the views of the members of the community.

It seems reasonable to believe that a strong sense of community will enhance the quality of education provided by a school. Conversely, disrupting a sense of community when it has been achieved is likely to harm the education of the children of South Elementary. The parents of South Elementary may well be right that the mandated changes in the school program will be harmful to the education of their children because it will undo the sense of community that has developed. But this does not altogether address the question. The authority of democratic legislatures over education does not rest on the claim that their judgments are inevitably the best and wisest decisions. American tradition (and much else) claims that political authority rests on the consent of the governed and in the right citizens have to have their interests fairly considered and to influence decisions that affect them. As we will see below, these rights are not "trumped" by claims that some other decision making institutions make better decisions.

Professionalism and Learning Communities

The teachers of South Elementary have claimed to be members of a different kind of community. They have claimed to be a learning community. They have also claimed to be professionals and have urged resistance to the board of education's mandates, arguing that these mandates are inconsistent with their professional judgment.

We view the idea that teachers are professionals and that they belong to learning communities as complementary ideas. The idea that someone is a member of a profession can mean various things. Here we view it as follows: A profession is an occupation that is characterized by a particular form of accountability. Performing the work of a professional depends on judgments that are rooted in specialized knowledge and extensive experience. Professionals require considerable training to become competent. Those who lack this training are not able to adequately judge the work of professionals. Hence one mark of a profession is autonomy. The profession is responsible for educating and certifying new members. Professions set their own standards. Professionals are the ones who judge whether other members of the profession are competent and when they have behaved incompetently or unprofessionally. This must be the case, because others are not in a position to adequately judge the performance of professionals.

Because professionals must be self-regulated, their practice must also be guided by an ethic that they have internalized. This ethic has two crucial features. First, professionals are obligated to respect and be guided by the knowledge base in which their practice is grounded. Second, professionals must be guided by the welfare of their clients. Such an ethic is expected to guide both the individual professional and the profession itself when it acts as a collectivity, as it may when engaging in such activities as setting educational standards or judging cases of alleged malpractice.

That the expertise of members of a profession is rooted in a specialized knowledge base does not mean that professionals possess a kind of internal rule book that tells them how to behave in each case. It may be that professional knowledge enables the professional to see things or see the relevance of things that the untrained would miss, or that the professional is able to make inferences that the untrained mind would be unlikely to make. If this is correct, then it is also true that collaboration, consultation, and discussion among professionals are important. Professionals are able to learn from one another and from their collective experience.

It is this collaborative element that connects the idea of teaching as a profession with the notion of learning communities. Teachers when they function as a learning community are not only guided by a knowledge base and by their professional experience, they are able to learn from other professionals and to make collaborative and collegial decisions in the best interests of their clients. Collegiality should also be a part of the ethics of a professional.

It is to ideals of this sort that the teachers of South Elementary appeal when they claim the authority of a profession and claim to be a learning community. They are asserting a right to some measure of autonomy rooted in their expertise and in their internalization of a client-centered ethic. In effect, they are saying to the school board and the state legislature that it is they and not these legislatures who are entitled to make educational decisions because it is they and not these legislatures who possess the knowledge required to make good decisions. They are arguing that they should be accountable primarily to themselves because they are the only ones who are able to judge whether they are doing what is best for children and because they can be trusted to decide in the interest of these children.

There are a number of reasons to be suspicious of such claims. First, it is unclear whether teaching and leadership are professions in the sense required. While educational research may have taught us many important things about education, it is far from clear that it has provided us with the kind of extensive and well-accepted knowledge base that a genuine profession requires to justify autonomy. Most claims about teaching strategies are controversial, and many teachers seem to be able to perform well without extensive knowledge of this research. Moreover, few states have recognized teaching or administration as self-governing professions.

Second, even if teaching and leadership are professions, we should not overstate the extent to which autonomy is warranted. We have learned that members of professions are capable of being self-serving, and governments have taken this into account in regulating professions. Physicians, for example, must have informed consent for any procedure they perform and they may be held accountable for malpractice to courts and juries of laypeople. They are able to set professional standards only with the recognition and consent of state legislatures. We should also note that the professional societies that claim to represent professionals represent not only their professional judgments on professional matters, but also represent the economic and political interests of their members. In the case of teachers this is clear. The NEA, for example, is both a professional society and a union. We are not opposed to this or to collective bargaining for teachers. Nevertheless, only the most naive would believe that professional societies always assert the welfare of clients over the economic interests of their members.

Finally, it is crucial to note that when professionals assert an inherent right to self-regulation because they and not others possess a specialized knowledge base, they are appealing to that most undemocratic of political principles, "Those who know should rule." This is the principle asserted by Plato in ancient Athens to justify the rule of philosopher kings and to claim that democracy was the rule of ignorance, of the passions, and of the mob. Societies that are democratic may recognize the need for professional autonomy when specialized knowledge is genuinely involved in decision making, but they will view this autonomy as ceded to the profession and exercised under the scrutiny of the legislature. If we apply this view to our case, the conclusion we must draw is that it might indeed be a good thing were the school board and the legislature to respect the professional judgment of the teachers, but they are not bound to do so. Moreover, unless we are to accept the idea that those who know should rule over the democratic creed that legitimate authority depends on the consent of the governed, we will have to agree that when the enactments of the legislature are inconsistent with the professional views of teachers, the views of the legislature must take precedence, not just because resistance is likely to be futile, but because the legislature has the right to rule.

There is much to be respected in the arguments of the parents and the teachers of South Elementary. While we have not accepted the claim of the parents to be a polity, we have said that the community they have formed serves important values and that the education of the children of South Elementary may well be harmed if this community is harmed. We also believe that it is a good thing that Fred Canter has been able to shape his teachers into a learning community and that it is quite possible that their professional judgment about what is best for the children is correct. What shall we make of this?

First, the authority of the legislature does not depend on the fact that its decisions are always right. It depends on the consent of the governed. Moreover, that a decision is wrong or thought to be wrong does not convey an entitlement either to citizens or to government employees to disobey it. Nor does it convey a right to some other group to substitute its judgment for that of the legislature. When citizens consent to be governed by a legislature, they do not consent one decision at a time. They consent to a way of making decisions. No democratic society could long survive if its citizens were to believe that they had a right to disobey any decision they believed to be wrong. The sovereignty of the legislature includes a right to err.

Fred Canter has the same privilege as any citizen. He has the right to present to the legislature the case that they are wrong and to urge them to change their policy. Perhaps as principal of South Elementary and as someone with special responsibilities for the welfare of its children, he has an especially strong obligation to do so.

The teachers and parents of South Elementary have intimated that he has another course of action. He may attempt to subvert or to work around the board's policy. This is an option that deserves more discussion than we are able to provide. Certainly Fred may attempt to implement the policy in a way that does as little harm as possible to the South Elementary program. He may seek to minimize its negative effects or take corrective action. At the same time, he should not lie to the board about what he is doing, he should not fail to implement the board's orders, and he should not be oppositional to the board's policies in a way that seeks to subvert them. (He may, of course, argue against them.) If he comes to feel that he can no longer in good conscience follow board policy, he should consider resigning. However, between the poles of seeking to mitigate damage and outright subversion, there are many nuanced issues we cannot discuss. For example, while Fred may not lie to the board, must he disclose all that he does? Is he entitled to continue to argue against board policy after it has become firm? May he do so publicly? Here we can only note that democratic societies depend on employees who respect the sovereignty of the legislature. The legislature is not sovereign if employees believe that they have the right to subvert policy when they believe it to be wrong. However, democratic societies also depend on vigorous debate, and governmental employees are often in a position to best know the consequences of policy for those whom they serve. Fred must find his way between these poles.

Return, for a moment, to our initial discussion of democracy. We suggested that two criteria characterize democratic decision making: people's interests must be respected and people must be able to influence decisions. And we suggested that these criteria expressed a conception of political equality. The idea of political equality, in turn, might be viewed as an expression of equal respect. Democracy, we believe, is the best form of government because, in viewing each citizen as entitled to equal respect, it affirms the equal value of each person and treats each person as an end, not a means. This argument does not justify democracy because it always makes the best decisions, but because it makes decisions in a just way. It does not appeal to the principle of benefit maximization. In contrast, the arguments we have considered for professionalism and for community tend to appeal to the principle of benefit maximization.

We believe that wise legislatures will take these arguments into account in their decision making and will delegate authority when and as appropriate. But these arguments are not morally basic. The chief value of democracy is that it treats each of us as free and equal. Good consequences may flow from that, but they are not the bedrock justification for democracy. Equal respect for person is.

ANALYSIS: OBJECTIVE MORAL REASONING

The incomplete part of our agenda is to ask if we have made a case that objective moral reasoning is possible. Certainly we have been able to provide reasons for all sorts of things. There seems to be some argument for each side of every case, even though we have tried to show that nonconsequentialism is a better basis for ethics than consequentialism. Are such issues ever decidable? If so, how?

It would be a mistake to conclude from the ambiguous character of the cases we analyzed and the others included in this book that moral deliberations can never be rationally concluded. In simpler cases, in our everyday lives as educators, we do reach reasonable and justifiable moral decisions about such things as plagiarism, theft, and honesty, for example. Our cases in this book have been constructed to be difficult and ambiguous. It is their ambiguity that makes them interesting and useful as a teaching tool. We are not even sure that each of our cases could be rationally and objectively decided in some conclusive way.

This is not decisive, however. We should be careful not to conclude too much from cases of moral ambiguity or moral disagreement. It is commonly argued that ethics are relative to culture because human beings disagree about moral questions and different societies have different moral points of view. The conclusion does not follow from the premises. It simply does not follow that if two people or two cultures disagree, no one is right. Different cultures have different views of medicine as well. However, we need not conclude that if some people believe that disease is caused by evil spirits, the germ theory of disease is incorrect. Nor need we conclude that the truth about medicine is relative to culture. It makes a good deal more sense to conclude that one of the views is incorrect.

Likewise, it does not follow from the fact that something is unknown that it is unknowable. If we do not currently know the answer to an ethical question, it does not follow that we may not be able to discover the answer by careful reflection and inquiry or that someone else at some later time may not solve the problem. If ethics is an area of human inquiry in which we search for the best principles that we can find to regulate human conduct, then we should expect that there will be ethical discoveries. Slavery was once morally controversial. Have not human beings "discovered" it to be wrong?

Finally, it is a mistake to expect a degree of precision from an inquiry that it is incapable of providing. In this century, even mathematics has been embarrassed by the discovery that there are mathematical questions that can be shown to be unanswerable. It does not follow that mathematical reasoning lacks objectivity or that mathematical truth is relative to culture. Likewise, it does not follow from the fact that some ethical questions are difficult or even undecidable that ethical reasoning has no point or that no ethical questions can be decided. In some cases, if nothing else, we make significant progress if we can become clearer about the nature of the difficulty itself. Sometimes, too, we can resolve a matter, at least for ourselves, by discovering that it connects with our basic principles in a certain way. If the process of moral deliberation is not always decisive or clear, or completely objective, it is also rarely fruitless. Moral reasoning and debate always gets us somewhere, and as moral agents we are obligated to participate in it.

If moral ambiguity and disagreement do not force us to conclude that ethical argument has no point, neither do they show us that, or how, legitimate moral argument is possible. Here we owe the reader at least a brief account of our view of moral methodology. Our position can be easily sketched, but not quite so easily defended. The central ideas are these: Moral decisions regarding choice and action require moral sensitivity, rationality, and the development of moral theory for which the initial evidence is our moral intuitions. Moral intuitions—that is, our intuitive sense of what is right and wrong—are important data for moral reasoning and the construction of moral theory.

Not every moral intuition is equally useful, however. We should begin with those that seem most compelling and least controversial. Constructing a moral theory, then, proceeds through attempts to formulate principles that account for these moral intuitions. It is not our intuitions themselves that are inconclusive. We must be able to describe the underlying moral concepts that generate our sense of right and wrong, to discover the implicit rules that cause us to feel the way we do. It is not just taking whatever pops into our hearts and heads as right or wrong; it is looking for the bases of our intuitions, describing and analyzing them, and then testing them to the best of our ability. In this way we move from simple intuition to a more sophisticated, objective, rational, and reflective approach to ethics.

In this respect, constructing a moral theory is much like attempting to describe the rules governing our sense of grammar. We have intuitions about how to use language correctly and meaningfully without necessarily being able to formulate the rules of our language. This sense of what is meaningful or correct to say provides the data against which to test sets of rules postulated to explain our sense of grammar. In fact, that is how grammarians do grammar. They will ask themselves such questions as "Why does 'all good boys eat cake' make sense and 'cake boys good eat all' not make sense?" Likewise, we must make clear and explicit the rules and principles that underlie our moral intuitions.

The analogy goes even deeper. Sometimes a deep understanding of the principles of language can lead us to revise our initial opinion about what is meaningful or correct. Understanding the principle can make clear and comprehensible an expression that seemed obscure or ambiguous, or it can lead us to see the awkwardness or obscurity of something that had appeared clear and simple. Likewise, a moral theory can change or overrule our intuitions about moral phenomena. Once we see more clearly what is assumed by our moral intuitions, we may wish to change our minds. Thus there is an interaction between moral theory and moral intuition in rational ethical reflection, each influencing the other. The trick is to achieve some point of reflective equilibrium between our moral sense and our moral theory. By reflective equilibrium we mean reaching a point in our deliberations where we feel that our moral intuitions and the moral theory that accounts for them are satisfactorily consistent and where the decisions we reach and actions we take can be objectively justified by our moral theory. Of course, as with scientific theory, new facts, events, and hypotheses can force us to reconsider and reformulate our moral theories and to alter our decisions and actions.

Moral theories must meet the standards common to judging theories of all sorts. They must explain the data appropriate to them. They must be consistent. Elegance, parsimony, and symmetry are nice, too, when they can be had. Moral theories must also be sensitive to knowledge in other domains. Factual matters and the theories of other disciplines are important to ethical theory, because they are important in knowing how moral abstractions are applied to concrete cases, but also because they can suggest new problems to be solved or alter the concepts by means of which ethical theories are articulated. Freud's discovery of the unconscious raised difficult questions about the notion of autonomy and posed new moral issues about psychological manipulations. The advances of physics and biology drove purposes from nature and required people to rethink the way in which values and purposes exist. These are things that any comprehensive moral theory must confront.

Having a comprehensive and well thought out moral theory is not enough. As feeling human beings we also need to be sensitive to the moral domain and draw upon our shared ability to empathize with and care about other persons. Our moral intuitions are rooted in our ability to feel and empathize as well as in our ability to think. We need emotion as well as reason to be moved to act morally and to care about rational moral arguments and their outcomes. Feelings interact with moral reasoning in several important ways. First, feelings help us to put ourselves in the place of others, to identify with them, to know what hurts and what helps. It will do little good to be committed to respecting the value and dignity of other persons if we cannot experience life from their point of view. How else shall we know how to respect them? How else shall we discover what counts as affirming their dignity?

Second, feelings provide motivation for right conduct. If one could build a computer capable of engaging in moral reasoning, its chief defect would probably be that it would not care about being moral. Knowing what is right and wanting to do it are different things. Our ability to empathize, to experience the wrong done to others as our hurt and the good done to others as our joy, is a large part of our desire to do right. Immanuel Kant, who had many wise things to say about ethics, said nothing wiser than that the only really good thing is a good will.

How, then, do we settle ethical arguments? We proceed first by trying to discover the moral principles that underlie our differing senses of right and wrong. When we see what it is that our moral intuitions assume, perhaps some of us will change our minds. If not, then we must test our conflicting moral principles by seeing what else follows from them. If we find that some proposed principle leads to an abhorrent or implausible result in certain cases, that is a reason to abandon it. Perhaps some will change their minds when they see what else they must agree to if they are to hold consistently to their current positions.

Where does our sense of right and wrong come from? This question would seem to bear on how possible it is to establish an objective, reflective equilibrium about ethical issues. Some philosophers have argued that our sense of morality is innate. Theologians may add that it is God-given. Others have suggested that moral intuitions are a kind of seeing. There are moral facts that we can see with our mind's eye, just as we see colors with our physical eye. Still others assume that we learn our moral principles, just as we learn our native language, from our culture. Does it matter? One might argue that if moral concepts are innate or God-given or involve seeing moral facts that have objective existence, then this certifies the objectivity of moral thought. Moral questions, like questions about the physical world, have answers. These answers are, somehow, grounded in the nature of reality. On the other hand, if we acquire those principles that generate our moral intuitions from our culture, this means that, fundamentally, relativism is still true. The best that moral reasoning could be expected to do in that case would be to produce a higher level of agreement among those who already agree about basic assumptions.

We cannot here resolve the issue of where our sense of right and wrong comes from. Instead, we want to suggest that the question of where our moral intuitions come from is not that decisive for the objectivity of moral reasoning. Seeing it as decisive rests on inflated demands for what will be permitted to count as objective knowledge and on an excessive pessimism about human commonalities. If we demand certainty of moral knowledge or if we demand that all legitimate knowledge somehow must be certain and beyond challenge and change in the light of new evidence, we may find knowledge difficult to come by—and not only about ethics. But if we insist only on establishing a provisional reflective equilibrium based on our best reasoned judgment at the time, we will have set a standard for objectivity that can often be met and will serve us well in our lives. What is the point of setting our standards for objective knowledge in a way that makes a fundamental and necessary human activity, that of reflecting on what we ought to do, appear impossible?

Moreover, even if our ethical intuitions are acquired from our society, it does not follow that reflective equilibrium among members of different societies is impossible. To the degree that societies are different, we may expect the search for reflective moral equilibrium to be difficult. To assume that it is impossible is to neglect the extent to which all societies are composed of people with a common biology, common fundamental needs and feelings, a common physical environment, and common aspirations. It is also to neglect the extent to which we live on a planet whose people are increasingly united by a common science and by common global problems. The commonalities are basic to our view of the source of the moral intuitions of human beings. We are not all so alike that reflective equilibrium about moral matters is likely to be easy. We are not all so different that it must be impossible. Some of us would even argue that we see writ large in human history a positive development toward a more humane and more broadly shared ethical point of view. There are, then, some good reasons to keep open the possibility of humanly arrived at ethical knowledge. We can be objective and reasonable even if we cannot be certain, and we can be tolerant and open to other points of view without being relativists.

Nevertheless, there is a common but misguided incentive for the prevalent modern belief in moral relativism. It is the human desire to be free, to be unencumbered by duties and obligations. If we may misparaphrase Dostoevsky, people seem to believe that if relativism is true, then everything is permitted. Each of us may do as we choose, and no one can tell us that we are wrong or that we must do something else. The idea is often captured in the suggestion that people who argue that something is genuinely right or wrong are, in reality, attempting to impose their views on others.

This response is both confused and problematic. It is confused in that it identifies compulsion with persuasion. When one person attempts to give reasons to another person, that act is not an attempt at coercion. Indeed, persuasion is a form of influence that recognizes individuals as free moral agents with rational minds and human feelings. To attempt to persuade someone is to assume that the choice is theirs and that as responsible moral agents they would wish to make it on the basis of the best reasons available. To give people reasons is to confirm their status as free individuals who have the right to choose for themselves.

Seeing persuasion as a kind of coercion ultimately rests on a failure to understand the ultimate moral basis of freedom. We are not free because we have no objective duties. Nothing about freedom follows from moral relativism, because nothing at all concerning ethical matters can follow from relativism. We are free because we are moral agents with the duty to decide for ourselves and because it is morally offensive to interfere arbitrarily with the liberty of a person who has the moral duty to make responsible choices.

It is often claimed that what sets human beings off from other living creatures is their ability to reason. From our point of view, we humans also share the distinctive capacity to have and choose to have obligations. To ask what moral obligations we should accept is to presume that we are free to choose and that good reasons can be given for some choices and against others. And the giving of reasons presumes that reasons provide objective grounds for reaching potential agreements and progressive states of reflective equilibrium and moral growth.

Relativism is problematic in that, if taken seriously, it can lead us to withhold resources that are important for moral growth. People do not learn to make responsible choices by being told that it does not matter what they decide, since one choice is as valid as another. They learn to make responsible choices by learning to appraise arguments and consider evidence relevant to what they have to decide. Such things are best learned by participating in a milieu in which ethical matters are seriously considered and debated. Moral relativism undermines the moral education appropriate to a free people.

Finally, we believe that moral relativism undermines the administrator's sense of his or her task. We see education as a profoundly moral enterprise. Its purpose is to develop educated citizens who can function as free people in a free and self-governing society. The moral commitments we have examined in this book—intellectual and personal liberty, equality, due process, and democracy—are more than simply concepts that provide handy vehicles for learning to think about ethical problems. They are more than concepts that are important to thinking about doing the work of an administrator. They are concepts that are central to our vision of ourselves as a free people. Thus they should be central to our view of education in a free society.

The administrator who is an ethical relativist cannot share in this vision. Such a person sees freedom, equality, and democracy as morally arbitrary, as things that some people happen to value, but that have no compelling objective justification. Such a view of these basic moral principles is hardly likely to inspire a reasoned commitment to them that guides daily decision making. The administrator who is an ethical relativist must either be uncommitted to the underlying principles of our society or irrationally committed to them. Neither seems especially desirable.

Finally, the administrator who believes in ethical relativism is likely to see administration as essentially a technical enterprise. If administrative behavior is to be based on objective knowledge, that knowledge can only be factual knowledge of how to accomplish given objectives. Values should not enter the picture. The relativistic administrator, thus, will concern himself or herself with how most efficiently to accomplish pre-identified goals. Such individuals quickly become manipulators of other human beings, unconcerned about the ethics of school administration and focused only on completing the tasks at hand. Such individuals also renounce responsibility for judging the educational and moral worth of the objectives and policies they are given by others. Like the administrators and guards of concentration camps, they only follow orders. Theirs is not to reason why. There is no point to moral reasoning.

CONCLUSION

The question of the possibility of objective moral reasoning is crucial both for our view of education and our view of administration. A belief in the possibility of moral reasoning permits a view of education that is itself moral in nature. It provides the grounds for administrators to pursue, with their staff and students, those moral commitments that define us as a free people in a free and democratic society. Ethical relativism, in contrast, leaves the administrator to pursue values that cannot be objectively chosen and thus, if operative at all, must be arbitrarily imposed. Moreover, relativism defines the administrative role as technical and manipulative. It treats people as means, not as ends, and views respect for persons as just one among many arbitrary value judgments. To us the choice is obvious. Moral relativism is a belief that no responsible and rational administrator can follow in practice.

ADDITIONAL CASES

Democracy in Action

"Who? Who the hell won?" Don Patterson, superintendent of Mayville public schools exploded. "Who are those people? They weren't even running! How could they have been elected to the school board?"

Patterson was sitting at the breakfast table with his wife and listening to the local news on the radio. He had turned it on to hear the results of yesterday's school board election. Actually, he had turned it on to hear what the turnout had been, not to find out who had won. The winners, he had thought, were a foregone conclusion. Three seats on Mayville's board of education had to be filled. The three persons who held those seats had sought reelection. They were running unopposed. Under those conditions, how could they not win?

Voter turnout, on the other hand, was very problematic. Like residents in most school districts in the United States, relatively few of Mayville's citizens bothered to vote in school board elections. Ordinarily, about 15% of those eligible actually cast ballots (a figure quite comparable to the national average). In the previous two elections, however, this percentage had declined even further; last year fewer than 8% of the town's citizens had gone to the polls.

These low turnouts were a matter of concern to Patterson. He had hoped that voters would begin to evidence a greater interest in their schools than they had in the recent past. Realistically, though, he knew there was little hope that this election would generate much interest. After all, there was no real choice to be made. Why go to the polls when the outcome was preordained? Apparently most of the good burghers of Mayville felt the same way; less than 4% of the citizens had voted in yesterday's election, according to the reporter.

Someone had obviously taken an interest in the election, however. The three incumbents had all been defeated by seemingly unknown, phantom candidates. Their defeat disturbed the superintendent considerably. The three incumbents had been good board members. They worked at their task, and they were not mouthpieces for any special interest group in the community. For example, they had stood firm during the last round of contract negotiations against union attempts to gain significant new controls over district policy making.

Patterson gave his full attention to the newscaster. She seemed as perplexed by the election as he. The three winners were Mary Rellihan, John Jacobson, and Henry Martin, all of whom were obviously as unknown to the reporter as they were to the superintendent. The three had been elected as write-in candidates, defeating the three incumbents by comfortable margins. The station was in the process of contacting the winners to obtain interviews and would have the full story in a later broadcast, the newscaster concluded.

"How could write-ins defeat people whose names are on the ballot?" Patterson asked his wife as he switched off the radio. "They'd have to mount a public campaign to get people to vote for them, and there hasn't been any such campaign. These people are completely unknown."

"Well, I don't know about two of them, but isn't Jacobson the fellow who helped the Mayville Teachers' Association write those position papers a few years back?" Patterson's wife asked.

The superintendent reflected a moment. "You know, I think you're right," he said. He leaned back in his chair and thought a few seconds longer. "In fact, now that you mention it, I'll bet that the MTA has had something to do with this. I'm going to get hold of Cleaver when I get to the office and find out."

An hour later Bill Cleaver, the president of the MTA, stood smiling at Patterson. "I had a hunch you'd want to talk to me this morning, Don," he said. "You've probably got a few questions about yesterday's election results"

In the next hour, Patterson got a lesson in practical politics from the union president, who was obviously feeling rather pleased with himself and his association.

Cleaver began by saying that the MTA had been very unhappy with the three incumbent board members who were running for reelection. Throughout their terms they had taken positions that the MTA considered "antiteacher." Further, they were articulate and persuasive. They always managed to convince at least one other person on the seven-member board of the correctness of their views. Hence the three had succeeded in getting a significant number of policy changes enacted that tilted the balance of power toward the board and away from the teachers. That the MTA should be unhappy with them hardly surprised Patterson. The union's method of handling its unhappiness was a surprise, however.

It seemed that several months ago the MTA executive council had made a deliberate decision not to publicly back a slate of candidates in opposition to the three incumbents. "This town's so anti-union that if the MTA backed Mother Teresa for the board, she'd lose," Cleaver had said. Therefore, rather than encouraging three persons to run and openly supporting them, the MTA had organized the write-in campaign. Cleaver insisted that this campaign had not been secret, however. "We simply didn't publicize it," he said. "The MTA isn't under any obligation to make its decisions and actions public."

The union had correctly foreseen that voter turnout would be low, especially if the three incumbents were thought to be running unopposed. Accordingly, its executive council had quietly sought out three persons in the community who were sympathetic to the MTA's position on various issues and who would agree to run as unannounced write-in candidates. Then, just a week prior to the election, the executive council had called a closed meeting of the entire MTA membership. It had presented its three candidates and explained its election strategy. Basically, it urged members to write in the names of the three and to get a few supportive family members and friends to do likewise. "We explained," Cleaver said, "that if each MTA member got only four other persons to write in our candidates' names, they would almost certainly win, as long as the voter turnout stayed below 5%. So," he concluded, "we told them not to 'get out the vote' but to get out four certain write-in voters. And we told them to keep a very low profile in doing so. It worked beautifully.

"A new era in teacher–board relations is about to begin," Cleaver concluded. "Instead of being at each other's throats, the MTA and the Mayville Board of Education can finally establish a cooperative and harmonious relationship. Education in this town is bound to improve." He paused and then laughed. "Of course, your job will probably be a little tougher, Don, now that the board's not in your pocket. But that's okay. That's why you superintendents get those fat salaries."

Some Questions

1. Earlier in this chapter, we said that a decision has been made democratically if two conditions are met. Has anything undemocratic happened in Mayville? If so, what?
2. The facts in the case regarding the low turnouts in school board elections in this country are correct. Why should low turnouts be characteristic of these elections? What does this say about "local control"?
3. Do low turnouts necessarily mean that many people's views are not represented on the school board? Does that mean that they do not have a fair influence on a decision?
4. What, if anything, should Patterson do regarding his three new board members? Should he say or do anything about the MTA's election strategy? If so, what?

A Problem of Policy: Retaining Pupils at Jackson Elementary[1]

"You did what?" Helen asked, barely controlling her anger. "You and your staff decided that district policy was a bad idea for the kids at Jackson, and you didn't implement it?"

"No, I didn't say that," Alex retorted. "We did implement it. But we modified it to fit the needs of our kids. For God's sake, Helen, you know the kind of children we have at Jackson. They come to us with all kinds of disadvantages. If I retained every pupil who read below grade level, half my school would spend an extra two years in elementary school. And most

---

1. This case is a slightly edited version of one appearing in Haller, E. J. and Strike, K. A., *An Introduction to Educational Administration: Social, Legal, and Ethical Perspectives.* Troy, NY: Educator's International Press, 1997. It is used by permission of the publisher.

of them would be our minority kids. Do you call that equality of educational opportunity? These kids need a break, not another kick in the butt from the school system.

"I know I'm responsible to you and to the board to implement board policy. And I've done that. At least I will have done it, as soon as we get the bugs worked out of our procedures. It's not what the policy says that's important; it's what its purpose is. And that's to ensure that our students learn to read. These nine kids will be OK if those damn teachers at the middle school do their jobs. But let's get it straight. Jackson isn't going to have a policy of automatic retention. That idea stinks. You said as much yourself when we first started talking about it. On top of that, it'll destroy the self-concepts of my kids."

The policy that had provoked the heated debate between Helen Aristeme, the superintendent of Centerville School District, and Alex Dumas, the principal of Andrew Jackson Elementary School, was simple and to the point. As passed by the district's board of education, it read:

1. It is the policy of this district that elementary school children who are seriously deficient in their reading skills not be promoted to the next grade.
2. Judgments regarding deficiency shall be made by a principal in consultation with the teacher concerned.
3. No elementary school student who reads more than two grade levels below district norms on the Comprehensive Test of Basic Skills shall enter the middle school in the district.
4. Notwithstanding Point 3, no student shall be retained more than twice during his or her elementary school years.

Alex was right about Helen's initial reaction. She had opposed the policy. It had originally been suggested by the board's president, and the full board had asked her to look into its merits and make a recommendation. She was unsure where the idea had originated, but she suspected that it came from some of the teachers and building administrators in the middle schools. For several years they had been complaining about the poor reading performance of many of the district's elementary school graduates. In any case, by the time Helen first heard of it, the board was already solidly behind the idea, as were many of her own staff. As nearly as she could tell, parents were, too. There had been substantial support for it from the community and, to the best of her knowledge, no opposition.

At the board's request, she had brought the idea to her administrative cabinet for study. After protracted discussion, a majority endorsed it. Given that endorsement and the strong support coming from all other sources, she had recommended the policy's adoption to the board. She had, however, conveyed her reservations and had succeeded in getting Point 4, the two-failure modification, included.

Now, two years later, it turned out that Alex had never really implemented the policy. Helen remembered Alex's impassioned objections to the policy when it was introduced at one of the weekly meetings of Centerville's cabinet. He had called it "elitist" and claimed that it would not work. He had collected the research on the subject and presented it to his colleagues. With only a few exceptions, that research did seem to show that retention seldom had the effect of improving test scores. In fact, one study concluded that it lowered them. Other studies claimed that retention had undesirable social effects. However, after all the discussion was over and the final policy hammered out, the board had unanimously adopted it. Helen had assumed that Alex, however reluctantly, had implemented it at Jackson. Obviously she had been wrong.

Instead, Dumas had instituted a special reading program of his own that he claimed would reach the same goal of improving reading skills. That program involved the adoption of a new reading series for the primary grades, a series that had the reputation of being especially good for disadvantaged kids. He had reduced other costs and used the money to hire a special reading teacher for his school. He had recruited a group of college student volunteers who worked with selected kids on a daily basis. And he had implemented an in-service program on reading instruction for his staff. But he had never retained a single pupil.

Nothing happened for two years. Then the whole issue surfaced again with the arrival of Susan White, Mark Stanford, and Josh Whittier at Centerville Middle School. When these students had entered in September, no one took any special notice of them. By the end of the month, however, their instructors began to notice that they were not doing very well academically. For example, in the course of reviewing fifth-grade arithmetic, Susan's math teacher discovered that she was unable to add fractions. Further informal testing revealed that ordinary multiplication and division of whole numbers were difficult operations for her. At about the same time, Mr. Peach, Susan's English teacher, noticed that she could barely read the short stories he assigned. In searching out the cause of Susan's difficulties, Mr. Peach examined her elementary school records. These showed that the girl had progressed normally and that although her marks were on the low side, she had never failed a grade.

It was her standardized test scores, however, that provoked Peach to turn the whole matter over to the principal, Margaret Hamilton. Susan's achievement tests all indicated that she was at least two years below grade level in every subject—and almost three in reading.

At about the same time that Susan's folder landed on Hamilton's desk, Mark Stanford's and Josh Whittier's arrived at the same place, forwarded by two different teachers. Essentially, their records showed the same problem as Susan's. They were well below grade level in all subjects, and more than two below in reading. It was Hamilton who noted that all three were graduates of Andrew Jackson.

Hamilton phoned her colleague Alex Dumas, the principal of Jackson, to find out what she could about the three students. What she learned caused her to check the records of all of the new seventh graders from that school and to pass the folders of nine of them up to superintendent Helen Aristeme with a lengthy memo of complaint. All nine were reading more than two years below grade level, and none had ever been retained.

The memo's closing paragraph suggested that the nine were just the tip of an iceberg that could sink the entire curriculum of Centerville Middle School. Hamilton wrote:

> We've spent the last couple of years revising our entire curriculum on the assumption that incoming elementary school students would be reasonably close to grade level in reading. We've adopted new texts on that assumption. The English Department has changed its entire program. What are we supposed to do if Dumas keeps sending kids here who can't read? Since when are principals free to adopt a whole new program without district approval? And since when are principals free to ignore board policy? Helen, you'd better get this mess at Jackson straightened out.

When Dumas left Aristeme's office, the issue was unresolved, and the superintendent was still angry. However, over the next hour she cooled down. She knew she would have to do something—but what? On the one hand, she was concerned about the problem of curriculum articulation; she was reluctant to permit Dumas to continue his own special program at Jackson, although it did seem to her that it might be a good one. And, of course, she could hardly countenance a seemingly obvious violation of board policy. On the other hand, she had never really believed that retention was the way to handle the learning problems of elementary school children. From the perspective of a professional educator, she thought that Dumas's program just might work. Perhaps she could smooth things over for a year or two and give it a chance. She considered setting up a formal program evaluation, perhaps using an outside consultant. If the Jackson program really was successful, such an evaluation might provide the basis for repealing the policy, and Dumas's program might serve as a model for the entire district.

Some Questions

1. Two years passed before the superintendent discovered that Dumas had ignored board policy. How could that happen?
2. Consider our discussion of the concept of democracy. Was the retention policy in Centerville arrived at democratically? Why or why not?
3. Schools are said to have an "egg crate structure." Teaching goes on in separate rooms, behind closed doors, and the failure of any one teacher has no immediate effect on the success or failure of another. Principals can directly observe and supervise teachers only a few hours each year. School buildings are geographically separated, so that what happens in one has no immediate effect on another. Superintendents are seldom able to visit a school more than a few times each year. How can a superintendent improve the possibility of supervising such a "loosely coupled" organization?
4. Make an argument that it is Aristeme, not Dumas, who has behaved unethically. What else might she have done?

Accountability Meets Community at Rubens Flats

In the deepening twilight Jack Diamond sat in his office and reflected on his career. Jack had been the principal of Rubens Flats High School for 12 years, but he'd been associated with the school much of his life. He was an unusual principal in many respects. He was the first student to enroll at Rubens Flats when the school was founded. Indeed, as an adolescent he had helped in that founding. After graduating from college he returned to his hometown, married, and become a social studies teacher in a nearby community. When a teaching job opened at Rubens Flats, he applied and was hired. He became one of the most successful teachers in the school's history, and through hard work and unusual leadership, he eventually became its principal. It was a job he loved. Indeed, he loved the school, its students, its parents, and the town itself.

Jack was also an unusual principal because of his leadership style. To a casual observer, students, faculty, and parents exercised more leadership at Rubens than did its principal. Jack seemed retiring, even shy. He spoke seldom and then so quietly that others had to listen carefully to hear him. In meetings he usually spent more time asking questions than providing answers. That same casual observer might miss the fact that Jack's questions were often precisely the ones that needed to be asked. After posing a question, he was quick to step back and let the group discuss it. Group members quickly learned that asking Jack's opinion usually elicited another question. Meetings with Jack were likely to be lengthy affairs. But Jack's style of leadership seemed to suit Rubens Flats perfectly.

Like its principal, Rubens Flats was unusual in several ways. Founded in the early 1970s by a group of "activist" parents, students, and educators, it was located in a small college town in the northeast. Its first students chose its name, after a farmer, Joshua Rubens, who in 1795 settled the area where the school now stood. It served a small student population, never much over 150, most of whom were transfers from Stevenson High, the district's regular high school of about 2,500 students. Many were children of college faculty members who craved more freedom and self-direction in their own education than Stevenson was able to provide.

In the beginning there was considerable suspicion and opposition to the school. But over the years Rubens had gradually gained the support of some of its initial critics. Now, more than three decades after its founding, it was a respected part of the public school system.

Formal tests played a very small part in student assessment at Rubens. Instead, portfolios and projects of various kinds figured heavily in assessing student achievement. While the state's regulations regarding curriculum and "Carnegie Units" were met, this was often accomplished in ways that had little to do with putting in "seat time" in regular classroom subjects. Often students' work required interaction with community issues, public service, individualized study with residents who were not teachers, or guided research with college faculty members. This sort of individualized curriculum simply wouldn't work for all subjects, and for these, especially ones requiring laboratories, students were bused back and forth to Stevenson during the day.

Another unusual aspect of the school was the way in which the student population was created. All potential students had to apply for admission. A committee consisting of Jack and several teachers, students, and parents interviewed them and their parents. A positive vote by the committee was required before the applicant could be enrolled. Jack's vote carried no more weight than that of any other committee member. Further, pupil discipline was handled by a similar committee, which had the ultimate authority to "expel" misbehaving students, meaning that they had to return to Stevenson. Since nearly all students were deeply absorbed into Rubens and its culture, the possibility of expulsion was taken very seriously.

Finally, parents were expected to take a serious interest in their children's schooling. "Serious interest" meant actually spending a specified amount of time on various school activities such as assisting teachers or students, contributing their expertise when that was needed, sitting on the governing council of the school, and representing it in the community. Thus, parents, too, came to feel themselves an integral part of the school community and to have an important commitment to Rubens's success. Coupled with its small size, all of these mechanisms helped to generate a strong sense of community in the school. Indeed, students were quick to defend Rubens from its critics and to informally "discipline" other students whose behavior was thought to reflect badly on Rubens Flats.

The phrase "the school as a community" has become a part of educators' rhetoric. Usually it has little or no substantive meaning. In the case of Rubens Flats, however, "community" was not an empty term. Indeed, an anthropologist at the college once referred to the school as having a "tribe-like culture." To a very large extent, this strong sense of community and a common culture were a product of Jack's efforts. Now, sitting in the growing darkness, Jack reflected that this strong, all-encompassing culture was part of Rubens's problem.

When authoritative groups outside the school began to apply goals and standards to it that the Rubens community viewed as subversive or illegitimate, reaction was swift, defensive, and often acerbic. The first serious instance of this began in the 1990s. In the previous decade the state legislature had instituted a massive educational reform effort as part of a move toward greater school accountability. As is usual in such efforts, a group of standardized achievement tests was developed and mandated for use in all schools. These were intended to measure students' mastery of required educational subjects. Needless to say, the Rubens community rejected these tests out of hand, claiming that they would seriously distort the school's purpose and curriculum (a perception that was undoubtedly correct). Besides, argued community members, the school was obviously successful, since nearly all of its graduates had gone on to college and were now embarked on useful careers. Test scores were less valid indicators of Rubens's success.

The state's response to this was sharp and to the point: Rubens Flats was not permitted to exempt itself from requirements established by the state legislature. The school could continue to use unconventional methods of instruction, but its students would have to demonstrate mastery of ninth-grade algebra, for example, and they would do so on the state's tests, not with projects and portfolios. What followed was several years of fruitless discussions with legislators and state officials. Finally, the Commissioner of Education declared that Rubens Flats had three years to prepare itself for the testing program, after which it must comply or its graduates would fail to receive a high school diploma. Now, two years after this ultimatum, little had been done, and the deadline was at hand. The school community faced giving up many of its cherished beliefs and making very substantial modifications in its curriculum and practices. To refuse was to risk the educational careers of its students, to say nothing of legal action.

The Commissioner of Education was not the only source of Rubens's problems. Its own board of education and superintendent had come to view the school as problematic. Essentially, the local issue concerned money. For several years Rubens's enrollment had been declining. From a high of 158 in 1992, it was now 112. This decline had occurred simultaneously with a decrease in the state's financial support of public schools and increasing resistance among residents to sharply rising tax rates. Budget shortfalls were a serious and ongoing difficulty. In this climate of fiscal restraint, Rubens Flats presented a target of opportunity. Certain expenses at the school were considerably higher than normal. For example, having a principal, secretary, and custodian for a school of 112 students created high administrative costs per student. The school was housed in a converted factory, so maintenance costs were high. Pupils needed to be bused to Stevenson throughout the day, and the state bore none of these transportation costs.

Some members of the administration, the board, and the public began to press for the consolidation of the school with Stevenson, in the belief that a substantial number of dollars would be saved. Others wondered how the district could justify spending more per student at Rubens than was spent at Stevenson, and this was especially so since many of Rubens's students were the children of college faculty. They hardly qualified as needy. The board offered to let Rubens operate as a "school within a school" at Stevenson, thereby helping to maintain Rubens's identity as an alternative institution. The Rubens community roundly rejected this idea, on the grounds that its tiny student body, its distinctive operating style, and its singular culture would necessarily be submerged and lost in the larger and more traditional Stevenson.

And now, as if all these troubles were not enough, an even more ominous development for Rubens appeared: Cracks in the heretofore seamless community began to emerge. Under pressure from all sides, the school first took on an "us versus them" mentality, and it developed an even more cohesive (and heated) culture. However, as the pressure on the school continued to grow, subsets of the Rubens community began to form around different approaches to the school's problems. Inevitably, some of these approaches centered on some sort of compromise: In return for maintaining autonomy in some aspect of Rubens's operations, a group would propose giving up autonomy in others. Just as inevitably, other members of the community saw these groups as "traitors" to Rubens's history and philosophy. With the stakes seemingly so high—the very survival of the school seemed to hang in the balance—discussions among various factions within the community became increasingly acrimonious. And perhaps most inevitably of all, Jack Diamond lost the support of virtually everyone.

Sitting in his darkened office, the building silent and empty, Jack thought about his long association with Rubens Flats. He'd been on hand at the school's creation. Now it seemed he'd be on hand at its demise. And at that moment he made his decision. If the school was to survive, it could only happen under someone else's leadership.

Some Questions

1. Someone once remarked, "Good leadership, long sustained, is impossible." That might be particularly the case in closely knit communities with very strong, pervasive cultures. Why might that be so?
2. Refer to our earlier discussion of a school community. Jack Diamond has been extraordinarily successful in creating a community at Rubens Flats. If a strong sense of community is a good thing, why is Rubens failing? (Before you blame a test-crazed society, a bullying state legislature, a craven Department of Education and a board of education that can't see beyond the bottom line, consider the defects of a strong school community.)
3. Consider a school with a strong sense of community that contains a faculty with a strong sense of itself as a professional body. Do you see any problems?

CHAPTER 7

Diversity: Multiculturalism and Religion

A CASE

Cassandra Lewis was an African American who was doing well by doing good. She was the Assistant Superintendent for Curriculum of the Midland School District. Midland was a city of several hundred thousand people. Ms. Lewis was a well educated member of the black middle class with a good job and in a position to help others. She had grown up poor but had been a good student in Midland's public schools and had received a lot of financial help in order to finish college and get an advanced degree. She understood what racism was about, but she also believed in the efforts U.S. society had made to provide equality of opportunity. *Brown v. Board of Education*, the 1964 Civil Rights Act, and affirmative action had worked for her. She had attended integrated public schools, a good college, and an elite graduate school. She had been rewarded for her achievement with good jobs in several school systems concluding with her job with Midland. She expected that with a few more years of experience she would become a superintendent. The American dream had worked for her. She believed in an integrated, multicultural society in which everyone had an equal chance to contribute and in which contributions from diverse cultures were blended in a larger culture available to every American. While the percentage of African Americans in Midland's population had grown dramatically over the last decade, and Ms. Lewis was concerned about the resulting de facto segregation in Midland's schools, that did not seem to her to be a reason to depart from those ideals. In fact, it seemed a reason to work harder to achieve them.

The legislature of the state in which Midland was located had recently approved a charter school statute. The new law provided for the creation of several new schools that would be proposed and developed by groups of parents and teachers. These schools would be exempt from many state and local regulations. Their purpose, according to the law, was to promote pedagogical experimentation. In Ms. Lewis's district proposals for new charter schools were to be evaluated by a committee of which she was chair. That was an important new responsibility that Ms. Lewis was pleased to accept.

At least she was pleased until she read the proposals. Several seemed unexceptional and reasonable. A few others would not fly because they were just ill-conceived. But two proposals caught her attention. They proposed program emphases that went well beyond her idea of pedagogical experimentation and that promised to be troublesome and controversial. Ms. Lewis was also struck by the fact that, while in some ways these two proposals seemed polar opposites, they also made some interestingly similar arguments.

The first was a proposal for the Harriet Tubman Middle School. It proposed a curriculum that would be "especially appropriate for African-American girls." It argued that the curriculum of most public schools was both Eurocentric and male-dominated. In neither case did most public schools help African-American girls develop a strong identity as African-American women. Instead schools often abetted their oppression and domination. A middle school was especially appropriate for a project emphasizing their needs, the proposal claimed, because early adolescence was the time when girls began to learn passivity and to subordinate their interests, plans, and lives to those of men. Since African-American women were subjected to both racism and sexism, the formation of a strong and distinct identity as African-American women was especially important for them. It required a special curriculum.

The second school, called The People of Faith school, was, if anything, even more unique. It proposed a curriculum that emphasized "the development of each student's religious understanding, tolerance, and spirituality through the study of the role of religion in society and culture in an atmosphere of tolerance and openness." While it claimed that its approach was secular in that it endorsed no religious outlook and insisted that it would make only secular use of sacred material, it also proposed that its curriculum would emphasize those religious sources of most interest to those students (African Americans) most likely to be represented in the student body. Its language program would give special attention to the scriptures of the Old and New Testaments as well as African spiritual sources. Its history courses would emphasize the religious history of the diverse peoples of the United States and would include discussion of the African roots of African-American spirituality, as well as the role of black churches in the civil rights movement. Its music program would emphasize religious music with a particular concern for black gospel music, and its science curriculum would discuss views on the relationship between faith and reason, would include the principles of African epistemology as well as European views, and would present controversial views on origins "so as to give equal weight to scientific naturalism and to the view that nature is ordered by a higher power as this idea appears in both European and African culture." It would, the proposal said, "recognize the scientific relevance of the experience of faith." While evolution would be taught, the curriculum would also provide space for what was described as "the Creation stories of diverse peoples." This science curriculum would be taught in a manner described as "open, unbiased, and offensive to no one." Ms. Lewis wondered at that. The prospects for a curriculum that dealt with religion and science in a culturally sensitive way and that was going to be neutral, tolerant, and inoffensive struck her as small.

Ms. Lewis's initial reaction to both schools was quite negative. On her first reading, one school seemed a segregation academy that was no less offensive to her by being black instead of white. The other was a religious school. Moreover, they seemed to offer different and conflicting pictures of the center of life for African Americans. They had a potential for much divisiveness. She doubted both their legality and their wisdom. She was prepared to support neither. However, as she read on her negative reaction softened. She began to be impressed with the care and thoughtfulness of the proposals. Although their authors were motivated to create a curriculum well targeted to their specific aspirations and the needs of a particular group of students as they saw them, they did not seemed motivated either by racial or sectarian hostility. She noted, for example, that both schools carefully characterized their uniqueness in terms of a curricular focus. And, while their curriculum was intended for a particular audience, neither group proposed to exclude anyone of any race or creed who was interested in the curriculum their school would provide. The Tubman School would take boys and students of all races if they applied and were interested. The People of Faith School had no requirements for admission other than an interest in religious studies, and it promised that those who had no faith would not be discriminated against in their academic work. Nor would they feel any pressure for religious conformity. Moreover, while the school would seek to accommodate private or group religious activities, the school would sponsor no religious services or practices.

Ultimately what came to bother Ms. Lewis was the abandonment of the vision of public schools as common schools. Ms. Lewis had thought of public schools as places where people of different races and creeds could come together to forge a common identity as Americans. She did not exactly think of schools as a melting pot. Differences were things to be respected and shared, not dissolved. At the same time, she had always believed that what people shared was more important than what divided them. People shared a common humanity and a common citizenship. But these proposals seemed to treat differences as more fundamental than these commonalities. They talked a lot about peoples' cultural, gender, or religious identities. They seemed to think that expressing and strengthening these different identities was more important than emphasizing what people had in common; that every truth was someone's truth and that what was important was to explore the truth of one's group and to avoid domination by others. And they seemed to view efforts to create common or shared identities as oppressive. Reveling in and strengthening distinct identities, Ms. Lewis thought, was not what the schools of a democratic society were for. (And, she noted, the proposal for the People of Faith School had some considerable difficulty with the diverse religious identity of African Americans. Its authors did not seem to have considered that many African Americans were Muslims.) African Americans had struggled hard to gain equal access to America's common schools, and there was still a considerable way to go. She was not sure that the curricular exclusiveness of these proposed schools was helpful. And she was uncomfortable about the way these proposals implicitly defined her. While she was both an African American and a religious person, neither of these cultures captured all of what she was. She had learned to think of herself as a human being first, an American second, and an African-American woman who was a member of an AME Zion church after that. Until now these different perceptions of who she was had not seemed at odds. And she was not quite ready to see her view as a sign that she had internalized the perspective of her oppressors. Moreover, the idea that every truth was someone's truth troubled her. Wasn't truth just truth?

She took a coin from her pocket and read the motto, *E pluribus Unum.* These proposals seemed to want to substitute *E pluribus pluribum.*

DISPUTE

A: One of the great things about our democracy is its pluralism. We have people from all races and religions, from all the countries and cultures of the world. We each learn from the other, and we all live together in peace and harmony.

B: Wait a minute! Our history, even our most recent history, is not full of peace and harmony. It is full of race riots, church burnings, ugly confrontations, marches, bombings, and FBI/ATF raids and sieges. Diversity is the catalyst not of peace but of hatred, discrimination, and the sanctioned use of brute force.

A: Yes, such things happen, but if you think of the country as a whole, these incidents are statistically insignificant. Ninety-nine percent of the population gets along with or at least is tolerant of others who are different. Tolerance is our solution to difference.

B: But just acknowledging and recognizing differences is the root of the problem. Ninety-nine percent of the time whites see blacks as different, and inwardly, unconsciously, see themselves as superior. Blacks learn early that they are different and feel a twinge of inferiority when treated in certain ways by whites. The same is true of Jews, born again Christians, Hispanics, Native Americans, Asians, and numerous other minority groups in our land. Young children pick up signals from their parents and other authority figures as well as from their peers. They learn to feel different by osmosis. We can try to teach tolerance in our schools, but the roots of difference have already grown deep and scar the souls of our children.

A: Very poetic! Yet your very description of the problem hints at its solution. Schools must be an oasis of tolerance, teaching it by example and osmosis. Different cultures need to be studied and their contributions appreciated. Different religions also have to be explored and understood as different ways human beings define the spiritual realm.

B: Oh, be realistic! There is not enough time to teach about all the cultures in the world. Even if there were, by whose cultural standards of judgment are we to determine what are *worthwhile* contributions? Standards differ in different cultures. Teaching about different religions can be dangerous too. Are all of them right in some sense? What happens to your own spiritual beliefs when you are asked to appreciate the contrary beliefs of others? Is there no true religion? Doesn't truth count?

A: Truth is not the point here. Tolerance and understanding are. What we need in a pluralistic, multicultural, democratic society is to learn to live peacefully together and respect difference, not tell the truth together.

B: Are you saying that truth is not important in our schools or in our democratic society? I can't believe it!

CONCEPTS AND ISSUES

Religious diversity and multiculturalism are complex issues. We aren't going to be able to do more than scratch the surface here. We want to focus on four connected issues. First is the issue of alienation and self-identity. The proposers of our two charter schools claim that many students are culturally alienated from America's common schools, which they do not see as common at all. Many minority students and many religious students feel that the school they attend isn't their school, that they don't belong, because their school seems to reject something about who they are. Second, there is an issue of truth and of who controls it. The official knowledge of the school, some claim, is that of secular, white, European-oriented, male elites. For many in America, school knowledge isn't their knowledge. Religious knowledge or the knowledge of non-European cultures is ignored, devalued, or disparaged. Do schools have a right to affirm some people's knowledge and marginalize that of others? Is truth just truth, or is there differential ownership of different truth? Who gets to decide what schools will view as the truth or what questions are open to debate? Third is the issue of dialogue. Ms. Lewis thinks of common schools as places where different ideas can be aired and debated. Perhaps she holds Mill's view that truth is best sought through free and open debate. Thus she would be dissatisfied with schools where students learn only their truth, but where interesting questions and arguments are avoided because someone might be offended, and, after all, there are multiple truths. But if schools are to be places for dialogue, a market place of ideas, who will set the rules for the discussion, and how will it be made a fair debate? Who owns the truth or the rules of discourse? Finally, there is the question of the one and the many. Should the school work to create a shared American culture? Or should it try to respect each culture equally? If it does the first, will not minorities be oppressed and alienated? If it does the second, will not our society become Balkanized and politically unstable? Is there a middle ground?

We have two purposes that we want to accomplish in this chapter. First, we want to develop some positions about these four issues concerning diversity. However, our second reason for raising these issues is that they pose an opportunity to ask some questions about the adequacy of some of the analytic concepts we have tried to teach throughout this book. We are thus going to revisit some ideas that we have developed in prior chapters in order to discuss some issues that have become important since the first edition of this book appeared: Not that we are going to recant (although we are going to reinterpret). But we think that you ought to have an opportunity to test these concepts against some objections that have become widespread. We originally developed this book as though it were a debate between two broad theories of ethics, a consequentialist view that emphasizes the principle of benefit maximization, and a nonconsequentialist view in which equal respect for all persons is central. We did this because we think that these are useful concepts for discussing ethical issues and because these are among the most general ways available to describe ethical theories. We still think this.

At the same time the views we have presented are two versions of what we might call the ethics of modernity. Modernity has been challenged by some philosophers who are sometimes called postmodernists. We can't do justice to this complicated debate here, but allow us a brief attempt to characterize it. Among the arguments that postmodernists have made is that the philosophies of modernity are insufficiently attentive to difference. These philosophies, they claim, want to bring everything under the sway of some grand unified theory Thus they make such claims as: regardless of how different we are, we are all the same in some important way and that it is this sameness that is the most important thing about us. We may differ in our views, in our religions, in our ethnicity, in our gender, in our history, but after all of these differences have been noted, we are all persons, or we are all utility maximizers (or both). Isn't our personhood the basis of our dignity and our rights? Don't we need to think about people as trying to maximize their happiness in order to evaluate the consequences of decisions?

Perhaps, however, our differences are more basic than our sameness. Indeed, perhaps our sameness is illusory. What after all is a person? Does our description of a person actually describe some real feature of every human being that is also central in our ethical lives? Perhaps this entity called a person is just a metaphysical delusion that names nothing. Even worse, perhaps a description of a person is really a characterization of people as Europeans see them. Perhaps it tries to universalize traits that are European, or male, or white, or Christian, but that are not really universal. If so, then an ethic that treats personhood as central may subtly impose the culture of some on others. Despite its claims of freedom and equality, it may be biased in favor of Europeans, or men, or heterosexuals. Analogously, perhaps the picture of human beings as utility or pleasure maximizers is the view of people conveniently held by capitalist economists. Thus it serves the interest of capitalism. Are these interests universal? Perhaps we need to abandon such ways of thinking entirely. We need to stop looking for some characteristic like personhood that is central and shared and to notice the importance of difference.

Consider the issue of truth. One of the things that many contemporary philosophers have argued is that people experience the world through the interpretive frameworks they receive through their cultures—we do not all see the world in the same way. Perhaps we live in irreducibly different worlds. Perhaps there is no Truth; there is only the experiences of women and men, of European Americans and African Americans and Hispanic Americans, of Jews and Christians and Muslims, only different truths—only different ways of seeing the world. The only truths we can have are truths that presuppose our background and that assume who we are. Thus all truths are partial and perspectival. No truth is the whole truth. Every truth assumes something about the perspective of the individual whose truth it is.

Notice how these two ideas connect. The idea that truth is partial and perspectival means that it is unlikely that we will ever achieve any ethical theories that are genuinely universal. We are irreducibly different. All theories assume someone's particular experience. Views that try to see us as persons or as utility maximizers end up imposing someone's truth as everyone's truth. Thus all attempts at ethical generalization are oppressive. They deny who we are, and they impose someone else's definition of what we should be on us.

These are not views we would accept in the form as we have stated them here. We do not believe that they promote tolerance or moral reflection. If taken in their extreme form, we believe that they undermine the grounds for tolerance and for moral dialogue. Yet we do take such claims seriously. First, we think that they pose an important challenge to the way we have proceeded. We think you should have a chance to consider them, and that there is something to be learned from them. Second, they provide an important warning to those who try to develop ethical theories. Even if there are some things that can be said about people in general and even if there are some important universal ethical claims that can be defended, we still need to be careful that we do not mistake the views of our culture or our own personal biases for these claims. We need to test any claims carefully. We need to be especially careful to do so when we are dealing with someone with a background that is significantly different from our own. Third, these concerns provide an especially useful window on the questions of pluralism and diversity that administrators must face in schools.

We will proceed by, first, describing a view of religious and cultural diversity that emphasizes the theme of alienation that was raised in our case, and that emphasizes radical difference and the perspectival nature of truth. We will then contrast this view with views of diversity developed from a nonconsequentialist and then a consequentialist perspective. We will then make a few comments on the strengths and weaknesses of each.

Radical Diversity

Are Americans one people? Should they be? Do schools have any obligation to take many and make them one? *E pluribus unum?*

In years past many educators thought they had just such an obligation. It was the job of the school to Americanize immigrants. People with diverse languages, religions, political beliefs, and customs were to pass through the school where they were to be made Americans by being stirred into the American melting pot. Not only was diversity not especially valued, it was to be dissolved and eliminated in the name of creating a new kind of person, an American.

Of course Americans have (in varying degrees) respected some kinds of diversity. The Bill of Rights included two phrases usually called the Establishment and Free Exercise Clauses that say "Congress shall make no law effecting an establishment of religion nor prohibiting the free exercise thereof." Historically, however, religious tolerance was limited in practice. Until the late 1960s many states required the school day to begin with readings from the Protestant Bible and recitation of the Lord's Prayer. Religious toleration, it seemed, often applied only to different kinds of Protestants. Catholic immigrants found public schools sufficiently unfriendly to their convictions that they began their own school system.

Other kinds of diversity were not respected. Africans were enslaved. Native Americans were driven west, persecuted sometimes to extinction, and confined to reservations that have, to this day, often been places of poverty and misery. Few minorities or immigrant populations have found America respectful of their culture, religion, or ethnicity. Some have found it viciously repressive and exploitative.

Public schools seem to have tried hard to make us one or to behave as though we were already one, and that one was often Protestant, white, and Northern European. Others were to be remade into this model or accommodate to it, or they were simply excluded.

Is this wrong? If so, why? The first answer we will explore emphasizes the importance of people's religion, culture, or ethnicity to their sense of identity and views the failure to respect their religion, culture, or ethnicity as a form of violence against this socially constructed self. (This account owes much to Taylor [1994]. However, we have made no effort to be faithful to the details of his account.)

In the case that opened this chapter, advocates of the charter schools claim that the common school has denied or failed to affirm something that is highly important to some students—their religion, their culture. But what's this got to do with who these students are, with their identity? The answer is that people's religion, culture, and ethnicity often are not just facts about them, but are central to their self-understanding, to who they are, to their own self-definitions. People are not just persons who happen to be Christians or women or African Americans. These characteristics are not possessions, like clothing, that can be shed or changed at will. Instead, people are Christians, women, or African Americans. If so, then one reason that can be given for respecting diversity is that to fail to do so is to reject who people are. It is to deny their worth. It does an especially insidious kind of violence to them.

Trying to respect diversity raises questions of truth, what is to count as truth, and who is to control what is to count as truth. Advocates for the People of Faith School seem concerned about how the school will treat questions about human origins. They want to teach evolution, but they also want to avoid teaching what they call "scientific naturalism" and to respect the creation stories of peoples of all cultures. Perhaps they might reason as follows: If religion is central to the identity of some people in the school, and if evolution is inconsistent with the religious convictions of some of these students, then teaching evolution may be experienced by these students as a rejection of who they are. Since peoples' stories about creation may be part of the literature that helps them form their identities, they want to respect these stories. Perhaps then the evolution versus creation debate is not just about biology. It may be about identity. Perhaps that is why people feel so strongly about it.

Similarly, it may be important to various groups in the United States to discuss their culture and history and to teach their contributions to the nation. When African-American students see the value of their culture acknowledged and find that they have made important contributions to the nation, they may feel affirmed. Their self-esteem may grow. If they define themselves as African Americans, then discovering that they have a valuable culture that has done something important might be expected to enhance their sense of self-worth.

But what if evolution is true? Can the People of Faith School find a way to respect different creation stories while also viewing them as myths? Does the role that these stories play in forming the identity of those whose stories they are, depend on their being viewed as true? What if some of the claims made about the contributions of African Americans or others are not true? What if much in conventional school history is there, not because it is true, but because it affirms the worth of dominant groups? Should students feel diminished by unpleasant truths? If they identify with some group, should they feel personally affirmed or diminished because of the accomplishments or failings of other, perhaps long-dead, members of their group? Perhaps it is a mistake to link one's sense of self-worth to claims about cultural values, stories about creation, or historical facts that may not stand up to examination. Are the contributions of all cultures equal? Must all of their stories be equally true? If not, are their members unequal on that account? Do people have a right to equal dignity? If so, and if the sense of equal worth is diminished by teaching such ideas as evolution or by failing to affirm various groups' cultures and contributions or by questioning valued historical accounts of them, does the school have a right to teach such offending doctrines? Must schools lie or hide the truth in order to affirm the equal worth of their students? This formulation seems intolerable.

But we might avoid the dilemma if we could also assert two other ideas. First, let us suppose that truth is relative either to religion or to culture. Second, let us assume that people have a right to control their own truth. If we affirm these two ideas, it will be impossible for members of one group to reject or overturn the truth of another.

Let's see how this might work out for Creationism and evolution. Many religious people do not reject evolution. They may claim that, while their creation stories are not literally the truth about creation, they contain some deeper truth about human beings or the human condition. Those religious people who do reject evolution, on the other hand, sometimes argue in the following way: They claim that much of the so-called evidence for the great age of the universe and for evolution is question-begging. It assumes that God does not exist. Consider, for example, an argument for the great age of the universe. If we are to believe what scientists tell us about the vast size of the universe and about the speed of light, then it seems that we can see objects that are so distant that their light must have been traveling for millions or billions of years to reach us. If so, then the universe must be more than a few thousand years old as some Creationists claim.

But Creationists have responded that when God created the universe, He may well have created the light from these distant stars and galaxies already in transit. The evolutionist's argument for the age of the universe assumes a universe without God. Thus the argument for the great age of the universe fails unless we already assume that it was not created by God.

Sometimes Creationists will generalize this argument. If we believe in God and that the universe and life are His creation, we can easily interpret all of the supposed evidence for evolution so as to be consistent with this belief. Evolutionists only see a universe in which chance and natural selection reign because they have already denied the possibility of God. But where evolutionists see chance and natural selection, Creationists can see purpose and design. We only need to believe in evolution if we have rejected God. However, if we choose to believe in God as our creator, then all of the evidence can be interpreted consistently with that belief. *Everythings depends on the assumptions with which we start.*

Then the next move: If truth is relative to our starting assumptions, why should the starting point of the evolutionist count for more than the starting point of the Creationist? What gives the evolutionist the right to try to dominate the minds of the children of Creationists? If this right is not grounded in the possession of the real Truth in the matter—and it has been shown that it cannot be—then it is nothing more than arbitrary power. What gives evolutionists the right to defame the views of people of faith? By what right do they compel people to send their children to public schools where they have a monopoly on what is to count as truth? Do not Creationists have the right to control their own truth?

The same argument can be made for the right of members of various cultures to control their own truth. They might argue that historical truth is a matter of interpretation, that they have the right to their own interpretation and to the final say about what picture of their group is presented in schools attended by their children. Indeed, since they have an interest not only in what their own children are taught, but also in what other children are taught about them, perhaps they have a broad right to control all the messages communicated about themselves.

If we generalize this argument the result is the following: Every culture has its own standards of value and of truth that are central to it. These standards are right for that culture. Since there is no general Truth about them, then one culture may not reasonably criticize another. Every culture owns its own standards and its own truth.

These arguments (if we accept them) tend to secure the dignity and worth of individuals by rendering their religion or their culture unassailable, by viewing all cultures as equally valuable, and by asserting a general rule that every religion or culture owns its own truth. Along the way, they also seem to lead to a radical pluralism. Societies are viewed as constituted primarily by difference and by groups characterized by their differences. There can be no question of subjecting one culture to the rule of another's truth. Difference rules.

Consequentialist and Nonconsequentialist Views on Diversity

Now we want to look at how nonconsequentialists and consequentialists might look at religious or cultural diversity.

A nonconsequentialist might reason about diversity as follows: The most important fact about people is not their ethnic identity or their religion, but their personhood. It is their status as persons, as moral agents, that is the basis of equal rights and of the respect we must show them.

However, if we are to respect people as moral agents, we must respect their choices. We cannot compel them to adopt our religion or our view of a good life, or our view of a worthy culture even if we think we are right and they are wrong. Respecting persons as responsible moral agents means nothing if we do not respect their choices. Moreover, we owe equal respect to different religions or cultures, not because they are equally true or equally valuable, but because they have been chosen by people who have equal rights.

Notice some features of this view. First, since rights are rooted in personhood and rights are enforceable, there are some moral views that we do not have to tolerate—at least if that means that we would not be allowed to work against them in schools or to prevent people from acting on them. (Perhaps we do have to acknowledge the right of people to hold them.) We do not have to tolerate racism, for example. We may argue for racial (or religious or ethnic) tolerance in schools, and we may prevent people from acting on their racism. What nonconsequentialists often say here is that people have a duty to be just, but that they are entitled to have and to pursue their own concept of a good life. It is this self-chosen sense of the good, which includes religion and culture, that we must respect even if we disagree or believe that ours is superior. Respecting peoples' religion or culture is required by equal respect for persons.

This means that nonconsequentialists do have a plausible approach to explaining what it is that people should have in common and how they may permissibly differ. Everyone should be just, and we may seek and enforce a shared view of justice. But we may not seek to regulate people's views of a good life. May we use the schools to make people Americans? Yes, if we mean that we may try to use schools to teach the essentials of a just constitution or to create the virtues (such as tolerance) that liberal democracies require of their citizens. No, if that means that we can use schools to promote a shared religion or a common culture beyond the political culture warranted by a just constitution.

This view does not root tolerance or pluralism in cultural relativism. We must tolerate other peoples' religion even if we are sure that it is false. We must respect other peoples' cultures even if we are convinced that ours is superior. What we are respecting is the right to choose, not the adequacy of the choice. On this view, tolerance does not trump truth. We are not necessarily intolerant if we reject something someone believes for religious reasons or if we deny some prized but dubious historical claim.

Also, in teaching tolerance, schools would need to be careful to help students to understand that they need to tolerate views and lifestyles even if they disapprove of them. But they would also have to respect students' right to disapproval. For example, schools might explain to students whose religion teaches that homosexuality is a sin that homosexuals are entitled to equal rights regardless of whether homosexuality is a sin. But schools need not insist that these students view homosexuality as merely an alternative lifestyle.

Respecting diverse cultures probably should be viewed as requiring that schools reflect the diversity of American cultures in their teaching. However, schools need not falsify or invent history in order to present a favorable view of every culture. Nor do they need to treat every aspect of every culture with approval. They owe their first obligation to the truth when they can find it. While truth may be difficult to find, it is not relative, at least not in the extreme form described above, and cultures do not own their own truth.

Nonconsequentialists can acknowledge that people may feel injured when they have to face something unpleasant about their group, their history, or their culture, and since this is a real harm, they should avoid causing such harm unnecessarily. But they can also argue that causing people this kind of injury is not the same as rejecting their worth as human beings. People's self-worth should depend on the fact that they are persons, moral agents, not on the truth of their religions or the achievements of their culture.

Nonconsequentialists might also note that the radical pluralist argument described above seems inconsistent with asking white people to acknowledge and rectify their oppression of minorities. After all, if truth is relative and if people own their own truth, why may not white people invent a history to their own liking? Arguably much of the history once taught (perhaps still taught) in public schools was written to support and justify white domination or white superiority and to minimize the fact of white oppression. Slavery has often been represented as benevolent paternalism. Was it? If white people choose to think so, isn't it useful to confront them with the truth?

This form of nonconsequentialist view does require public school teachers to walk a tight line with respect to their treatment of controversial views and diverse lifestyles, but there is a line to be walked.

We return to John Stuart Mill for a consequentialist view of diversity. Mill has argued for what he calls individuality by claiming that tolerating diversity has the consequence of promoting what he calls experiments in living. Just as free and open debate is necessary for seeking the truth, it is also the case that experiential evidence is necessary if we are to decide what are the best ways to live. Mill thus argues for individuality as a way to conduct experiments in living. We can only learn from one another about good ways to live if diversity and experimentation are valued and protected.

Mill presents several other arguments for diversity. For example, he argues that diversity in ways of life makes life more varied and interesting. Diversity adds to the intrinsic interest of societies. Mill also claims that while it is true that happiness is the good, it is also true that different people find their happiness in different ways. We have different tastes and needs. A society without diversity would require everyone to find their happiness in the same kinds of things. However, significant diversity allows people to find a way of living that fits their own happiness.

Thus, in a variety of ways, Mill argues that diversity contributes to the greatest good for the greatest number.

Mill wants to distinguish between areas of life over which government or society may assume control and those over which individuals are sovereign. However, he draws the distinction between the public sphere and the private sphere differently than nonconsequentialists. As a consequentialist, his views emphasize the consequences of actions or ideas more than respecting personal choice. However, we think that for most practical purposes Mill and most nonconsequentialists would regard the same things as appropriately under public control and the same kinds of things as private. Both Mill and nonconsequentialists would view speech, religion, culture, and lifestyle—people's conceptions of a good life—as their own business. However, they would do so in a way that rejects relativism. It may be especially worth noting that inquiry into the truth about ideas and about ways of life is an important goal for Mill. This requires intellectual liberty and experiments in living, open debate and experiential evidence, dialogue. Mill would regard two different attitudes towards truth as destructive of dialogue. One is certainty. If we are sure we have the truth, why dialogue? But the other is radical skepticism. If there is no truth to be found, why dialogue? He encourages an attitude of fallibalism—the view that inquiry into the truth has a point, but that we can never be certain that we have the truth.

Pros and Cons

We have now stated three different justifications for tolerating diversity. Consider some pros and cons about them. First some objections to the standard nonconsequentialist and consequentialist analyses.

We think that the story about respect for persons does not adequately reflect the extent to which the self is socially formed. Few of us think of ourselves as just abstract persons. We are rather "situated selves" formed by our histories, cultures, religions, and much else besides. Moreover, the story does not adequately reflect how we think about valuing people. Few of us wish to be valued merely because we are persons. (Of course, few of us wish to be valued merely because of our group identity either.) We want to be valued because of the particular people we happen to be. How affirmed are we likely to feel when we are informed by someone that our rights are respected because we are persons, but of course our religion is false, our culture worthless, and the achievements of our people and of ourselves insignificant? Heaven save us from such praise! A view that detaches the value of persons from their "situated selves" and attaches it only to abstract personhood has missed something. We may all be persons, but we are all also particular persons who need to be valued for that reason. Our particularity as well as our personhood needs to be considered in an adequate ethic.

While we do not think that the form of cultural relativism we have described above is defensible, we do think that something we shall call "modest relativism" can be defended. Modest relativism seeks to acknowledge two things. First, any adequate view of rationality has to acknowledge that the concepts that people acquire from their culture and their education influence and structure their perception of the world. Second, it is also true that what people take to be true is often colored not just by what it is reasonable to believe, but by their interests and biases. Sometimes reasoning can be nothing more than a way of pretending that our particular interests and biases are somehow rooted in the nature of things instead of our own interests.

Hillary Putnam (1983) puts the idea that thought always occurs within a context of shared concepts this way:

There are two points that must be balanced, both points that have been made by philosophers of many different kinds: (1) talk about what is "right" and "wrong" in any area only make sense against the background of an inherited tradition; but (2) traditions themselves can be criticized. (p. 234)

Notice, however, that the way Putnam puts the point is designed to show that all reasoning occurs within traditions of substantive ideas and concepts. However, it is not intended to show either that criticism and debate between traditions is impossible or fruitless or that what we take to be rationality is nothing more than an expression of our interests and biases. Indeed, we think that to accept Putnam's point is to see that dialogue and argument between different traditions, religions, or cultures is essential if we are to discover our blind spots and have our biases brought to light. It is the only way that we can learn to see in another way.

There is another aspect to our "moderate relativism." Mill's "experiments in living" argument does not assume that all differences in how people choose to live are just experiments in which eventually, when we get enough evidence, we will learn what the best way to live really is. Mill also believes that people find their happiness in different ways. If this is true, and if happiness is the good, then a society that permits people to pursue their happiness as they experience it will be more conducive to the greatest good for the greatest number.

There is much to be said for this view, but its weakness (in this context) is that it does not express a clear sense of the extent to which what people experience as valuable in their lives is significantly a function of their culture. It is not only our concepts, but our happiness that is socially formed. If so, two things may follow. First, perhaps it is at least equally important for us to value pluralism as it is to value individuality. To value pluralism is to value more than just diversity. It is to recognize that religion, culture—the things that not only make us diverse, but divide us into groups—provide the resources that make diversity and choice possible. They form both our ways of valuing and the objects of our values. Pluralism is a precondition of diversity. We need a more groupish vision of diversity than Mill's conception of individualism provides.

Second, a recognition of cultural variation in standards of value may help us to avoid biased cultural critique. Perhaps this point can be made clearer if we express it as an objection to Mill. Experiments are judged successful or not according to some standards. How are we to judge experiments in living? What standards of success shall we use? Where do they come from? Are we to use the standards of Englishmen of the 19th century? Mill's country and his century were notorious in judging other people's "experiments in living" as failures when compared with their own.

Moreover, when they judged others to be "primitives" or "barbarians," they found justification for imperialism and domination and the right to civilize and rule, which they called the white man's burden. Mill himself gives way to such sentiments in *On Liberty* where he argues that paternalism is appropriate both for children and barbarians. Arguably, if we do not have a sense of the extent to which standards of value are socially formed and what counts as happiness is culturally dependent, we will end up uncritically using the standards of our culture to judge others, and we will fail to respect or learn from their experience.

Is this not cultural relativism? No. At least not in the sense we described above. We have not denied the possibility of criticizing other cultures or of learning from them. That different cultures have different standards of value is not inconsistent with either critique or mutual learning. However, recognizing the variability of cultural standards of value should help us in avoiding naive or biased critique, from seeing our values as absolute, and in finding a middle ground between absolutism and relativism.

Mill's view also suggests that we should not assume that there must always be a right and a wrong about differences or in how people seek their happiness. Taste in food is a useful example. People's taste in food is obviously a matter of what is valued and served in their family or in their culture. They may learn to like other kinds of food as well. Or perhaps they will not. But it remains true that tastes are not just a function of some innate tendency to like some things and not others. Tastes are a cultural product. Tastes are not merely individual likings. They are culturally packaged. Even if we learn to like the food of other cultures, the standards of taste we develop from our own will condition what we learn to like in other food. Again, Mill's argument for individualism might be viewed as an argument for pluralism. We must respect the tastes of different cultures simply because they constitute both the standards of value and the objects of value of these cultures in a way that is not always amenable to judgments of inferiority or superiority—truth or error. Culture is often the reason why people find their good in different ways.

Thus, we do believe that an adequate ethical theory needs to come to terms both with the extent to which selves are more than persons and with the "concept embeddedness" of perception, thought, and value. But we also think that the formulation of the argument for radical pluralism we described above, while it does take these things into account, has some serious flaws.

One weakness of radical pluralism is that it has difficulty explaining why we should regard people as equal and as possessed of equal rights. Cultural relativism seeks to make all people equal by making all cultures equal. It does this by denying that there are any criteria that could be discovered that could be used to appraise different cultures. But how does this make either individuals or cultures equal? Indeed, since cultures need respect only their own standards of value, what is it that requires people to suspend these standards of value when judging other cultures? Is it not at least equally plausible to judge others by the standards of one's own culture even when that leads to a negative view of other cultures? Why not?

The cultural relativist cannot say that we must tolerate other cultures because tolerance is an objective value. Nor can the relativist claim that equality is an objective value. There are no objective values. There are only the values of particular cultures to which their members are entitled. Suppose culture A holds values that lead A's to find the culture of B's worthless and the members of B inferior. What are the grounds for asserting equality and tolerance against the views of the A's? If cultural relativism is true, there can be no such grounds that are not just the values of a particular culture and thus there can be no grounds that the A's should accept.

In fact cultural relativism seems parasitic on a tradition of tolerance and equality that derives from the ethics of modernity. It insists that we value other people and other cultures as equals and claims that the ethics of modernity fails to do so. But it can provide no grounds of its own for either tolerance or equality and seems to have no argument to make to intolerant cultures.

Consider that the kind of relativism that makes all truth the truth of some group or culture undermines the very meaningfulness of appraisals of value. If standards of value are entirely relative, then every culture's standards of value are equally arbitrary.

To assert that something is valuable makes a claim about that thing that goes beyond the mere fact that we happen to value it. It is to claim that this object meets standards of appraisal that have a claim on others for their consideration. Consider an example. Suppose that someone in a romantic mood calls someone else beautiful. Is this a real compliment if we believe that there are no standards of beauty? "Darling, there are no objective standards of beauty, and you are beautiful," lacks something as a compliment. We might believe that there are objective standards of beauty and also consistently believe that beauty comes in different forms. We might believe that it can be expressed or seen differently in different cultures. We might believe that we can come to see beauty in different ways. We might believe that had we been taught or encultured differently, we might find something to be beautiful that does not seem so to us now. In short we might believe many things about beauty that permit it to have significant cultural variation. But all of these things also suggest that other ways of seeing beauty might have a claim on us. We might come to appreciate what other people see as beauty. They could explain it. We could come to understand. Not only does cultural relativism not support such views, it undermines them by making all standards of value entirely arbitrary.

What we cannot do is to say (in effect), "My beloved, there are no objective standards of beauty, and I think you are beautiful." Cultural relativism says nothing about a given "value" other than that a given culture holds it. But this makes no claim on us for considering this value in any of the ways suggested above. Instead of earning our respect for this value, it destroys any possibility of that respect by also claiming that nothing could be pointed to about that value that could have a claim on anyone else.

Relativism also undermines criticism often where it is most important. If truth is relative and every culture owns its own truth, then it is impossible to criticize the values of other cultures. Indeed, this is the intent of the position. It is designed to liberate minorities from the majority's making their standards obligatory for everyone. However, it also undermines our capacity to criticize minorities or majorities when criticism seems important or warranted. Some cultural practices we might want to criticize are slavery, economic exploitation, sexually degrading views and practices, and religious intolerance and persecution. If all truth is relative to a given culture and if cultures own their own truth, on what basis do we reject or criticize these? Indeed, radical pluralism may be used as a warrant for oppressive cultures to insist that it is their right to hold and act on their views. (Some Nazis made similar arguments.)

Finally, radical pluralism is anti-dialogical. We would like to recommend the view that cultural conflict should be resolved through a kind of dialogue that views everyone as an equal participant and insists that the outcome should depend on the evidence, not only on power or on who is the majority. If we believe that people's cultures significantly influence how they see the world, and that people have a right to their own culture so long as they respect the equal rights of others, we may find that we have reason to listen carefully to what others different from ourselves have to say, and we may be cautious before we assume that we know the truth or that our values are superior. We may encounter other cultures with a willingness both to criticize and to learn. However, if we are to engage in dialogue of this sort, we will also have to believe that it has a point. We will have to believe that we can give others reasons to change their minds and that they can give us reasons that may change our minds.

Cultural relativism, however, denies that there are any reasons that have validity between cultures. What then is the point of dialogue?

What kind of view do we need? We need a view that acknowledges the importance of our "situatedness" both to our sense of self—one in which we are not just persons—and one that acknowledges that our sense of the good is significantly dependent on our culture. But this view must do this while at the same time (1) providing some reasons for belief in equality and tolerance that can be viewed as objective, (2) not undermining the very possibility of value, (3) not undermining the possibility of criticizing injustice, and (4) not undercutting the meaningfulness of dialogue.

Persons and Citizens

To suggest some features of a view that succeeds on these criteria, we want to reconsider an interpretation of personhood that is central to an ethic that emphasizes freedom and equality, but that also allows us to recognize that people are situated and have selves that are more than just persons. (These views are significantly indebted to John Rawls [1993]. Again we have developed our own account of these views and have not tried to be faithful to the details of his.)

In this book we have tried to describe what it means to be a person in terms of the human capacities that describe personhood. We are not describing some mysterious entity or essence that inhabits all human beings, or some "metaphysical" features of people that are independent of what we can observe about them. Instead, in characterizing persons, we are describing capacities that all normal human beings acquire given adequate nurturance. People have a capacity for a sense of justice, and they have a capacity for forming a conception of their own good.

While it is clear that peoples' views of justice and of their good are rooted in their own cultures, it is important to our concept of a person that people have the capacity to view their understanding of justice and of the good as objects of criticism and to change their minds given good reasons. Whatever a self is, it is not situated in culture in such a way as to be inconsistent with achieving the distance required for reflection and criticism. This capacity for critical distance is an important part of what we mean by calling people responsible moral agents. Thus, our conception of a person is not "metaphysical." It is rooted in moral capacities and moral experience.

It is thus an error to assume that any one description of these capacities is required. However, it is also a mistake to claim that the very idea that there are such capacities is itself an expression of the experience of some particular group, white European men, perhaps. This view suggests the rather insulting conclusion that some groups are incapable of reflecting on the moral content they receive from their culture.

It is also important to notice that the ethical concepts we have discussed in the previous chapters—due process, intellectual liberty, equality—are all concepts that have legal standing in our society and in all liberal democracies. We do not view these concepts as the whole of ethics so much as a civic ethic, and we have emphasized a civic ethic in this book because we are writing a book on ethics for people who will work in public schools where the civic ethic must be central.

Similarly, we think that our view of a person is the view of human beings that needs to be emphasized in a civic ethic. Indeed, it is precisely the conception of human beings that is important to the civic ethic of a pluralistic society. Why must this be?

The reason is that in many civic contexts we need a concept of persons that abstracts from differences. The reason isn't that people aren't different or that these differences aren't important in civic contexts. It is instead that the civic ethic needs to be devised in such a way that it is not biased against people because of their group memberships or their particularities. It needs to be impartial between the conflicting interests, views, and values of different religions, races, ethnic groups, and genders.

Impartiality doesn't mean that the distinctive features of people can't be considered in public contexts. It means that the basic rules and standards society functions by can't be devised to inherently benefit one group over another. We can't prefer Catholics to Protestants, Jews, or Muslims. We can't prefer men to women. We can't prefer white people to African Americans, Native Americans, or Asians.

Think of what is required as analogous to a sporting event. Impartiality doesn't require that we ignore who is stronger, faster, or more skilled. It requires that the rules not be rigged in ways that are irrelevant to the point of the game. Similarly, we need a view of social justice that gives people a fair chance to pursue their own conception of their own good without rigging the game to prefer the interests of some over others.

A concept of human beings as persons, as moral agents who because they are moral agents are to be viewed as free and equal and who are therefore entitled to equal liberty and equal treatment, helps us to conceive and sustain a society that respects pluralism. It does so by focusing attention on the status that people have as citizens and making that central to a concept of social justice. And it does this by abstracting from those features of people that make them different, not because they are irrelevant in all contexts, even civil contexts, but because rooting the basic rules of our society in a concept of persons allows us to have a view of the basic rules that is fair and unbiased, in that it does not assume that any one group is privileged in society.

Does this concept of a person describe some essence people have prior to being socialized? No. Indeed, development of the capacities involved in personhood requires socialization. Does it deny that people are situated or the ethical relevance of their situatedness? No. Their situatedness is an important aspect of who real people are, which needs to be taken into account in dealing with them. Is it a view that subtly makes the characteristics of some particular group, white males perhaps, normative for everyone? We don't think so. One needs to be careful of the details, and open criticism and dialogue are important to the process of taking care that this isn't so.

Thus we think that properly formulated, the notion of personhood and the civic ethic toward which it points is defensible. Indeed, it seems to us to be crucial for a defensible pluralism. But we also think that the fact that people are social beings, that they are not just persons but situated particular beings, and that religion, culture, ethnicity, and gender are important to that particular person whom each of us is, are important facts about people that need to be recognized. They are especially important to take into account in a view of moral dialogue, because they remind us that we need to be sensitive to different voices and to be careful to not universalize our own particularities.

And what now shall we say about our case? Should Cassandra Lewis approve the Tubman School and the People of Faith School because they affirm differences that are real and important in peoples' lives? We aren't going to answer this question for you. Not only is that not our role, we haven't provided enough detail about these schools to permit all of the issues they raise to be fully aired. But we do think we can say something about the criteria on which they should be judged. We suggest four criteria.

1. People need educational opportunities that allow them to pursue and develop that which is distinctive about them. They need to learn their own religion, study their own culture, form their own conception of the good in cooperation with others who share it. Thus we believe that there is nothing inherently wrong with an educational system, even a public one, that recognizes that differences are important and provides space for people with shared interests or a shared background to meet together and to explore the meaning of their commonalities.

2. People need educational opportunities that allow them to acquire the public ethic. They need a sense of justice that includes tolerance of difference and respect for the equal rights of other citizens.

3. The need for students to acquire the public ethic and a sense of justice must be distinguished from the attempt to view the culture of one group as normative for others. Creating a shared civic life is a legitimate aspiration for the schools of a liberal democracy. Creating a common culture is not.

4. People need the opportunity to learn from one another and to learn about one another. No education that functions to isolate people from differences or to isolate their views from criticism is a good education.

One of the things that makes these criteria hard to apply is that they are difficult to succeed on simultaneously. Perhaps the more we emphasize the first, the more we put the second and so forth at risk. Nevertheless, we think that a fully adequate education must find ways to balance these criteria. You might find it useful to return to the case and ask how you would apply these criteria to the facts we have provided.

ADDITIONAL CASES

A Christmas Quarrel

Tenderville is a well-established middle-class community. Its roots go back to the early 1800s, but it didn't become a full-fledged township until 1936. World War II gave it a growth spurt, and it boomed in the 1950s. Its citizens were proud of its excellent school system, good library, and extensive community services. In the 1960s and 1970s it attracted many white-collar workers from the nearby big city as a tranquil haven and good place to raise children. It was one of the first northern towns to voluntarily and successfully desegregate its schools. Everyone seemed to get along very well together. Because of its openness and friendliness, a Jewish community moved in, establishing its own synagogue. In the 1980s and 1990s many Asians were also attracted to Tenderville. It seemed to be a haven of tolerance and real democracy.

Then it happened.

The acute sensitivity to the worth of others and the great and genuine tolerance of difference that permeated the town stimulated a seriously responsible school board to raise the issue of Christmas in the schools. Christmas, they noted, had always been celebrated with Nativity plays, Christmas caroling, decorated trees, exchanges of presents, and of course, the Christmas vacation. But the Board began to wonder out loud about how this civic celebration of a major Christian event would feel to those who were Jews, Muslims, Buddhists, Confucianists, or whatever? There seemed to be something askew here. Just as Tenderville had grown from a small Christian community to a larger multicultural and multireligious community, should not the school system do the same? But how?

There were a number of suggestions made at the Board meeting. Here are some of them and some of the objections to them voiced by the participants.

The superintendent suggested that for starters, he could issue a policy that the schools should not have any decorations, songs, activities, or talk, written or oral, about Christmas. The holiday vacation name could be officially changed to Winter Recess. No gift giving in school would be allowed. All trappings of Christmas then would just disappear, thereby solving the problem. The superintendent said that he and his principals would strictly enforce this no-Christmas policy, if the Board agreed to his plan.

Some felt, however, that this would be impossible to do. It is hard to ban Christmas with the attention given to it in the environment outside of school. Besides, the kids are full of it. Maybe it would be better to recognize and teach about Christmas and also about Chanukah as major religious holidays of winter. After all, the combined population of Christians and Jews in Tenderville was over 85%. But, some wondered, what about the mix of other religions in the remaining 15%? Should they not also get their due and have one of their major religious holidays celebrated in school?

Someone quickly raised the question of separation of church and state. Isn't the school constitutionally obliged to stay away from religious teaching, either directly or indirectly? "But," someone else interjected, "doesn't being tolerant require understanding another's point of view? How is that possible if you don't learn about what others believe?"

The meeting went on well past midnight. The remarkable thing was that there was no venom, no "we" against "them," no unalterable oppositions. It was a genuine attempt by a board and its superintendent to find a sensible and sound way to continue the good feeling of a community of inclusion, but the solution always seemed just out of reach.

Some Questions

1. If you had attended this meeting as the superintendent, what suggestions would you have made?
2. Does the separation of church and state doctrine disallow any talk or teaching about religion in the public schools? What does it allow?
3. Does practicing tolerance require understanding the basis of differences or just respecting difference even if you don't understand the grounds for it?
4. There are multicultural as well as multireligious differences in the school population of Tenderville. Should different cultures also be addressed in school policy and the school's curriculum? How?

Understanding Infibulation

Joshua Logan smiled inwardly at the irony of the situation. Sitting in his office were a delegation of upper-middle-class, politically liberal, and very angry parents complaining about one of his teachers, John Muth. Although Logan was sure that they wouldn't put it this way, these parents were complaining not because Muth was a bad teacher, but because he was an extraordinarily good one. Further, he had accomplished exactly what they had asked him to accomplish: Kids were gaining an understanding of vastly different cultural practices from their own. Unfortunately, they may have become more understanding than their parents liked, and the practices involved weren't exactly the ones the parents had in mind.

Logan was the principal of Middlebury High, located in a wealthy suburban community in the Midwest. Muth, a young teacher who had majored in anthropology at Yale before taking an M.A.T. at the state university, had been at Middlebury only three years teaching twelfth-grade social studies. In that brief time, however, he had gained a reputation as perhaps the best teacher in the school. He was extremely popular with students, and, at least until the present time, with parents as well. This year, however, he had introduced a new course, "Understanding Other Cultures: An Anthropological Approach," an elective open only to seniors. Its purpose was "to help students gain an appreciation of different peoples and their cultures and to see things from others' perspectives." Students were to learn "that every group faces similar problems, e.g., subsistence and governance, but their solutions to these problems might differ dramatically from the way Americans addressed them." Those differences were rooted in the situations in which people lived and in their histories and beliefs, Thus, Muth argued, judgments of others' ways of living should be delayed until we understand those situations, histories, and beliefs. Developing that understanding was the principal goal of social studies. "If students are to really understand other cultures, they needed first to walk in other peoples' shoes, not rush to judgment," Muth had said.

When Muth first proposed the course to Middlebury's curriculum committee (on which several parents sat), there was unanimous agreement that such a course was important and badly needed in a community whose citizens were almost entirely of Anglo-Saxon Protestant or Jewish backgrounds. Middlebury's youth needed to learn about people unlike themselves, since they certainly didn't meet them in their schools, churches, and temples, or in the streets of their town. Ultimately, the Middlebury Board of Education had approved the offering on a one-year trial basis, after which a decision would be made whether it should become a regular part of Middlebury High's curriculum.

When school opened in the fall, it became almost immediately obvious that Muth's strategy for teaching the course would be highly effective and often dramatic. He had deliberately selected for study cultures that were vastly different from our own, cultures with practices and beliefs that his students would find strange, bizarre, even repulsive. He dug out original materials, usually written by members of the culture, that presented their views of those beliefs and practices. Where the cultures were preliterate, firsthand accounts of sympathetic westerners or cultural anthropologists were located for students to read. For every unit Muth tried to bring in at least one representative of the culture, sometimes at his own expense, to talk with his class and to answer questions. Where that was impossible, Muth himself would read extensively on the culture, don the attire of one of its members, and appear before his class to represent that culture as convincingly as possible for his students. Not only was Muth an excellent teacher, he was a talented actor, and it was his first appearances as a member of another culture that brought him immediate notoriety in the school and in the community.

The class had been studying the culture of the aboriginal peoples of Australia. Since there were no Aborigines in Middlebury, Muth appeared before his class one day with blackened skin, wearing only a loincloth and carrying a spear and boomerang. During his discussion of aboriginals' culture, he had turned to the subject of food. "Because my people are nomadic, we have no crops or domesticated animals to eat—except dogs, of course. In the deserts of central Australia, we must eat what is available. Often this means eating something that is quite good and very nourishing, but that isn't considered food here in Middlebury." To demonstrate, Muth paused dramatically and then untied a skin sack from his waist (made from a kangaroo's testicles, he remarked), and removed several thumb-sized, white, and squirming grubs. He ate these, one at a time, smacking his lips and explaining to his shocked pupils that the grubs were really "quite good. They taste like cashews," he claimed. Student reaction was swift: Three dashed from the room violently ill, and many of the pale, gasping, and visibly shaken remainder seemed on the verge of joining their departed friends.

Had he stopped there, the lesson might have passed as overly theatrical but not otherwise objectionable. Muth, however, went on to offer a grub to any student who would like to try one, "in the interest of better understanding our cultural biases concerning food." Four of the more adventurous students took him up on his offer, and most pronounced the taste as "not bad." One, showing off for his classmates, asked for seconds. While Muth's performance certainly broadened his students' understanding of aboriginal culture and their own cultural biases regarding food, the lesson had provoked angry phone calls from the parents of two of the imbibing students. One objected to serving grubs to his son on grounds of sanitation, the second because grubs weren't kosher.

Later that year Muth provoked an even stronger parental reaction when he presented a unit on "The Culture of Anti-Semitism," choosing prewar Germany as the specific site of inquiry. His class read numerous explicitly anti-Semitic documents from the period including sections of *Mein Kampf*, *The Protocols of the Elders of Zion*, and translations of popular accounts of sensational trials supposedly of gruesome ritual Jewish murders of gentile boys. Virtually every student was deeply offended by these readings. Muth insisted, however, that students step back and examine the documents as cultural artifacts, and that they treat anti-Semitic beliefs as a cultural anthropologist might, that is, nonjudgmentally, as something to be explained, and with a goal of trying to understand why so many Germans held them. As the culminating event in this unit, Muth appeared as a Nazi Brown Shirt, a swastika on his arm, and gave a matter-of-fact account of many Germans' antipathy to Jews, following as closely as he could contemporary accounts of anti-Semitic beliefs. Muth made it very clear that in no way was he justifying or condoning anti-Semitism, but he wanted his students to see those beliefs from the cultural perspective of a German living in 1933.

Since Middlebury contained a large Jewish population, and many of its residents had lost parents and grandparents in the Holocaust, the reaction was swift and angry. "This sort of despicable crap has caused the deaths of millions of people," one person said to Logan, referring to the *Protocols*. "The public schools have no business teaching children that they should be 'neutral' to hate literature. Don't think for a minute that some of these impressionable students haven't learned to be tolerant of anti-Semitism. They have, and that's a catastrophe in a democratic, multicultural society." Logan managed to calm the furor, but he made it clear to Muth that if "Understanding Other Cultures" was offered next year, there would be a serious reconsideration of the topics covered.

Despite the warning, in the spring of the year Muth stepped firmly over the boundary of what even the most liberal residents of Middlebury would tolerate. The topic was the Lesotho culture of Somalia. While there were many interesting (and prosaic) aspects of that culture that Muth discussed, one that he considered at length was the Lesotho practice of female circumcision. While this practice was common among certain Muslim peoples in Djibouti, Sierra Leone, Sudan, Ethiopia, and Eritrea, as well as Somalia, the Lesotho practiced a particularly drastic form of it, infibulation. Indeed, in the United States infibulation is usually referred to as female genital mutilation. Without anesthetics and using ordinary, unsterile razor blades, the clitoris and labia minora of four-year-old girls were excised. The labia majora were then scraped, cut back and sewn together with twine, so that, after healing, only a small opening was left for the passage of urine and menstrual blood. At marriage the labia were cut apart, thus permitting intercourse. Besides the extensive damage to the girls' genitals, the practice sometimes caused serious infections and long-term complications, including chronic pelvic infections and infertility.

Of course Muth's students were horrified. He insisted, however, that they withhold judgment until they understood the social context of infibulation. "If you are going to truly understand other peoples and their cultures, you can't simply rush to a decision that something is good or bad on the basis of your own particular cultural biases. You must stop, reflect, put yourself in others' places. That's especially necessary when you find a practice that offends you. You need to see why many cultures practice some form of female circumcision. For example, you need to understand the importance of virginity at marriage in poverty-stricken cultures generally and in poor Muslim cultures especially, hence to the Lesotho people. Surely some of you think virginity at marriage is an important value." (Muth noted that several of his students nodded almost imperceptibly.) "Infibulation virtually guarantees virginity. It is quite analogous to a chastity belt, a device that was common in Europe not long ago and which, incidentally, often caused severe physical harm to women. Further, you have to understand the critical significance of the incest taboo in all societies, and the problem it creates in those where whole families must live crowded into one-room huts. Finally, while it may be true that female circumcision serves to reinforce male domination of women, you should ask what social functions are served by male domination. We need to talk about these things before you make judgments." Then he said something that would, figuratively, bring the Middlebury roof down on his head. "After all," he went on, "infibulation is really no different than male circumcision. For example, Bris, the ritual circumcision of young boys, is a rite that is widely practiced in the Jewish community right here in Middlebury. Both consist of the deliberate surgical mutilation of perfectly healthy genital tissue, solely for cultural reasons."

In the ensuing community uproar Muth mounted a spirited defense of his teaching and of "Understanding Other Cultures." In June, at a packed session of the Board of Education called to consider the continuation of the course, he said that he had designed it so that it successfully did exactly what the Curriculum Committee, the Board, and the people of the community said they wanted done: Students were to become more tolerant of different cultures and ideas. He presented evidence to support his assertion. In addition, in a letter to the Board, a large number of his students claimed to have benefited in exactly this way. Muth said that he had chosen his materials deliberately and sequenced them with a clear purpose in mind. "I went from the easy-to-understand point that our definition of what counts as food is purely a cultural matter, to the much more difficult point that beliefs we find abhorrent, such as anti-Semitism, are also a cultural matter. They don't develop and flourish because people are stupid or depraved, but because of the circumstances in which those people find themselves. Finally, I asked my students to understand a practice that I knew all of them would find horrific, infibulation. If you truly want our young people to be tolerant of other cultures, you have to present them with cultures and ideas that challenge that tolerance. You must find practices that stretch their preconceived notions of right and wrong. You don't create tolerance by asking Jewish kids to hang ornaments on Christmas trees and Gentile kids to spin dreidels and read about Chanukah. That's not teaching multiculturalism. It's teaching pap. I don't teach pap; I stretched my students' beliefs and challenged the values they grew up with. The fact that I'm standing here today defending my course is proof that I succeeded."

Some Questions

1. If you were on the Middlebury Board of Education, would you support Muth and "Understanding Other Cultures"? Why or why not?
2. If you object to the course, consider each of the three beliefs and practices described in our case: food prejudice, ethnic prejudice, and sexual prejudice. Is the first appropriate to the course's purposes? If it is, why not the second and third?
3. Is there a danger, as one Middlebury citizen claimed, that teaching students to withhold judgment of practices and beliefs that are highly objectionable in our culture will lead them to be tolerant, even accepting, of those practices and beliefs? If so, is that an acceptable outcome for public schools to seek? Why or why not?
4. Would it be appropriate to require Muth to couple his class's study of highly objectionable practices with a study of the reasons we find those practices objectionable? For example, should the objective study of anti-Semitic beliefs be paired with an equally objective study of Americans' belief in the value of every individual and the need to respect every person? Why or why not? Can we be "objective" about our own culture?
5. Has Muth got his pedagogy right? Is it necessary to challenge students' beliefs with objective and dispassionate study of deeply offensive practices, if we are to make them tolerant?
6. Does the age of these students make any difference? That is, one goal of "Understanding Other Cultures" was to get students to "think like anthropologists," i.e., to think objectively about practices and beliefs that are highly offensive in our culture. Maybe that's necessary for anthropologists, who are, after all, adults. But Muth's students are minors and are not anthropologists-in-training. Does that make any difference?

The People of the Corn

The Public School Textbook Committee had been in session only a few hours when it hit its first snag. The Committee was charged with the responsibility of approving textbooks that could be used in any public school in the State of Texas. The idea behind the Committee was straightforward: By creating a list of approved textbooks from which each school district must select its texts, the State was in a position to order books for its schools in very large quantities. Publishers, of course, were anxious to have their books placed on the approved list, since it had the potential for generating millions of dollars in sales. As a consequence Texas could demand (and get) very substantial discounts from publishers, and thereby save taxpayers a great deal of money. Each year the Committee considered different textbook series. Last year it had selected math and science texts; this year it was doing history and English.

The Textbook Committee was a large body, most of whose members were teachers, administrators, and school board members, but it also contained a sprinkling of business persons, religious leaders, and members of the general public. For years the Committee had functioned in obscurity; it received book nominations from school districts and from publishers, it listened to publishers' representatives and the occasional comments from interested citizens, it perused the nominated books more or less closely, and then it made its decision whether to place the series on the approved text list. Aside from school administrators who checked the list before ordering texts, few in the general public even knew of the Committee's existence.

Its emergence into the public limelight had taken place a decade ago, and its meetings had sometimes become raucous and the center of media attention. Various groups had appeared at the Committee's deliberations and sought to influence its decisions. For example, two years ago during the consideration of middle school health texts, a group representing a coalition of Pentecostal churches had appeared to protest the "neutral attitude" toward homosexuality taken by several of the books. They had nothing against homosexuals, they said. Homosexuals were among God's children, and therefore they should be welcomed into Christian fellowship. However, homosexuality was a sin. To teach their children to be neutral toward sin was to undermine their faith, and the State of Texas had no business doing that. In response, a group calling itself The Gay and Lesbian Task Force argued that anything less than a favorable attitude toward homosexuality would simply promote homophobia in the young. Neutrality was not satisfactory, they said. That particular meeting had turned into a shouting match, the police had to be called, and it provided both *Time* and *Newsweek* with pictures and a full column of text—to the embarrassment of most Texans. Last year a variation on the same theme resurfaced, when high school biology texts were adopted. This time a group representing Southern Baptist churches had argued that creationism should be included in the texts, as an alternative theory to Darwinian evolution. This position was countered by biology professors from the state university, who pointed out that creationism had no scientific standing, and therefore it had no place in science textbooks. In the first case the Committee had decided that neutrality toward homosexuality was appropriate (thereby pleasing neither Pentecostal nor the Gay and Lesbian Task Force), and in the second case it had agreed with the professors and decided that publishers should not be required to include unscientific beliefs in their books.

This year the problem arose from within the Committee itself. The texts being considered were history books intended for high school use. Several of the series contained accounts of the histories and cultures of various Native American tribes. These accounts were extensive, amply illustrated, and told the stories of the Indian peoples with understanding and often from an Indian point of view. The culture of various tribes was described sympathetically, and sometimes quite movingly. In addition, several texts provided one of the standard anthropological and geological explanations of the origin of Native Americans. That is, they said that many scientists believed that Native Americans had come here from Asia roughly ten thousand years ago, over a land bridge across what is now the Bering Strait. Indeed, one text series from Alchemy Publishing Company referred to Native Americans as "our nation's first wave of immigrants." These immigrants, the Alchemy authors said, were later driven off their land, often with violence, by the "second wave of immigrants," that is, Europeans.

There was little comment from the public following the publishers' presentations, and the Committee seemed on the verge of approving the texts, when Michael Spotted Cloud rose to speak. He did so quietly but with obvious conviction. "I want to thank the Committee, and especially the publishers of all of these books," he began. "I want you to know that as a Native American, I and my people appreciate your attempt to honestly tell children the history of our country and the nature of the westward migration of Europeans. Our land was taken, usually by force or duplicity, and our past is replete with broken treaties and discriminatory practices that have reduced many of us to poverty. For years our children were taught in your schools that their forebears were savages and deserving of their fate." He paused. "But that is in the past. It is time to move forward, to right past wrongs, and to heal old wounds. These books are surely a step in that direction, and I and my people applaud that.

"However," he went on, "there is a matter that I ask you to consider. Several books state that our people came to North America from Asia, across the Bering Strait. I recognize that you believe that. However, that is not what we ourselves believe. Every tribe has its own story of its origins. For example, my people, the 'People of the Corn,' as we call ourselves, believe that when God created the world, He sowed a miraculous plant, corn, in a holy spot, not far from this very place. Knowing that the corn would need to be tended and made into food, he caused just two of the seeds to sprout into a man and a woman, our tribe's first members. We have faithfully tended His gift ever since. Thus, we do not believe that we came from Asia, but that we have always been here, right from the beginning of the earth. Wouldn't it be possible," Mr. Spotted Cloud asked, "to include a paragraph or two in the books to explain this important aspect of our beliefs? In truth, the 'Gift of Corn' story is really quite beautiful, and it is central to our culture. A few paragraphs to tell our story—or the stories of other tribes, if you so choose—would add to white children's understanding of our history and would help us in the task of preserving our own heritage in our children's minds. Thank you for your consideration." With that Mr. Spotted Cloud sat down.

The representative of Alchemy Publishers immediately jumped to his feet. "I want to assure the Committee and Mr. Spotted Cloud that such a change in our textbook series would be easily accomplished. Alchemy Publishers thinks the point is very well taken, and we would be happy to comply. Clearly our books would better represent the history of Native Americans and improve the education of all children, regardless of their backgrounds."

With that, the matter seemed settled. Most of the Committee members were nodding in agreement and seemed ready to vote, when Reverend Thomas spoke up. Samuel Thomas was an Episcopal priest and the head of the largest church in the state. He had served on the Public School Textbook Committee for seven years and was highly respected by everyone on the Committee. "Before we vote," he said, "we should consider something. Last year we rejected the request of my friends of the Baptist persuasion that creationism be included in our biology texts. We did that because, we said, creationism has no standing as a scientific theory or fact. With all respect to Mr. Spotted Bear, I'm sure that the Corn Story, too, has no standing as scientific theory or fact in the way that the Bering Strait theory does. Shouldn't history books present the truth as best as we are able to discern it in the same way that science books do? On what principled grounds do we include the Corn Story and not the Genesis Story? Finally, with respect to the aesthetic aspects of both accounts of man's creation, while I'm sure that the Corn Story is beautiful, I'm told that the Genesis story is not without its divine qualities."

Some Questions

1. Is there a principled difference between the Corn Story and the Genesis account of the creation of man that permits the first to be included in textbooks but not the second?
2. Does it make any difference that the creationists wanted their story told in a science book, while the People of the Corn want theirs told in a history book? If so, why?
3. If you answered "Yes" to the previous question, are you making a distinction between "scientific truth" and "historical truth?" If so, what is it?
4. If you would approve of including the Corn Story because the culture of groups should be treated with respect, shouldn't you show similar respect to Southern Baptists? If not, why not?

CHAPTER 8

Supplemental Cases

In this book we have emphasized two principles, benefit maximization and respect for persons. We have done this for two reasons. First, these principles are central to what are probably the two most important philosophical views on ethics of the last century or so, utilitarianism and Kantianism. The cornerstone of utilitarianism is that people should act so as to maximize the average happiness or average utility. The keys to Kant's ethics are the categorical imperative (or the Golden Rule) and the notion of respect for persons. Second, we believe that these principles continue to provide useful lenses for trying to understand what is at stake in ethical issues. Most people employ some variation of these two principles intuitively. The idea that respecting others and the idea that seeking good results is important are both commonplace. Utilitarianism and Kantianism should be viewed as attempts by philosophers to deepen our understanding of these intuitive approaches. It is also significant that these ideas are historical competitors. While in many cases a reasonable application of either benefit maximization or respect for persons will produce a similar result, sometimes, particularly in hard cases, they can generate different outcomes. Looking at ethical issues through these lenses sometimes helps us to understand what makes a case a hard case.

We do not, however, believe, that everything that is of moral relevance is captured by these two principles. There are several other current ethical theories that have "lead principles" of their own. Shortly we will discuss some of them. But first, we want to comment briefly on what we mean by the word *principle*. We think it important that you not assume that we mean too much. We use the word to denote some idea that asserts that some factor (benefit maximization, respect for persons) needs to be taken into account in ethical deliberation. We do not mean to say anything more profound or complicated. Here *principle* is not a term of art. We are not, for example, saying that ethics can be reduced to a set of rules or that all ethical reasoning can be reduced to the application of rules to cases. In fact we think otherwise. For example, we think that ethical reasoning

core values

involves such activities as striking a balance or discovering a mean and that it requires virtues such as wisdom.

Other ethical principles (or important ethical considerations) might include an emphasis on relationships, or on community, or on personal growth. Consider each of these:

1. *Relationships.* One of the things that adds value to our lives is the relationships we form with others. Relationships such as friendship, companionship, caring, and love are intrinsically worthwhile, and they add value to other things that are intrinsically worthwhile. Sporting events and concerts are better when we share them. We all enjoy a good conversation. Moreover, that we exist in such relationships provides the context in which nurturance is provided. Without nurturance children cannot grow into healthy competent adults. Thus, it is important to consider the effect of our decisions and actions on our relationships.

2. *Community.* We might think of community in two ways. First, a community could be viewed as a network of relationships. However, communities are often formed to pursue certain goods or values: religious communities may exist to serve God or save souls; tennis clubs exist to further a sport and allow members of the community to enjoy each other's company while playing it; schools exist to promote learning. Given this, some activities can be viewed as unethical in that they disrupt community. This might mean that they destroy the relationships on which community depends. It might also mean that they undermine the values the community exists to serve. Someone who cheats at tennis undermines the values internal to the sport and will erode personal relationships as well. Schools serve such values as learning and the pursuit of truth. They are disrupted by such vices as intellectual dishonesty and censorship. We can often appraise actions by asking whether they maintain community.

3. *Character development.* In acting we create ourselves. We form habits and tendencies to respond through our actions. We make ourselves more or less sensitive to the needs of others when we respond to their suffering or when we ignore it. If we cheat, not only do we do something dishonest, we begin the process of becoming dishonest persons. Often, "I am an honest person, so I will only cheat just this once" is a serious form of self-delusion. It ignores the extent to which we create ourselves through our actions. If this is true, then we can also judge our choices and our actions by the kinds of persons they make us into. We might ask, "Do I want to be the kind of person who does this?"

Each of these three "principles" provides fresh insight into things that are of ethical import in judging actions and decisions. Perhaps they are implicit in much of what we have said before in this book. (They all might be considered forms of consequentialism.) But they are also aspects of recent ethical views that have seen themselves as critical of Kantianism or utilitarianism. Some feminists have developed ethics of care and relationships, and have worried that the importance of these has been missed by the philosophical tradition. Communitarians have accused the tradition of ignoring the values of community. Those who emphasize the importance of virtues in ethics have thought that Kantianism and utilitarianism favor a cognitive approach to moral judgment over character. It is not our purpose to comment on these theoretical disputes any more than we already have. But we do think that the kinds of considerations that these views have built into them are of ethical significance and deserve serious consideration.

Below we provide a number of additional cases for you to consider or to write on. We hope that you will continue to use some of the concepts we have emphasized in this book as tools to consider them. But we also want to encourage you to ask questions like "How does this effect relationships?" "Is community strengthened or eroded?" and "How does this effect moral growth?"

And we do not think that these three "additional perspectives" exhaust the domain of factors that are morally relevant in ethical judgment. As you consider these additional cases, you might ask yourself whether there are additional moral principles that are useful in reflecting on ethical issues.

CASE #1: FRIENDLY SUPPORT OR SEXUAL HARASSMENT?

It had happened again. She felt very uncomfortable, but maybe it was all in her mind. Maria Sanchez was in her third probationary year at Bonnville High School. Her tenure decision was in process, and Mr. Alsop, her principal, kept her informed of its progress as best he could given the confidentiality required by district policy.

Maria was a modestly good teacher of social studies. Her subject matter background was a little thin in European history and she had worked hard to improve it. She had a few discipline problems in two of her first-year classes, but that, too, had improved. All but one of her bi-yearly evaluations were satisfactory. She thought she had a good chance to earn tenure.

She needed the strong support of Mr. Alsop, though, and there was the problem. Many of the women teachers talked about his insensitivity. He sometimes would tell off-color jokes at faculty meetings without a clue that some women blushed. In public, he would put his arm around male and female teachers alike in gestures of fun and colleagueship but sometimes a little fondling would seem to go on. Rumor had it that he slept around a lot. Some women said he made their skin crawl. But he was a good, efficient, well-meaning principal, and his judgment was respected by the higher administration.

Maria felt a little intimidated by him. Maybe it was her imagination, but it seemed that ever since this year began, Mr. Alsop always managed to sit next to her at district and staff meetings; his knee would gently touch hers; sometimes in a gesture of comfort he would pat the back of her hand; sometimes he would just look at her and smile.

When they met in his office in March to discuss how her tenure review was going, he made it clear that he had to keep certain things confidential, but that he was the kind who with a good dinner and wine sometimes told more than he should. He wondered if they could have dinner together. They could discuss European history, teaching, and school politics. Nothing personal of course! Except perhaps her tenure review.

He reached for her hand and said, "Please? Tonight?"

Some Questions

1. Do you think Mr. Alsop was sexually harassing Maria or just being a supportive principal?
2. Do you think Maria had reason to feel uncomfortable? Is feeling uncomfortable the same as being sexually harassed?
3. What kinds of things constitute sexual harassment in a school setting?
4. Do you think every school should have a policy against sexual harassment? If yes, what should it be and what procedures should be provided to enforce it? If no, why not?

CASE #2: ABUSE? NEGLECT? OR NOTHING TO WORRY ABOUT?

After class, Mary Sue came to Ms. Broudy looking a little frightened. She confessed that perhaps she shouldn't be doing this to her friend, but she was worried about her and had to tell somebody. It seems that when Mary Sue and her friend Kim were at a sleepover together on the weekend, Kim showed her some cuts on her lower arm and told her that she couldn't stand it at home anymore. It had something to do with her father, but she wouldn't say what it was. Mary Sue was worried that Kim might be being molested, or beaten, or maybe even inflicting wounds on herself as a prelude to suicide. She had heard that Asians were more prone to suicide and Kim's mother was Korean.

Ms. Broudy assured Mary Sue that she would speak to Kim and go to the school counselor if things really were as bad as Mary Sue had said. The next day Ms. Broudy asked Kim to stay at the end of class. She asked Kim if everything was alright at home. Kim said it was fine. She asked if she got along with her father, who was a principal of an elementary school in the district. Kim blushed and said, of course. But when Ms. Broudy asked to see Kim's arms, she refused to show them saying it was personal and none of her business. Ms. Broudy did notice Band-Aids on the inside of both of Kim's wrists, but Kim just said it was poison ivy. Did she need help in any way? Kim said, "No."

Ms. Broudy had some doubts. There was a clear school policy that even the mere suspicion of child abuse must be reported to the school counselor and principal. Ms. Broudy didn't hesitate. She went to both and told them the whole story. The principal knew Kim's father as a fellow principal and just laughed. He couldn't believe anything like that of him. The counselor said she would talk to Kim.

A week passed. Kim seemed to get even more distant in class and one day appeared with a bruise on her cheek. Ms. Broudy went to the counselor to find out what had happened with Kim's interview. The counselor said in her professional opinion there was nothing solid she could report to the authorities. She had called the parents to see what they thought was going on at home. The mother had nothing to say. The father said Kim was just being moody and would grow out of it. The counselor told Ms. Broudy that she had reported all this to the principal. He agreed that there was insufficient evidence to go to the authorities.

Ms. Broudy returned to her room to find Mary Sue. Mary Sue was crying. She said Kim had finally told her that her father had abused her. Kim was getting desperate. Mary Sue was worried that Kim might do something to herself. Ms. Broudy went back to the principal telling him the latest. He asked if she had any better evidence of abuse than she had had before. He wanted to know if there was anything more concrete to go on than the secondhand word of an imaginative teenager. Ms. Broudy said, "No," but she felt something more should be done. The principal assured her that she had done her duty and he had done his. There was nothing more to do than keep an eye on things. He asked her to keep him informed.

Some Questions

1. Do you agree with the principal's handling of this case? Why or why not?
2. If this turns out not to be a case of child abuse, is it possibly a case of child neglect? Were the parents neglecting the clear signs that Kim was having serious problems? Is there a difference between neglect and abuse? Does a teacher or the principal of a school have any obligation to report child neglect? To whom?

3. Is due process a consideration in delicate cases of possible child abuse or neglect? Wouldn't strict adherence to due process disfavor the child?
4. Do/should parents have the right to physically strike their children?

CASE #3: THE RUMORS ABOUT TAYLOR ROBERTS

"What did you say your new math teacher's name was?" asked Trevor Hunt.

"Roberts, Taylor Roberts," responded Sam. "We were really lucky to find him. We were stuck when Lucinda Kramer had to quit suddenly in mid-year because her pregnancy became problematic. I thought we were going to have to fill in with substitutes for four months. You know what a disaster that can be, especially in subjects like mathematics, where good teachers are hard to find and good substitutes are non-existent. I figured the district was going to have to make do with a series of babysitters until next September when I'd have a shot at getting someone fully certified in math. Roberts, who has math certification in Missouri, just walked in off the street one day and said he was looking for a job."

Sam Ketchum and Trevor Hunt were old friends. They had been undergraduates together at the University of Nebraska, where both had studied education. After college Sam and Trevor had taken teaching jobs in the same district, Valdosta, the former in English and the latter in physical education. After several years, both began taking graduate courses in educational administration at the U. of N. while continuing to teach. Each had earned a master's and shortly thereafter Sam was offered his first administrative position—an assistant principalship at one of Valdosta's middle schools. A year later Trevor was offered a similar position in a small town in Missouri. Over the years the careers of each had prospered, and both were now superintendents—Sam in Valdosta, where he had remained, and Trevor in Ironton, Missouri. Despite their geographical separation, they had kept in close contact in the intervening years. Their wives and children were friends, and they frequently visited one another during vacations. It was on one of these occasions, while sitting on Sam's patio having a drink, that the subject of Taylor Roberts came up.

"Well, you know we had a Taylor Roberts who taught math for us for several years," Trevor remarked. "A good teacher, but he left us under a considerable cloud: He was accused of molesting one of his students, a girl of fourteen. I don't suppose it's the same guy, though. That was four or five years ago. I'm not sure where Roberts went when he left. I never heard anything more about him. Sure caused a hell of a furor in my district, though." He paused. "You did check this guy's references though, right?"

Sam was looking a little worried. "Well, of course, I checked his references. He'd been teaching in Crayton, a small, rural district down around Cape Girardeau. They said he was a fine teacher and had caused no problems. I have letters supporting him from both his former superintendent and his principal." He paused. "On the other hand, there can't be too many certified math teachers from Missouri named Taylor Roberts. I think I'd better check into this."

The next day Sam called Roberts into his office and asked him straight out whether he had ever worked in Ironton, Missouri. Roberts's face fell.

"Damnit," he cried. "What do I have to do, get a job in Mongolia? That lousy story is going to follow me the rest of my life!" He went on to claim that he'd never molested any student. He said that the girl involved had developed a crush on him. "The way teenagers sometimes do with their teachers," he said. "I discouraged her, but she became even more persistent, sent me romantic notes, called me at night, and even started to follow me around. Finally I got angry and told her to stop or I'd speak to her parents. That's when she began to circulate lies about our relationship, telling people that I'd propositioned her, stuff like that. It was plain revenge because I'd rejected her. But there was no way I could defend myself against rumors. My life became such a hell that I had to get out. That's when I went to Crayton."

"Why'd you leave there?" asked Sam.

"I left because after four years the Ironton story somehow reached Crayton, and people began to gossip. Parents went to the principal and asked that their kids not be assigned to my classes; my friends began to shun me; other teachers stopped sitting with me in the lounge. And then a couple of suggestible, attention-starved girls started saying that I'd made improper remarks to them. My life became a living hell all over again. So I went to the superintendent and offered to resign, if he'd give me a favorable recommendation. He agreed, and that's how I arrived in Valdosta."

He paused and looked Sam in the eye. "I was never convicted of anything, not in Ironton and not in Crayton. I was never even officially charged with anything. Because of one mixed-up adolescent, am I going to have to spend my life traipsing from one job to another? Well, I'm not. I've had it," he almost shouted. "The only way I'm leaving here is if you fire me!" He spun on his heel and stormed out of the office.

Some Questions

1.   Well, that's a possibility. Because Roberts is new to Valdosta, he doesn't have tenure. In most states that means he can be fired for any reason or no reason. Thus, Sam could fire Roberts without having to say why or make an issue of it. Would you do that? Why or why not?

2. If you fired him, what would you write in a letter of recommendation when asked for one when Roberts applied for his next job? Would you ignore the rumors about his sexual proclivities?
3. If you decide not to fire Roberts, how do you meet your responsibilities to protect your students from harm?

CASE #4: HONORS COURSES AND BOARD POLICY

Phillip Wallace was the superintendent of Jamestown City School District, a large urban system in a northeastern state. Jamestown had many of the problems associated with large cities, but it also had a stable, middle-class population of both white and minority parents, a high level of community support for schools, and an excellent stream of revenues from the many banks, insurance companies, and other financial institutions that made their home in Jamestown.

The trouble for Dr. Wallace began when John Rayner's family moved across town during the summer before John's senior year. John had attended West High School, and as a consequence of his move had transferred to East High. He was black, an extraordinarily gifted student with a straight "A" record since junior high, Preliminary Scholastic Aptitude scores over seven hundred and fifty in both verbal and math, a lettered athlete in three sports, and the president of his class. He was a shoo-in for any Ivy League school that he cared to attend, and he had set his heart on Yale, where he intended to major in physics. On the opening day of school he had met with his advisor to pick up his schedule. It was then that he discovered that he had been placed in "Physics-E" rather than "Honors Physics," the course he would have taken had he remained at West High School. He was unfamiliar with this way of labeling courses, and so had inquired of his advisor what it meant. His advisor explained that the "E" meant that the course would be "enriched" for exceptional students like John. "Is Physics-E the same as Honors Physics?" he asked. "Pretty much," his advisor explained. "At East we don't call them honors courses the way they do at the other high schools in Jamestown. It's a new system we're experimenting with this year."

John was satisfied with this explanation, and the first week or two of school went smoothly. Indeed, he was pleased with the obvious attention Mrs. Kramer, his physics teacher, paid to ensuring that he was given challenging material to read, additional experiments to carry out, and access to the laboratory during his free time to work on his own. John also noticed that there were three other students in the class who were receiving similar attention. It was the rest of the students in the course and Mrs. Kramer's regular lessons that bothered him. The students were all bright and motivated, but they were obviously not in John's intellectual league. This didn't bother him particularly—since first grade he had always been at the top of his class. He was used to that, and he didn't have an inflated ego because of his academic talents. However, they certainly weren't honors students. Of more concern was Mrs. Kramer's teaching, the textbooks, and the other curricular materials. These were geared to the level of the majority of the class, and hence John often found himself waiting while the rest of the class wrestled with a concept that he had grasped immediately. Since John had been told the course would be like an honors-level class, this surprised him. Physics-E certainly wasn't like the Honors Biology and Chemistry courses that he'd taken at West High.

After two weeks John described his Physics course to his parents. Fred Rayer was surprised. "Of course there's an Honors course at East High School. It's Board policy that there be such courses in every major subject at all high schools. There's something fishy here. I'm going to check with the principal." While he didn't say so to John, he suspected that what was fishy was simple racism: John was being barred from an honors course because of his race.

Fred made an appointment with Dr. Susan Salinsky, East's principal. It turned out that John was correct. There was no honors physics at East. Nevertheless, race was certainly involved in the matter. East had offered honors courses in physics, chemistry, and biology. However, last year the science department had decided that it needed to face up to the fact that its honors courses seemed to be racially discriminatory. While minority students made up 34% of the student body, they represented just 2% of the total honors program. Students were admitted to an honors course on the basis of grades, test scores, and their teachers' recommendations. However, even relaxing these requirements would do little to change their racial composition, the faculty decided, unless the course was radically expanded in size. That, however, would also make impossible the highly individualized instruction and "project orientation" of the honors classes. Further, operating the honors program resulted in pulling out all of the most gifted students from the department's regular offerings. Teachers viewed this result as highly undesirable: They all agreed that the regular biology, chemistry, and physics courses were much better when they contained the gifted students. So, with Dr. Salinsky's approval, the Department had decided to end its Honors Courses, fold all gifted students back into its regular courses, and develop an extensive series of enrichment activities for those students who would ordinarily be enrolled in the Honors Program. "That way," Dr. Salinsky concluded, "everyone benefits. Gifted students like John have a highly enriched program and other students benefit from having them in their classes."

"But I thought that the Board of Education's policy was to offer honors courses in major subjects like science in every high school," said Fred.

"Well, technically that's true," responded Dr. Salinsky. "But our enriched program serves the same purpose and falls well within Board policy."

"And did the Board approve your interpretation of its policy?" he asked.

"Well, not specifically." Salinsky said. "However, it's clearly within our right to make this interpretation. Jamestown's Board of Education has adopted a site-based management style for the district. That gives individual schools considerable latitude in making their own decisions regarding their curriculum and operations. Our faculty determined that honors courses were inappropriate for East High School."

"Let me see if I understand," said Fred. "The Board of Education, which represents the people of Jamestown, makes policies that govern the schools. Presumably these policies represent the will of Jamestown's residents. One such policy was to have every high school offer honors courses in all major academic subjects. Then they made a policy that says that decisions should be made as closely as possible to the level at which those decisions are carried out—what you called 'site-based management.' Now you claim that the second policy gives your faculty the right to ignore any of the policies that the Board itself makes, that is, policies that represent the wishes of the community. And all of this comes down to depriving my son of the kind of courses that he would be entitled to at every other high school in town and the kinds of courses, honors courses, that any college admissions committee will recognize. Is this description correct?"

"Well, yes," said Dr. Salinsky, "but you miss . . ."

"I think I need to talk to the superintendent," replied Mr. Rayner, as he got up to leave.

The next day the issue, in the person of a visibly upset Fred Rayner, arrived at Dr. Wallace's office.

Some Questions

1   If you were the superintendent, Dr. Wallace, how would you handle Mr. Rayner's complaint?
2.   Have the science teachers at East High violated any democratic principles by dropping honors courses from their curriculum? What principles? Why or why not?
3.   Suppose that East High has established a "management council," a board composed of teachers, the principal, and representatives of parents. This council was intended to operate in an analogous fashion to the districts' Board of Education (i.e., to make policy for East High). Suppose further that this council had authorized dropping honors science. Would this make legitimate the teachers' action? Why or why not?

4.   There is a potential for problems to arise when school districts authorize site-based management plans for schools, as happened in this case. How might school districts minimize the chances for these problems to occur?

CASE #5: A MATTER OF HONESTY

Mr. Blain enjoyed looking through travel guides. He especially liked looking through guides to warm and sunny spots when the temperature at home was below zero and the snow was piled up to his office windows. Northern Minnesota had many things to commend it as a place to live and work. In Mr. Blain's opinion, however, February wasn't one of them.

Fortunately, the Board of Education of Allen Federated Schools provided its superintendent with a generous allowance for professional improvement. This allowance could be used to pay for travel to professional meetings. Generally it was enough to cover airfare to remote and warm spots such as Florida, Arizona, and southern California. It would even stretch to include a week in a good hotel and some first-rate dinners.

The trick was to find a good professional meeting in the right place at the right time. Fortunately, those folk who organized conferences for superintendents were attentive to the pleasant effects of warmth and available sunshine on conference attendance. In the winter there was always something plausible going on down South.

Of course, Mr. Blain had to admit that once or twice he had gone to conferences that were of little interest to him. There was the trip to the Urban Education Society meetings last year. His district was hardly urban. Indeed, the local deer population outnumbered the student population. And then there was the conference on artificial intelligence five years back. He had not understood a word of the one session he had attended. Still, there was something to be said for attending a conference that was of minimal interest to him. It interfered less with his recreation.

Not that Mr. Blain was entirely inattentive to his superintendently duties while he was away. He generally took along some work, and he went to conference sessions when they seemed to deal with something of potential value for his district. Indeed, Mr. Blain felt that the district got its money's worth. He often learned something of use, and when he did not he came back warm and rested and was able to devote more time and effort to the welfare of his school system. It was a fair trade.

Nor was the arrangement likely to cause trouble. The board of education always approved his trips even though their recreational potential was evident. He made no attempt to hide his tan on return. The arrangement had evolved into a kind of fringe benefit. It was good for him, did not hurt his district, and no one raised objections. Why shouldn't he use his professional development money for a midwinter vacation?

Some Questions

1. Do you believe that Mr. Blain is acting dishonestly or unethically? Why or why not?
2. Does the fact that the board of education has tacitly accepted his midwinter vacation justify it? If they simply granted him a paid midwinter vacation as a fringe benefit would that justify it?
3. Suppose it really is true that Mr. Blain is a more effective superintendent because of his midwinter vacation. Does that justify it?

CASE #6: A MATTER OF INTEGRITY

Her orders were clear. She had done her best to change the decision, but the board would not agree. She was required to implement it. But she could not. She was deeply convinced not only that it was a mistake, but that it was wrong.

Sandra Jones had been the principal of the New Hope alternative middle school for about 15 years. During that time she had forged a successful alternative school that served the children electing to attend it very well. The children who attended it came from a variety of backgrounds and possessed an enormous range of abilities. They had one thing in common. They did not function well in the usual classroom. Some of the students were conventional behavior problems. They were not academically talented and had rebelled against schools that seemed persistently interested in demonstrating their inferiority to others. Some of her students were, however, enormously talented. But they had difficulty seeing why they should learn what someone else had picked for them instead of pursuing their own interests. Mrs. Jones's students were the academically alienated.

She ran a school with few rules, many of which students worked out for themselves. Students' programs were highly individualized. The only real requirement was that students spend their time profitably. Persistent goofing off was not long tolerated. Older or more gifted students were used to teach younger or less gifted ones. The teachers provided much individual instruction and even more individual counseling.

Sandra Jones considered her school a great success. She had built a school community. Old students helped initiate new students into the life of the school. Many students were reclaimed, going on to become good citizens and productive people. The achievement scores for her students were only slightly below the district average. Given the students she worked with, some of whom simply filled out standardized tests randomly to express their distaste for testing, she thought this to be remarkable.

Unhappily, the board of education and the new superintendent were not similarly impressed. What they were impressed by was the demand for excellence, which meant to them higher expectations, more discipline, more required courses and more testing. They had not been pleased with what they saw at New Hope. Its program was not consistent with their concept of excellence.

Last year, the board had decided to study New Hope. They had appointed a subcommittee headed by the new superintendent. The subcommittee had recently reported and made its recommendations. The report bemoaned the lack of excellence at New Hope. While they recommended that it continue to exist, that it function as the alternative school for the district, and that Sandra Jones continue to be its principal, they also recommended that New Hope conform to the curriculum and the discipline practices followed elsewhere in the district. Despite her vigorous protests, the board adopted the recommendations. The new superintendent assured the board that they would be strictly followed.

Sandra knew that these new policies would destroy the program she had carefully constructed. She believed that it would destroy many of New Hope's students, and some of its teachers as well. She simply could not implement the board's recommendations.

She had intended to resign. She could not follow board policy with a clear conscience. When she had expressed her intent to some of her teachers, however, they suggested another alternative. They suggested that she seek to subvert board policy. One teacher suggested, "Why not just tell them what they want to hear and do what you want?" Within a few days she had heard essentially the same message from a number of teachers and students.

She thought that this might just be possible. There was a great deal of ambiguity in the language of the recommendations. Moreover, neither the board nor the superintendent had shown much inclination to come to New Hope for inspection trips. She was their main source of information. It would be possible to make a few cosmetic changes and continue with business as usual. At least she could give it a try.

The trouble was that this strategy felt wrong. She would be being devious and would be subverting board policy. She felt uncomfortable about both of those. On the other hand, her school had become crucial to the lives of many of her students. Was it right to quit and abandon them to someone who would enforce board policy with enthusiasm? Perhaps with a bit of guile she could salvage much of her program. Should she try?

Some Questions

1. Does Sandra Jones have a moral obligation to resign her position if she believes that she cannot conscientiously implement board policy? Why might this be the case?
2. Is it wrong for her to attempt to subvert board policy if the results of doing so are genuinely beneficial for her students? Why or why not?
3. What would you advise Sandra Jones to do?

CASE #7: MERIT OR MERCY?

Teddy Clemens vaguely remembered that he had been in favor of merit pay. That was before he had had to administer it. As principal of Red Bluff Elementary School, it had fallen to him to pick a few teachers to receive special merit raises this year. Moreover, this year the board had really gotten into the idea of merit pay. The merit bonuses were large enough to be worth having.

It was less easy to decide who was meritorious. Teddy had dutifully solicited the advice of his faculty on how he should proceed. They had made it clear that it was his choice. Apparently the matter was sufficiently contentious that the teachers wished to make sure that some administrator had to take the rap. The teachers were unwilling to participate directly in the decision He had, however, asked that they submit letters to him suggesting who might be awarded the merit bonuses.

The teachers had willingly submitted letters. He had found the results surprising and informative. The teachers were in reasonable agreement about who the genuinely excellent teachers among them were. Only one case bothered him. That was Ann Bently.

Ann was a young teacher. She had only recently gotten tenure, and the decision was close. It was the fact that she had improved consistently over her three years' probation rather than her teaching ability per se that had persuaded Teddy to recommend her. With continued improvement, she would probably become a satisfactory teacher.

But she had not been satisfactory this year. Her teaching had deteriorated significantly. Parent complaints were on the rise. Her evaluations had been poor. She had decidedly not been meritorious. Yet she was frequently mentioned by the faculty as deserving a merit raise.

Teddy thought he understood. Ann had had a disastrous year personally. Her husband had been killed in an automobile accident. He had left her with two small children, little insurance, and a large pile of unpaid bills. He knew that Ann was financially desperate. Apparently, so did everyone else. Ann talked freely about her problems. Teddy thought that was probably healthy. But she had a unique mix of charm and vulnerability that easily roused the concern and sympathy of others. She had received a good deal of mothering and fathering from the older members of his staff. Teddy thought that was commendable. His teachers were good people. They cared about each other.

But it was clear that Ann had been the beneficiary of a sympathy vote. No one really thought her to be an excellent teacher, but everyone wanted to help her out. Thus his staff was trying to suggest subtly that he give the poor kid a break. As one letter had said, "Under the circumstances she's done well, and some extra money right now would certainly help her concentrate on her teaching."

Perhaps this was the right idea. If he gave Ann the money, it might just help her concentrate more on her job. And she certainly needed it. There was much to commend the idea. But shouldn't merit raises go to those who earn them, not to those who need them?

Some Questions

1. If you were Teddy Clemens, what would you do in this case? Why?
2. Are there cases in which, as an administrator, it is more important to consider people's needs than to give them what they deserve? Can you name a few? Why, in these cases, is humane treatment more important than just treatment?

CASE #8: A CONFLICT OF INTEREST

John Tobin, the superintendent of Claymont public schools, listened with interest to Philip McDuff's speech to the other members of the board. McDuff was giving a rather impassioned speech about how poorly paid Claymont's teachers were. McDuff should know. He was married to one of them.

McDuff was reciting a litany that had by now become familiar to almost everyone in public education. Teachers were underpaid. The teaching profession could no longer attract the best and brightest undergraduates. It could not pay them as well as science, medicine, or law. Moreover, Claymont had fallen behind other comparable districts in its pay scale. It was in danger of not being able to attract the kinds of teachers it needed. McDuff was proposing a whopping 8% increase for each of the next three years. If Tobin recalled correctly, the rate of inflation last year had been less than 2%.

It was not that Tobin was against these raises. Indeed, he was inclined to agree that his teachers were entitled to them. Moreover, high salaries made his job as an administrator easier. What made Tobin uneasy was the fact that McDuff had emerged as the leader of the "big raise" faction of the board. McDuff often allied himself with the "tax savers" rather than the spenders. Arguing for a salary increase that would require a hefty tax increase was a bit out of character. Tobin could not help but wonder if the fact that McDuff's wife would be a recipient of one of these raises had not influenced his judgment in the matter.

Of course, the fact that McDuff's wife was a teacher sometimes seemed to be an asset. McDuff often seemed to have a clearer idea of what actually went on in Claymont's classrooms than did other board members. In this case, however, it seemed to Tobin that McDuff had too much of a personal stake in the salary raises. He might at least be a bit more tactful about the matter and be quiet.

Some Questions

1. Does McDuff have a conflict of interest in this case?
2. If he does, should he avoid participating in the discussion of teacher salaries? Should he abstain from voting on them? Should he be required to abstain?
3. If McDuff's wife came up for tenure while he was on the board, how should he behave?
4. Are there other issues on which McDuff should abstain? Should teachers or their immediate families be excluded from membership on school boards?
5. Suppose you were John Tobin and that you were asked to write a policy indicating what board members should do in order to avoid such conflicts of interest. What would you suggest?

CASE #9: EXPLOITATION

"Mr. Place, I've put up with this pay for five years, but now I have a kid in college and I need the money, not just the job. You need to pay me for the work I do. I'm tired of working a full-time job for part-time wages."

Mr. Place was unsympathetic. Laura Connors had taken the job knowing quite well what it paid and what the work was. She had no right to complain now just because she thought she needed money. He felt that he was doing women like Laura Connors a service by making work available.

Laura Connors was one of a dozen women who worked in the evening division of Agamemnon High School. The evening division offered a variety of courses to the citizens of Agamemnon. Courses in photography, macramé, and oil painting were part of its fare. Laura Connors worked in the second-chance program. This program helped pregnant teens continue work toward their high school diploma.

All of the programs in the evening division were staffed in the same way. They were taught by women who worked part-time and at an hourly rate. No one was permitted to work more than 20 hours a week, since as long as they worked less than 20 hours, the school district did not have to pay them benefits. The hourly rates were low. The combined wages of two part-time teachers who worked a total of 40 hours per week were about two-thirds of the salary of one of the teachers who taught full time in the school district. Usually the teachers in the evening division had qualifications similar to the full-timers. All were college graduates, most were certified teachers, and many had master's degrees.

Even these facts were somewhat misleading so far as pay rates were concerned, for the part-time teachers generally worked more hours than they were paid. They were not actually paid for the number of hours they put in. Instead, they were paid for the number of hours at which the job was rated. The rating for the jobs generally included only the number of hours teachers were scheduled to be in the classroom, plus an hour per week of preparation time. Teachers, however, usually spent far more than one hour per week preparing for their teaching. Moreover, any time spent working with students before or after class was not compensated. It was not unusual for a teacher whose job was rated at 20 hours to actually work 30.

Mr. Place, of course, understood how Laura Connors felt. Yet he felt that his main responsibility was to provide the program. Many of its students needed the program desperately. This was especially true of the second-chance program. But the district simply could not afford these programs if it paid its part-timers at the same real wage it paid its full-time teachers. The use of low-paid part-time teachers made it possible to provide a much more extensive program than would have been otherwise possible. He felt he could not responsibly raise the pay rates and cut back the program.

Finally, he felt that wages should be determined by the market. The fact was that the Agamemnon School District had a surfeit of well-educated women. They were the wives of Agamemnon's numerous professionals. Having the research division of one the world's largest computer companies in one's district had its benefits. Most of these women were not really interested in the money. They worked because they wished for something worthwhile to do outside the home. Mr. Place could replace Laura a dozen times. If wages should be set by the market, Laura was overpaid.

He had tried to explain this to Laura. "Laura, I'm sorry I can't pay you what you're worth, but if I increased the wages of all of the people in the evening division, I'd have to cut back the program. I don't think you would want me to do that. You are a capable person. Perhaps if you really need the money, you should look for a better-paying job."

Some Questions

1. Is Laura Connors exploited?
2. How should one go about deciding what counts as fair pay? Is it important that Laura agreed to accept the job and that she could probably find a better-paying job if she wished?
3. In education, part-time positions of the sort that Laura Connors occupies are predominately held by women. Is the practice of cutting costs by hiring part-timers a kind of gender discrimination?

CASE #10: BORROWED PROPERTY?

Tom Wicks had not been at Scottsdale High for more than a few months when he realized that his colleague, Fred Trevor, freely borrowed school property. But he thought that *poached* was a more accurate word.

Scottsdale was a large school, with over 3,000 students, and it had two vice-principals. Tom held one of these posts. It was his first administrative position. While his job had an impressive title, Dean of Students, actually, of course, he spent most of his time on pupil discipline. It was probably the worst job in school administration, but Tom wanted to do well at it. Someday, he hoped, he would have a school of his own.

Fred, who had been at Scottsdale for a number of years, had once been its dean of students. He had been promoted and was now its dean of instruction. That was, in Tom's judgment, an infinitely more rewarding job. Fred was responsible for curriculum, teacher evaluation, and staff development. Both Fred and Tom reported to Harry McIverson, the principal.

One Friday afternoon, shortly after Tom had arrived at Scottsdale, he and Fred happened to be walking together across the staff parking lot at the end of the school day. Fred had been trying to juggle a large box, his briefcase, and a gym bag, while getting his car keys from his pocket. Tom had offered to help by holding the box but in the process of taking it, the carton had fallen to the ground and broken open. Inside, among other things, were several reams of paper, a couple of staplers, a tape dispenser, and several sheets of first-class postage stamps. Fred had seemed a bit embarrassed, but explained that he did much of his work at home and that he needed the supplies and equipment to do so. That seemed reasonable to Tom.

A couple of months later, when Tom was working late one evening, he glanced out his window and saw Fred on his way out of the building with a large desk lamp. Tom recognized the lamp immediately. It was one of those that had been used in the school's mechanical drawing classroom. That classroom had recently been refurbished and made into a computer room. The old equipment, including 20 or so architect's desk lamps, was currently stored in the school's basement awaiting disposition.

It was true that these lamps were now surplus. It was even possible that the district might decide to give them away to any staff members who wanted one. Nevertheless, the lamps were still district property and were worth a fair sum of money. (New, they sold for well over $100 apiece.) Tom doubted the propriety of simply appropriating one of them for home use. On the other hand, since Fred said he worked at home a lot, it was possible to argue that the district should provide him with all of the equipment he needed. Certainly a light was needed equipment; he could not be expected to work in the dark.

Last night, however, Tom had recognized that his senior colleague's borrowing exceeded the limits of propriety. Fred and his wife had thrown a cocktail party and invited Tom. A large crowd had circulated freely about the Trevors' home. During the course of the evening Tom had asked directions to a bathroom and had been routed upstairs. Walking down the hallway, he had passed an open door and noticed Chris, Fred's son, bent intently over a personal computer. Tom had stopped to say hello, and Chris had invited him in to try his hand at defeating the galactic invaders swarming over the monitor's screen. As Tom had sat down in front of the machine, he noticed the lamp angled over Chris's desk. It was a large architect's light, obviously one of those from school. Then he looked at the powerful and expensive computer in front of him. Riveted to its front panel was a tag: Property of Scottsdale Board of Education.

Some Questions

1. How would you handle this matter? Would you inform McIverson, the school principal? Why or why not?
2. If you would not, are you not, in effect, an accomplice to an act of theft?
3. What procedures might a school district implement to curtail theft of the public's property by a few employees, while still treating the vast majority of its staff as honest people?
4. Are Tom Wicks's personal motives relevant to informing his superior of Fred's actions? If so, how?

CASE #11: AN OFFICE AFFAIR

Susan Matheson wasn't sure when her feelings about Bill had become something more than professional. Perhaps it was when she observed him for the first time in his classroom. He was simply a superb teacher. That was obvious. It wasn't just that his lessons were carefully wrought and thoughtfully presented. They were also served up with a charm and wit that captivated his students. He was somehow able to appear at one with his class, a first among equals, and simultaneously to be the acknowledged authority and leader of a very difficult group of students.

Perhaps it had happened even earlier, when he had interviewed for the position at Lublow Junior High. Susan had been impressed with his boyish, fresh-out-of-college eagerness and his patent commitment to serving poor and minority pupils.

Regardless of when her feelings had changed, it was obvious now that they had. Now, not only Bill's pupils loved him. Susan did, too.

For his part, Bill had been slow to respond. Later, he had confessed to Susan that he thought that the signs of her attraction to him were figments of his imagination. How could an accomplished and very proper professional woman, especially such an attractive one, find him appealing? He had also been slow to react even after he recognized Susan's actions for what they were. After all, she was his boss. Getting sexually involved with your principal perhaps was not a good idea for a brand-new teacher.

For her part, Susan had resisted strenuously her growing attraction to Bill. It wasn't just that she was his principal, with all that that implied for their professional association. There was the matter of the rest of her staff. Were it to become known that she and Bill were having an affair, her relationship with her faculty would surely be damaged. Finally, there was the matter of her own family. While her marriage had been troubled for a long time, she had no intention of dissolving it.

Susan was under no illusions about the permanence of her affair. She knew that eventually it would end. But in the meantime, her life had been transformed. It was infused with a kind of enchantment she hadn't felt in years and might never feel again. Why should she give that up? Further, the salutary effects of the affair were not simply personal. She looked forward to each day at work with a new enthusiasm that was beginning to show in the operation of the school itself. Lublow Junior High was humming in a way that it had not in years. Surely that was a good thing.

Some Questions

1. People—both married and unmarried—have affairs all the time. Is there anything about an affair between educators that makes it more problematic than most others?
2. Superiors and subordinates also have affairs all the time. Is there anything about such a relationship between principal and teacher that makes it especially problematic?

3. Suppose it is true that Bill is a superb teacher and that Lublow Junior High is actually running better because of its principal's dalliance. If you were Susan Matheson, how would you handle this situation?

CASE #12: SOCIETAL AND INDIVIDUAL GOOD

It had the worst reputation in the city. Nestor High suffered from a 60% drop-out rate, open drug trafficking, student violence, vandalism, and the lowest achievement scores in the state. When Emanuel Diaz had arrived as principal just five years ago, no one thought he could turn the place around. Mr. Diaz started with the community. He went to the local merchants, owners of small businesses, and local factories. They all agreed with him that something had to be done for the neighborhood. Amazingly, Mr. Diaz convinced them that they were the key. He arranged enough work-study opportunities so that any student who wanted one could almost pick his or her occupational "experiment." Teachers soon joined in the cause and linked their teaching as much as possible to the work experiences students were having. Practical math and science, history of technology and labor, literature of workers, and all sorts of other "applied" aspects of the school subjects were being taught. And it was like a communicable disease. Students infected with good experiences at work and school spread their enthusiasm to others, and Mr. Diaz worked hard to make sure his "clinic" had spaces for the new patients.

And now Nestor High was among the best urban schools in the state as measured by reading scores, dropout rate, vandalism, crime, drug abuse, and subjective assessments of "atmosphere."

There was one problem, however; the few students from Nestor who applied to highly selective colleges were being turned down. Admissions officers claimed that the courses at Nestor were not academic enough and that the experience was too narrowly vocational to really prepare people for college. Mr. Diaz wondered if he had really done good for his school and its students, or if he had merely created a social salvage machine that could produce workers but not provide opportunity for true upward mobility and individual fulfillment.

Some Questions

1. Is the societal good created by Mr. Diaz's changes at Nestor in conflict with individual good? Is there an ethical issue here?
2. Are the school's primary obligations to society or to the individual? What is the nature of these obligations? Contractual? Legal? Constitutional? Traditional? Ethical? Discuss.

CASE #13: JOB REFERENCES FOR STUDENTS

In the large system in which Mrs. Goode had trained as assistant principal, school counselors handled all local calls for outside references. But here in the Bush Hills Consolidated School District, it fell to her as part of her job as principal to respond to requests from prospective local employers of students. It was a little difficult at first, because she didn't know the students too well. Still, discreet conversations with a student's teachers usually provided Mrs. Goode with enough information to satisfy her sense of a real and useful appraisal—something "canned" recommendations too often failed to provide. She felt she had an obligation to provide prospective employers with an honest appraisal of a student's job-related characteristics and his or her school record. After all, this was a public school and should serve the public.

Then she got the call from the electricians union. They needed a reference for Fred Fredricks. He had applied to become an apprentice. Mrs. Goode said she would call back, but already she knew she had a problem. Fred was probably the most notorious senior at Bush Hills. He bullied the young kids, cut classes, didn't do his homework, and was always being sent to the principal's office. And he wasn't too bright.

On the other hand, she had gathered some firsthand information on his background that mitigated the situation. His mother was an alcoholic and on welfare. His father had abused Fred and currently was serving a term in jail for housebreaking. Fred had had little care growing up and had rebelled against his family. All through the years before Mrs. Goode had come to Bush Hills, the teachers had tried to help him overcome his antisocial behavior and at least learn enough to pass each grade. They knew he needed help. In fact, it looked like he would even graduate, albeit with the absolutely lowest average anyone had ever had in the history of the school.

If Mrs. Goode told the union of his grades, his absentee record, and his lack of application to schoolwork, she knew they would turn him down. But this might be Fred's only chance to make something of his life, to become a responsible adult. She was leaning toward giving a "canned," noncommittal recommendation until she remembered that just last week there had been a story in the paper about a house that had burned down because a careless worker had crossed wires when installing a switch.

In one last, desperate effort to find a legitimate basis for helping Fred, she went to his shop teacher, only to find that Fred wasn't too handy with tools either, was sloppy finishing up work, and tended to cut corners.

Some Questions

1. What would you do if you were Mrs. Goode? How would you justify your decision?

2. Should schools serve as society's sorter? Does the school have an obligation to respond to requests for information about students? Are there any limits?

CASE #14: CONFIDENTIALITY, OBLIGATIONS, AND FRIENDSHIP

Henry Hendricks had made it a point to get to know the staff at his school personally. He remembered the warnings of his professors of school administration that if proper professional distance were not maintained, subjective personal feelings would enter into what should be impersonal, objective, professional decisions.

But Henry had always been a gregarious type; his style of leadership was personal, and it worked. He had been at Grover Cleveland High for only five years, but it was a changed place. Faculty morale was high, and an atmosphere of good, warm feelings pervaded the halls. The faculty liked him, and they worked hard.

All this went through Henry's mind as he sat across the desk from Jim Austin, the head of Cleveland's physical education department, who had asked for a confidential meeting with Henry. He and Jim had become good friends as early morning jogging companions. Henry couldn't figure out why Jim hadn't just talked to him that morning about whatever was on his mind. Jim didn't take long to get to the point now, however. First, he made it clear that this was to be a confidential talk, that if he hadn't come to respect Henry as a friend as well as a principal, he wouldn't be here. He had just found he had AIDS and wanted to stay at his job without anyone's knowing for as long as he could.

Henry's first thought was that he wished the board had a policy on AIDS; then he felt embarrassed for thinking first of himself and a way out rather than of Jim's grappling with his death notice.

Henry's next inclination was to respond to Jim as his friend and tell him he would keep his secret and let him stay on. But then Henry wondered about his obligations to his students and staff. Jim was a physical education instructor, and things might happen that would allow the virus to be spread. He wished he knew more about AIDS, but this was a little late to get an education. He needed to make a decision.

Some Questions

1. If you were Henry, what would you decide? How would you justify your decision? Did the nature of the disease influence your decision?

2.   Are personal relations and any degree of friendship between adminis-
     trators and staff best avoided? Discuss.

CASE #15: LOYALTY

It had taken many years of hard work and team effort. Nancy Reilly had
risen through the ranks in the Milford school system with the help of
many colleagues to become the first female superintendent of schools in
the county. She was proud of her accomplishment, but she also knew that
overcoming the sex barrier in this town required the support of many un-
sung heroes (and heroines) working behind the scenes over many years.
Now Nancy could repay all that effort, encouragement, and trust by being the best superintendent the Milford schools ever had. It might take
a few years, but she knew that she had the support of the teachers and
of the parents' Coalition for Better Schools and that all would turn out
well because she was dedicated to the task, as all her supporters knew.
At least that's what she and they thought until "the offer" came along.
It seemed that the majority party in the state felt that the only way they
could win the next gubernatorial election was finally to face the charge
of antifeminism by putting a woman high up in the administration. The
job of Commissioner of Education was opening up and they had heard
of the talent and dedication of Nancy Reilly, first female superintendent
in Milford. She was just right for the job; the timing and publicity were
perfect.

They contacted Nancy and offered her the position. She was torn
between loyalty to Milford and to the feminist cause, not to mention her
own ambition. She would have to think about it, she told them.

Some Questions

1.   What would you do if you were Nancy? Is loyalty a moral virtue or
     just a personal disposition?
2.   Are contracts made to be broken? Doesn't an individual have a right
     to advance his or her own career?

CASE #16: ARE SCHOOLS MORE IMPORTANT THAN SEWERS?

Editor,
Urbanville Star *Tribune*
Urbanville, New York 14850

Dear Sir:

We, the teachers of the Urbanville Teachers' Association, must protest the recent action of the school board that froze teacher hiring for
next year. We recognize that the board has had little choice in the matter,
given the recent unconscionable decision of the Urbanville City Council.
Nevertheless, as professional educators responsible to the children of this
city, we cannot let the board's action go unchallenged.

It is important that readers of the Star *Tribune* understand exactly
what is at issue. The Urbanville School District is a fiscally dependent
one. That means that the school board must submit its budget to the city
council for approval, along with submissions from all other departments
of city government, for example, Parks and Recreation, Human Services,
Sanitation, and Streets and Sewers. On September 15 of last year the city
council cut almost $2 million from the district's original submission. After
negotiation, the district was able to get some of this money restored, but
next year's budget is still almost $1.5 million lower than this year. The os-
tensible reason for this draconian cut was the disrepair of the city's sewers.
The city council claimed that Urbanville's sewers are in such poor condition that money must be diverted from other city services to repair and
replace them because taxes could not be raised any further. In effect, the
council has claimed that sewers are more important than schools.

In response to this cut in its budget, the school board has had to find
a way to reduce the services it offers to the children of Urbanville. It has
chosen to freeze staff hiring for next year. Since 45 teachers are expected to
retire or otherwise leave the system in June, the pupils of those teachers will
have to be absorbed into the classes of those of us who remain. We estimate
that the average class size in the district will increase by nearly five pupils.

We doubt that either the school board or the public fully understands
the impact of this change. Already our classes are too large, and it is extremely difficult to provide the individual attention pupils need. Next year,
with even larger classes, it will be impossible. As just one example of the cut's
effects, careful grading of all assignments will become a hopeless task.

In order to demonstrate to the public the consequences of the board's
decision, the members of the teachers' association have voted to take a drastic
action. Beginning next week, we will cease giving assignments that require
a large amount of out-of-school time to grade. For example, weekly essays
will no longer be assigned in ninth-grade English, and senior themes will
not be required. Next year, with even larger classes than we currently have,
such assignments will not be feasible. We teachers are willing to tighten our
belts and contribute our share to the solution of the city's fiscal crisis. We are
unwilling to pay for sewer repairs with time taken from our own families.

We deeply regret taking this action. However, we have been given no choice. We think that the Board's decision is unjustified. We believe that the school board, instead of meekly submitting to the ill-considered actions of the city council, has the duty to resist these cuts; we demand that the children of Urbanville receive the education they deserve. Education is more important than sewers!

Respectfully,

Allan A. Grimshaw
President, UTA

Some Questions

1. Well, is that true? Is education more important than sewers? How do you know? How are such questions decided in a democracy?
2. What role do experts have in such decisions? Specifically, what is the proper role of teachers in deciding the relative importance of education compared to other governmental services?
3. We have said that government policies almost always contain factual as well as valuational premises. Thus elected representatives can democratically and collectively make a mistake. What are professional educators to do when a community democratically arrives at a mistaken judgment about what is educationally worthwhile?
4. Urbanville's teachers are set to engage in a kind of job action often called a "slowdown," a collective action occupying a middle ground between doing nothing and striking. Are such actions appropriate for professional employees?
5. Fiscal dependency is relatively uncommon among U.S. school districts. (Most school boards adopt a budget and levy whatever taxes that budget requires.) Make a case for fiscal dependency as a mode for funding schools. That is, argue that city councils, not school boards, should set school budgets.

CASE #17: BANG! ZERO TOLERANCE

It was a gun—a real gun. James had brought a gun to school. Ms. Hesston couldn't believe it. James was a shy kid who seemed to get along with everyone. It was hard to imagine him as a gang member, drug dealer, or aspirant hit man. It was hard to imagine him as anything other than a nice fourth grade boy. What did he want with a gun? But there it was. She had seen the bulge under his jacket, which he refused to take off. She had asked him what he had under his coat. James was not good at weapons conceal-ment. He had taken it out and put it on her desk. And it was a real gun. He had taken it from his father's dresser drawer.

Thank God, it wasn't loaded. James had not intended to shoot any-one. In fact, he had carefully removed all the bullets before he brought the gun to school. But apparently he had intended to threaten some-one. She got the story out of him bit by bit. Every day after school, two bigger boys met James. They demanded his money. If he refused, they took it anyway. If he didn't have any money, they punched him and shoved him around. James only had his lunch money to bring to school. So in order to have something to give them, he had stopped eating lunch. "Why didn't you tell me about this, James?" Ms. Hesston asked. "Or why didn't you tell your parents?" James just shrugged. "I didn't think you would be able to do anything," he said. "If you tried to protect me, they would get me later and hurt me worse. Can you protect me all the time? Are you going to put them in jail?" His point was well taken. The school didn't manage bullying well. Ms Hesston suspected that the point of the gun wasn't really to threaten the bullies. It was to get the school to take his problem seriously. Perhaps he would succeed in this.

But what James didn't know about was the school district's zero-toler-ance policy. Neither Ms. Hesston nor the school's principal, Mr. Quayle, had any discretion about what to do with James. So she took him to Mr. Quayle's office, explained the whole situation, and left the problem with him, muttering to herself as she went out the door, "I'm glad he has to call the police and not me!" Mr. Quayle was stunned. He knew what he had to do, but James's infraction was full of mitigating circumstances that cried out for understanding and compassion and not just for enforcement. If he called the police, James would be expelled and placed in an "alterna-tive program." Mr. Quayle thought that at least James would have a hear-ing in juvenile court, but he didn't know if the court had any discretion about what happens to James. The school obviously had no choice. This is what zero tolerance means—no discretion, no taking circumstances into account. There would not be a discussion with James's parents about what was best for him, and there would not be a discussion about the educa-tional consequences of what was decided. Zero tolerance was mandated by state law pursuant to requirements of federal legislation. James was going to have a tough time.

Unless he could handle it discreetly and privately and persuade Ms. Hesston, who seemed sympathetic, to keep it quiet for James's sake. No, he couldn't do that. Ignoring the gun was illegal. Why couldn't he just sit down with James, his parents, and Ms. Hesston and decide what to do? Isn't that how problems like this should be solved?

Some Questions:

1. Teachers and administrators often claim to want discretion over such matters so that they can consider mitigating circumstances and so that they can take the best interests of the child into consideration. Are these good reasons for giving them more discretion? Is this how such discretion is likely to be used?
2. Here are two arguments for zero-tolerance policies.
    a. We need to send a message that drugs and guns aren't tolerated. Tough penalties and no exceptions send this message. Kids will hear it. Letting educators work things out with parents sends the message that kids can get away with drugs and guns in school.
    b. Educators are self-serving and soft-hearted. It's nice to say that they should have discretion about appropriate penalties, but it's always more convenient for them to let kids off, and educators always think kids need one more chance. We need to do the same thing with educators that we did with judges who are too soft on crime—take away their discretion and make them hand out tough penalties.

    Is either of these arguments a good argument?
3. Is it morally permissible for Mr. Quayle to violate the law to protect James?
4. Is expulsion a fair penalty for James's crime?
5. Suppose that expulsion isn't fair to James, but that tough zero-tolerance policies do reduce shooting incidents and drug usage, does that justify such policies?

CASE #18: HIDING BAD NEWS AT HINDEMITH HIGH

Hindemith was the sole high school in the small community of Oakdale, a suburb of a major northwestern city. While Oakdale wasn't large, it was notable. It had the highest per capita income of any town in the state. Nearly all residents had graduated from college, and many held advanced degrees from the likes of Stanford, Yale, and Princeton. Most worked as top executives or engineers at a well-known software firm nearby, or they were doctors, lawyers, or other professionals in the city.

As might be expected, these well-educated and wealthy citizens placed a great deal of importance on the community's schools, and they were willing and able to support the Oakdale Public School System extremely well. The OPS had the highest expenditure per pupil of any district in the state. Its budgets had never been defeated at the polls. Its teachers' and administrators' salaries were the envy of educators throughout the region.

If Oakdale's residents spent fulsomely on their schools, they also expected those schools to provide a top-notch education for their children. And by all the usual measures the OPS met these expectations handsomely. Hindemith High, in particular, stood out. Almost all of Hindemith's graduates went on to higher education, many to the same schools their parents had attended. Virtually no one dropped out. Their scores on the SAT were substantially above average. Hindemith High was always among the top schools on the state's achievement tests. Every year the superintendent, Sarah Adams, collected these statistics and made them available to the school board as well as to the local papers. And each year the board, educators, and residents of Oakdale, perhaps a bit smugly, congratulated themselves on the quality of their schools.

In addition to test results, each year the state also published a vast array of other measures of the performance and characteristics of every public school within its borders. These included, as just a few examples: pupil-teacher ratios, the number of reported cases of serious student violence and drug use, per-pupil expenditures for teacher and administrator salaries, average socioeconomic data for each school's parents, and the number of pupils classified as having special needs. This massive data set was made publicly available by the State Education Department on its web site, allowing anyone to make specific and direct comparisons of a particular school with any other school—or with all other schools—in the state. Indeed, that was precisely the Education Department's purpose.

The Department reasoned that if schools were to be held accountable by parents and citizens, these parties needed to have readily available objective and current measures of a wide array of school inputs, characteristics, and outcomes, measures that would allow them to compare their school with others. The state's data set made it possible for parents to easily ask and answer some highly specific, comparative questions about their school. For example they could ask, "Were police called to my kid's school more often last year than to other schools in the district?" Such a question could be answered in a few minutes by anyone with access to a computer.

Unfortunately, few citizens even knew of this data set, much less its uses. Further, educators have long recognized a basic problem with making such comparisons: Many factors besides the quality of a school's efforts have substantial effects on student performance, and these other factors must be considered when making comparisons among schools.

What many educators have not recognized, however, is that recently statisticians have made considerable progress in developing techniques for taking into account these other factors, thereby making direct comparisons across schools much more defensible. And it was these techniques, which go under the formidable title of "hierarchical linear modeling," that led to Superintendent Adams's problem.

It began when Nicole Florentine, a music teacher at Hindemith High, took a course, "Topics in Multivariate Analysis," at the state university. Nicole was a talented musician, and, like many musicians, she was also talented in mathematics. She enjoyed math, liked to do quantitative research, and hoped one day to take the position of head of the Office of Program Planning and Evaluation in Oakdale's central office. In fact, Superintendent Adams had her eye on Nicole for exactly that job.

Two things happened in "Topics in Multivariate Analysis:" Nicole learned how to use hierarchical linear models, and she recognized their potential for analyzing the massive and largely unused data sets on the State Education Department's web site. After discussing the idea with her instructor, she undertook to prepare a term paper assessing the performance in algebra of Hindemith's ninth graders compared to ninth graders in the other schools in the state.

Her results were surprising. Hindemith students' algebra achievement was certainly better than average. But it was not that much better, given their personal and family advantages and the rich resources of their school. Less advantaged students in a number of schools with considerably fewer resources seemed to outperform their counterparts at Hindemith. Nicole reported these findings carefully, and concluded the paper by strongly urging greater use of the state's data set by citizens interested in evaluating the performance of their schools. When the paper was returned to her at the end of the semester, her instructor, Professor McCabe, was profuse in his laudatory written comments in its margins. He thought that she had correctly structured the paper's central question, that she had carried out her analysis thoughtfully and defensibly, and that her findings were compelling. He gave her an "A" and wrote that if she ever thought of returning to full-time graduate work in educational research and statistics, to come to see him.

Pleased, Nicole brought the paper to Hindemith's principal, John Isaacs, with the suggestion that he'd be interested in its findings. She explained that she'd used her university course to develop a method that would help the school and the community make data-based decisions about school programs, and that she'd used Hindemith's algebra program as a test case. Further, she suggested that he should share the paper with Superintendent Adams and the school board when he finished with it. Isaacs agreed to do so and took the paper home to read.

When he finished, he was not pleased. He fully understood Nicole's findings, and he didn't like them at all. He considered his school to be an exceptionally good one, and its programs, including its algebra program, to be outstanding. All of the test results he'd ever seen showed that. He simply didn't believe that Hindemith's students were achieving, on average, only "moderately above state means," as Nicole concluded. Worse, he didn't understand how Nicole arrived at this conclusion. He hadn't the faintest idea what hierarchical linear modeling was, and he had no desire to learn. As far as he was concerned, the paper had "too damn many squiggles in it" (his term for all mathematical symbols).

A few days later Isaacs sent the paper to the superintendent, as he had promised, and the following week he met privately with Sarah Adams to discuss it. Adams was also surprised by the paper's findings and was equally in the dark as to its methods. The two administrators put their heads together and agreed that the paper should not be forwarded to the board. They reasoned that it would certainly become public and possibly become the subject of an article in the local paper. Further, regardless of Nicole's findings regarding algebra, they saw no reason to draw the public's attention to the easy availability of the state's data set and the possible comparisons it offered. This was especially true in Oakdale, they felt, a community chock-full of Ph.D. scientists and engineers fully capable of doing the kind of analysis carried out by Nicole, the analysis Adams and Isaacs found so incomprehensible. They also reasoned that, despite Professor McCabe's favorable evaluation, the paper's findings could be in error, and there was no point in promulgating error. Finally, they thought it was unfair to single out Hindemith's math department for criticism, on the sole grounds that its data were available and met the required statistical assumptions. Nicole, they noted, did not choose to compare her own department, music, to those of other schools.

The next day Adams wrote a thoughtful and pleasant letter to Nicole. She thanked her for sending the paper. She said she'd found it highly informative. She commented that she'd been aware of the state's web site but not of a statistical technique that seemed to permit fair cross-school comparisons. She was grateful to Nicole for bringing it to her attention. She wrote that she was very pleased that Nicole had put her newly learned skills to use in serving the school district. And she strongly encouraged Nicole to follow Professor McCabe's advice and continue her graduate work. Finally, she noted that the school board was in the middle of its budgeting process and that negotiations with the teachers' association were under way, so it wasn't going to be possible to present the paper to the school board anytime in the near future. Instead, she suggested that Nicole discuss the paper, confidentially, with the math faculty at Hindemith. Superintendent Adams did not mention that if the paper went to the Board of Education, it would be sometime after her retirement. Also, she didn't mention that she no longer thought of Nicole as a good candidate to head the Office of Planning and Evaluation. That position necessarily required a great deal of discretion.

Some Questions

1. It's not uncommon for heads of organizations, including schools, to bury unfavorable information rather than make it public. Have you experienced such situations? Aside from the ethics of this behavior, what is its likely effect on the ability of boards to hold schools (and school administrators) accountable?
2. Under what conditions, if any, do you think a superintendent would be obligated to present unfavorable information to a school board? Under what conditions, if any, would a superintendent be obligated *not* to present unfavorable information to a school board?
3. Arguably, Sarah Adams has handled this situation adroitly; Nicole has very likely been quieted and a potentially embarrassing report has been buried. But has she behaved ethically? Could Adams have handled this situation better?
4. Refer to our discussion of the nature of a profession. Now consider the following argument: Many, probably most, practicing administrators are simply unable to read with critical understanding the research that undergirds their professional practice. This situation undermines any claims that educational administration is a field of professional practice, and hence any claims that administrators' judgments are due any special deference from the public because of their professional expertise. How would you respond to this argument?
5. Consider another kind of argument: The professional model just doesn't apply to school administrators (or teachers either, for that matter), because they do not possess any specialized body of technical knowledge in the sense that physicians, lawyers, or engineers do. Instead, they simply possess the kind of knowledge that accumulates from their experience in educational organizations. That experience alone justifies a level of deference to their opinions. Claims to be professionals simply confuse the issue, and they have an odor of occupational self-aggrandizement.

Annotated Bibliography

Achinstein, B. (2002). *Community, diversity, and conflict among school teachers: The ties that blind.* New York: Teachers College Press.
    A study of teachers in two similar, multicultural middle schools who seek the formation of community out of diversity but handle the inevitable conflicts that arise with diversity differently. An eye-opener showing that the climate of a school is as much or more important than the espoused mission of a school.
Ackerman, B. (1980). *Social justice in the liberal state.* New Haven, CT: Yale University Press.
    An argument for liberalism with a strong emphasis on neutrality and dialogue.
Appiah, K. A. (1994). Identity, authenticity, survival: Multicultural societies and social reproduction. In A. Gutmann (Ed.), *Multiculturalism: Examining the politics of recognition.* Princeton, NJ: Princeton University Press.
    A discussion of identity and multiculturalism.
Aristotle. (1980). *Nicomachean ethics* (W. D. Ross, Trans.). New York: Oxford University Press.
    An important classical text on the nature of virtues.
Arkes, H. (1981). *The philosopher in the city.* Princeton, NJ: Princeton University Press.
    An excellent treatment of ethical issues that arise in urban politics. Contains a section on education.
Arons, S. (1997). *Short route to chaos.* Amherst: University of Massachusetts Press.
    A critique of standards-driven reform emphasizing the importance of local community in education.
Baier, A. (1995). *Moral prejudices.* Cambridge, MA: Harvard University Press.
    A collection of essays on ethics that includes two important discussions of trust.
Banks, J. A. (1996). *Multicultural education, transformative knowledge, and action.* New York: Teachers College Press.
    A discussion of the nature of multiculturalism.
Barber, B. (1992). *An aristocracy of everyone.* New York: Oxford University Press.
    A discussion of citizenship and the education of citizens from the foremost advocate of strong democracy.
Bellah, R. (1985). *Habits of the heart.* Berkeley: University of California Press.
    A classic discussion of the importance of community.
Benhabib, S. (1992). *Situating the self: Gender, community and postmodernism in contemporary ethics.* New York: Routledge, Chapman & Hall.
    A feminist statement of discourse ethics.

Berlin, I. (1969). *Four essays on liberty.* London: Oxford University Press.
A classic discussion of the nature and importance of individual liberty.
Bok, S. (1979). *Lying: Moral choice in public and private life.* New York: Vintage.
Addresses the possible justifications and consequences of withholding the truth.
Bok, S. (1982). *Secrets.* New York: Pantheon.
Discusses the right and obligation to keep secrets and those situations in which keeping secrets may not be justified.
Bonhoeffer, D. (1949). *Ethics.* New York: Macmillan.
A discussion of Christian ethics from a German theologian who died in a Nazi concentration camp for his opposition to Hitler.
Boyd, L., & Miretzky, D. (Eds.). (2003). *American educational governance on trial: Change and challenges.* Chicago, IL: University of Chicago Press.
A discussion of educational governance with a number of useful essays on topics such as community, accountability, and school choice.
Brighouse, H. (2000). *School choice and social justice.* New York: Oxford University Press.
A normative discussion of school choice that emphasizes the centrality of autonomy and equality.
Bryk, A. S., Lee, V. E., & Holland, P. B. (1993). *Catholic schools and the common good.* Cambridge, MA: Harvard University Press.
A discussion of schools as communities in the context of Catholic education.
Callan, E. (1997). *Educating citizens.* New York: Oxford University Press.
A discussion of the connection between liberal political theory and education for citizenship.
Dewey, J. (1957). *Reconstruction in philosophy.* Boston: Beacon Press.
A good description of Dewey's views on science and philosophy, together with his views on the application of the scientific method to ethical problems.
Dworkin, R. (1977). *Taking rights seriously.* Cambridge, MA: Harvard University Press.
A discussion of legal and ethical philosophy, with a good chapter on affirmative action.
Etzioni, A. (1993). *The spirit of community: Rights, responsibilities, and the communitarian agenda.* New York: Crown Publishers.
A statement of a communitarian view.
Feinberg, W. (1989). *Common schools and uncommon identities.* New Haven, CT: Yale University Press.
A discussion of how to balance pluralism and the need for a shared American identity.
Fischer, L., Schimmel, D., & Stellman, R. (2003). *Teachers and the law.* Boston: Allyn and Bacon.
A good summary of education law, valuable for teachers and administrators.
Fullinwider, R. (Ed.). (1996). *Public education in a multicultural society.* New York: Cambridge University Press.
An excellent collection of essays on multicultural education.
Gilligan, C. (1982). *In a different voice.* Cambridge, MA: Harvard University Press.
A feminist critique and alternative to current views on moral development.

Glendon, M. A. (1995). *Seedbeds of virtue: Sources of competence, character, and citizenship in American society.* Lanham, MD: Madison Books.
> A discussion of civic virtue and the importance of community in producing it.

Gutmann, A. (1987). *Democratic education.* Princeton, NJ: Princeton University Press.
> This work develops a democratic theory of education and applies it to a wide range of educational issues.

Habermas, J. (1984). *The theory of communicative action.* Boston: Beacon Press.
> The classic statement of discourse ethics.

Haller, E. J., & Strike, K. A. (1997). *An introduction to educational administration: Social, legal, and ethical perspectives.* Troy, NY: Educator's International Press.
> An extensive treatment of common administrative problems from three different perspectives.

Hare, R. M. (1972). *Applications of moral philosophy.* Berkeley: University of California Press.
> A lucid treatment of many moral concerns, including such issues as relativism, the moral development of adolescents, the morality of governmental acts, and peace; deals with such questions as "What is life?" and "Can I be blamed for following orders?"

Hodgkinson, C. (1978). *Toward a philosophy of administration.* New York: St. Martin's Press.
> A treatment of a variety of philosophic issues, including ethical ones, as they apply to educational administration.

Howe, K. R. (1997). *Understanding equal educational opportunity.* New York: Teachers College Press.
> An excellent discussion of equal educational opportunity.

Kant, I. (1956). *Critique of practical reason* (L. W. Beck, Trans.). Indianapolis, IN: Bobbs-Merrill.
> The classical statement and defense of a nonconsequentialist ethical position. Hard reading, but worthwhile.

Kimbrough, R. B. (1985). *Ethics.* Arlington, VA: American Association of School Administrators.
> A brief treatment of central topics in educational administration.

Kittay, E. (1999). *Love's labor.* New York: Routledge.
> A discussion of dependency and justice with particular relevance to the ethics of special education.

Kymlicka, W. (1995). *Multicultural citizenship: A liberal theory of minority rights.* Oxford, England: Clarendon Press.
> A discussion of the question of whether there are group rights.

Lickona, T. (1991). *Educating for character: How our schools can teach respect and responsibility.* New York: Bantam.
> A important source for ideas and materials about character education.

MacIntyre, A. (1982). *After virtue.* South Bend, IN: University of Notre Dame Press.
> A recent influential critique of modern ethical theories and a defense of an Aristotelian viewpoint.

Mill, J. S. (1956). *On liberty.* Indianapolis, IN: Bobbs-Merrill.
   The classic arguments for freedom of opinion and lifestyle.
Mill, J. S. (1973). Utilitarianism. In J. Bentham & J. S. Mill (Eds.), *The utilitarians.* Garden City, NY: Academic Press, Doubleday.
   An excellent and brief statement of utilitarianism.
Nash, R. J. (1996). *"Real world" ethics: Frameworks for educators and human service professionals.* New York: Teachers College Press.
   A discussion of how professional ethics should be taught in university settings.
Nash, R. J. (1997). *Answering the "virtuecrats": A moral conversation on character education.* New York: Teachers College Press.
   A critical discussion of virtue ethics and character education as they have been promoted in educational settings.
Niebuhr, R. (1932). *Moral man and immoral society.* New York: Charles Scribner & Sons.
   A classical discussion of social ethics from a religious perspective.
Noddings, N. (1984). *Caring. A feminine approach to ethics and moral education.* Berkeley: University of California Press.
   A feminist approach to ethics and moral education.
Noddings, N. (1992). *The challenge to care in schools: An alternative approach to education.* New York: Teachers College Press.
   The application of Noddings's theory of caring to schooling.
Okin, S. M. (1989). *Justice, gender, and the family.* New York: Basic Books.
   A feminist viewpoint on justice with an important discussion of socialization for equality.
Peters, R. S. (1970). *Ethics and education.* London: George Allen & Unwin.
   A discussion of several ethical concepts, such as punishment, respect for persons, freedom, and equality, in an educational context.
Rawls, J. (1971). *A theory of justice.* Cambridge, MA: Harvard University Press.
   Possibly the best contemporary statement of a liberal theory of social justice.
Rawls, J. (1993). *Political liberalism.* New York: Columbia University Press.
   An updating of Rawls's work in *A Theory of Justice.*
Rich, J. M. (1984). *Professional ethics in education.* Springfield, IL: Charles C. Thomas.
   Deals with various issues in professional ethics. Thoroughly researched. A good place to begin research on a variety of topics.
Robinson, G. M., & Moulton, J. (1985). *Ethical problems in higher education.* Englewood Cliffs, NJ: Prentice Hall.
   An excellent treatment of central ethical issues in higher education.
Rosenblum, N. (1998). *Membership and morals.* Princeton, NJ: Princeton University Press.
   A discussion of the importance of community membership for the ethical life.
Sandel, M. (1982). *Liberalism and the limits of justice.* Cambridge, England: Cambridge University Press.
   A communitarian criticism of liberalism.
Sergiovani, T. J. (1993). *Building community in schools.* San Francisco: Jossey-Bass.
   A discussion of the importance of community in schooling.

Shaver, J. P., & Strong, W. (1982). *Facing value decisions* (2nd ed.). New York: Teachers College Press.
> Explores values education within a democratic context and the rational foundations of values.

Sola, P. A. (Ed.). (1984). *Ethics, education, and administrative decisions.* New York: Peter Lang.
> A collection of papers on a variety of issues concerning administrative ethics.

Strike, K. A. (1982). *Educational policy and the just society.* Urbana: University of Illinois Press.
> A discussion of the concepts of liberty, equality, and rationality as applied to a range of educational problems.

Strike, K. A. (1982). *Liberty and learning.* New York: St. Martin's Press.
> Develops a theory of liberty for education. Contains chapters on academic freedom and students' rights.

Strike, K. A. (1996). The moral responsibilities of educators. In T. J. Buttery & E. Guyton (Eds.), *Handbook of research on teacher education* (2nd ed.; pp. 869–892). New York: Macmillan.
> A discussion of the role of professional ethics in the education of teachers.

Strike, K., Anderson, M., Curren, R., van Geel, T., Pritchard, I., & Robertson, E. (2002). *Ethical standards of the American Educational Research Association: Cases and commentary.* Washington, D.C.: American Educational Research Association.
> A discussion of research ethics rooted in AERA's code of ethics and employing a case method.

Strike, K., & Moss, P. (2003). *The ethics of college student life.* Boston: Allyn and Bacon, 2003.
> A book on ethics for college students, using cases, with discussions of topics such as cheating, tolerance, and sex.

Strike, K. A., & Soltis, J. F. (2004). *The ethics of teaching (4th edition).* New York: Teachers College Press.
> A book, similar in purpose and organization to *The Ethics of School Administration*, but focused on ethical issues in teaching.

Taylor, C. (1994). The politics of recognition. In A. Gutmann (Ed.), *Multiculturalism: Examining the politics of recognition.* Princeton, NJ: Princeton University Press.
> One of the most important works on multiculturalism by a philosopher.

Tomasi, J. (2001). *Liberalism beyond justice.* Princeton, NJ: Princeton University Press.
> This book discusses the consequences of liberalism and argues for the need to accommodate groups such as religious conservatives.

White, P. (1996). *Civic virtues and public schooling.* New York: Teachers College Press.
> A discussion of the cultivation of virtues such as trust and honesty in schools.

Williams, B. (1985). *Ethics and the limits of philosophy.* Cambridge, MA: Harvard University Press.
> An important discussion of the limits of ethical reasoning.

Young, I. (1990). *Justice and the politics of difference.* Princeton, NJ: Princeton University Press.
> Young discusses the view that oppression and domination are not issues of distributive justice and argues for a politics of difference.

About the Authors

Kenneth A. Strike is Professor of Cultural Foundations of Education at Syracuse University and Professor Emeritus of Education at Cornell University. He has his Ph.D. from Northwestern. He has also taught at the University of Wisconsin and been a department chair at the University of Maryland. His research emphasizes professional ethics and political philosophy as it applies to matters of educational policy. He has authored, coauthored, or edited over a dozen books and about 150 articles and book chapters. He is a past president of the Philosophy of Education Society and has been elected a member of the National Academy of Education. He lives in Thendara, New York, a small village in the Adirondack Mountains, in a house on the shore of the Moose River on which he regularly canoes and kayaks and where he only occasionally bothers the fish.

Emil J. Haller is Professor Emeritus of Educational Administration at Cornell University. After earning his Ph.D. at the University of Chicago, he taught at the Ontario Institute for Studies in Education and then joined the faculty of Cornell University. In addition he has taught at the University of Oregon and the University of British Columbia. He is the coauthor of three books and the author or coauthor of numerous research reports and journal articles. Most of this research has been empirical in nature and has centered on the possible effects of students' race and social class on teacher decision making, on the social and political issues surrounding small and rural schools, and on the effects of graduate training on administrative practice. When not occupied with these tasks, he spends much of his time traveling; canoeing or kayaking; and fly fishing for trout, salmon, or steelhead. He and his wife live in Ithaca, NY.

Jonas F. Soltis is William Heard Kilpatrick Professor of Philosophy and Education Emeritus at Teachers College, Columbia University and is past president of both the John Dewey Society and the Philosophy of Education Society. He was an early pioneer in the development of professional ethics case studies for educators, and is coauthor of *The Ethics of Teaching* as well as *The Ethics of School Administration*. He served as editor of the *Teachers College Record* and as lead editor of the NSSE Yearbook, *Philosophy and Education*. He also served as a seminar leader for the Christian A. Johnson Foundation's Educational Leadership Program. Currently he is the series editor of Teachers College Press's Advances in Contemporary Educational Thought Series, and also serves as series editor and coauthor of the Thinking About Education Series, a collection of five foundations texts for pre- and in-service teachers which focus on case studies in teaching, learning, curriculum, ethics, and school and society.